LOOKING UP AT THE SKY

First Edition

Published in 2017 by

Woodfield Publishing Ltd
www.woodfieldpublishing.co.uk

ISBN 978-1-84683-184-3

Printed and bound in England

Typesetting & page design: Nic Pastorius
Cover design: Klaus Schaffer

Source document
Looking Up at the Sky - Adcock (final)

Looking Up at the Sky

My 50 Years Flying with the RAF 1960-2010

a memoir by

C.B. 'SID' ADCOCK

Woodfield Publishing Ltd

Bognor Regis ~ West Sussex ~ England ~ PO21 5EL

tel 01243 821234 ~ **e/m** info@woodfieldpublishing.co.uk

Interesting and informative books on a variety of subjects

For full details of all our published titles, visit our website at
www.woodfieldpublishing.co.uk

For Breda

The Graduation of 81st Entry RAF College Cranwell, July 1962. The Author is in the front rank, second from the right.

"When once you have tasted flight,
you will forever walk the Earth with your eyes turned skyward,
for there you have been,
and there you will always long to return."

Leonardo da Vinci

The photo which appeared on the front cover of the RAF Newton Station Magazine in 1993 following my appointment as Station Commander.

Contents

A Qualified Flying Instructor (QFI), 1966 (see p.51).

Foreword

By Air Chief Marshal **Sir Andrew Wilson** KCB AFC ADC FRAeS RAF (Retd)

When the author and I graduated from the Royal Air Force College Cranwell in July 1962, as fellow Flight Cadets of No 81 Entry, the Service we joined as Junior Officers was a vastly different organisation from the one that exists today. With the Cold War at its most intense, the primary role of the RAF was to maintain Britain's nuclear deterrent. It also contributed to the NATO alliance through the Second Tactical Air Force based in Germany. In addition, it supported various treaty organisations in the Near East, the Middle East and the Far East. Finally, it provided the air element necessary for imperial policing. To fulfil these roles it maintained a vast network of airfields extending from the United Kingdom in the west to Singapore and Hong Kong in the east. This network provided a basis for the operational, training, maintenance and support functions necessary for the application of air power in response to various political and military events around the world.

While the size and scope of the RAF in the 1960s exposed junior aircrew to a wide variety of experiences, life was in other ways much more constrained. Society was still organised on a very hierarchical basis, it being customary to show respect for those in positions of authority such as teachers, policemen, politicians and members of the establishment. As very few people owned a car, travel was mostly by bus and by train. There were no charter flights, and air travel was both exclusive and expensive. Those posted abroad were unlikely to return home in the course of their tour of duty unless they could secure an indulgence passage on a military flight. Servicemen were also poorly paid. The digital revolution was still some way off and there were no computers, no mobile telephones and no social networks. The upshot of these lifestyle limitations was that social life centred around the Mess, with military communities being close-knit and largely self sufficient in terms of entertainment.

Within the 50 years covered by the author's flying career in the RAF, all this was to change beyond recognition. Britain withdrew from its commitments 'East of Suez' and began its slow metamorphosis from imperial grandee to a partner in the Commonwealth of Nations. The concomitant reduction in size of the armed forces was accelerated by the ending of the Cold War as the nation sought a 'peace dividend'. The RAF, which had numbered nearly a quarter of a million men and women when the story starts in the 1950s, found itself by the story's end in 2010 with fewer than 40,000 personnel. Economic difficulties and the exponential rise in the cost of aircraft and equipment called for drastic measures to reduce expenditure. Long-standing and often historic airfields at home and overseas were closed at an ever-increasing rate as the RAF concentrated itself into a handful of large bases within the United Kingdom. These constraints notwithstanding, the RAF remained then, and still remains today, a potent military force, owing to advances in aircraft design and technology and a vast improvement in the accuracy of its weapons.

One thing that has remained constant throughout the turbulent political, military and social changes that provide a backdrop to the story told in this book is the continuing demand for high performance and professionalism from RAF aircrew. Vast improvements in the design and performance of aircraft, and the ever-increasing complexity of the environment in which they operate, calls for constant updating of the knowledge and skills of those who fly them. To meet this challenge, old shibboleths about doctrine, training and leadership have to be regularly reviewed and, where necessary replaced by new approaches. There is no room for complacency.

Through his unique achievement of serving as a pilot in the RAF for more than 50 years, the author has been involved in all aspects of these complex developments. In this book, he tells the story with humour, insight and compassion. The resulting narrative presents a significant and heartwarming chapter in the history of the Royal Air Force, and I commend it to you.

CHAPTER ONE

The Formative Years

NO YOUNG PERSON growing up in the 1950s could fail to be aware of the tremendous developments that were taking place in the world of aviation. At that time very few homes had access to television, but the newspapers and radio broadcasts were full of stories of the latest acts of derring-do. Only a few years earlier, in October 1947, an American rocket-powered Bell X-1 research vehicle, launched from the belly of a B-29 Superfortress, and piloted by 'Chuck' Yeager, had broken the so-called 'sound barrier' for the first time. As scientists, aerodynamicists and engineers began to understand and come to terms with the problems of transonic flight, and as the design and technology of the recently-introduced jet-engine improved, new aircraft of hitherto unheard of performance began to appear in the skies. Initially, these advances were confined to military aviation. In 1952, however, a Mk 1 De Havilland Comet inaugurated the world's first jet scheduled commercial flight from London to Johannesburg. This service was to herald the massive increase in global commercial aviation that would occur in the latter half of the twentieth century.

The surge of general interest in these remarkable developments was picked up and exploited by the media. The film industry, in particular, produced some classic examples of the genre. The film *Sound Barrier* directed by David Lean and released in 1952, captured not only the entrepreneurial spirit of the age but also the enthusiasm and excitement with which each technical advance was greeted by the public at large. In addition, there were films which glorified wartime feats of aviation. *The Dambusters* released in 1955, told the epic story of the raid by 617 Squadron on the Mohne and Eder dams during the Second World War. This hugely popular and successful film was followed in 1957 by *Reach for the Sky*, the story of Douglas Bader, the famous legless wartime pilot. Meanwhile, on the other side of the Atlantic, Hollywood was producing a vast number of films in which aviation played a central theme. Nor was this enthusiasm for aviation restricted to the cinema; in the Eagle comic, Dan Dare, and his faithful batman, Digby, explored the boundaries of space in exciting weekly instalments.

From the perspective of a young boy, the most striking feature of these events was that they seemed to be enacted not by a race of supermen but by ordinary people who had found themselves living in extraordinary times and had risen to the challenge. In particular, the RAF personnel depicted in the films were noteworthy for the insouciance with which they approached the dire circumstances of wartime operations and the cheerful good humour with which they went about their tasks. Even then, in those early years, it seemed not beyond the bounds of possibility that an individual from a modest background might aspire one day to join them. As the years went by, and adulthood beckoned, it became more and more fixed in my mind that to join that band of brothers and wear those coveted RAF wings on my chest was the one true path to lasting happiness. Meanwhile, at the sound of a propeller or the scream of a jet, my friends and I would search the sky until we spotted the aircraft creating the noise. Then we would follow its progress until it became so small that it vanished from sight, leaving us looking up at the empty sky above.

My own specific interest in aviation had been sparked at an early age when I stayed with one of my aunts during the summer holidays in a village not far from Desford Aerodrome in Leicestershire, at that time one of the RAF's flying training schools. In the fine summer weather, taking a packed lunch with us, a couple of friends from the village and I would cheerfully walk the few miles to the aerodrome. There we would ensconce ourselves on one of several disused air raid shelters on the edge of the grass airfield, from where we had a grandstand view of the aircraft taking off and landing. Today's children would regard such activities as commonplace, if not banal, but in those far off days they were sufficiently novel to keep us interested for much of the day. And whenever there was a lull in the proceedings, our air raid shelter would become a fort, or some other symbol of boyhood imagination, and that would keep us occupied until flying operations started again. Although I did not know it at the time, the aircraft we were observing were Tiger Moths, the mainstay of RAF ab initio pilot training for many years. Nor was I aware, as we made our way home along the hot, dusty country lanes, that within a few years I would myself be taught to fly on just such an aircraft type.

Around about this time I lived with my family in a Leicestershire village not far from what was then the RAF station at Cottesmore. One day, the attention of my elder brother and I was drawn to a poster advertising an Air Display at the base. On the appointed day, we duly set off on our bicycles and rode the ten miles or so to the airfield. Then as now, air displays were hugely popular events, and we soon found ourselves amongst a vast throng of excited spectators. In those immediate post-war years, there was little or no security to speak of, and we found that we could climb into the cockpit of the latest jet fighters and waggle the controls around to our hearts content. I also recall climbing into the fuselage of a Lancaster bomber and making my way forward over the main spar and through a dark tunnel until I reached the cockpit. Like many other spectators, I was duly impressed by the immense size of the aircraft and the vast array of dials, gauges and levers that were obviously necessary to coax the machine into the air. My nose was also assailed by an unforgettable smell of warm leather, engine oil and aviation gasoline, a smell that even now, 60 years later, takes me instantly back to my early flying days. As we cycled home through the late afternoon sunshine, our young minds thrilled by what we had seen and heard in the course of the day, I was not to know that within few years I would carry out my first operational tour on an aircraft not dissimilar in type to the one that had so impressed me during the visit.

At the age of 13 I was sent along with my elder brother to be a boarder at Loughborough College School. In an establishment comprising some 600 pupils, there were only about 40 boarders, so we formed a small but elite group in the school population. More important, in the context of my military flying career, was that the school ran a squadron, No 132 Squadron of the Air Training Corps (ATC). The squadron was run in a somewhat ramshackle way by three members of staff, Mr Modral, Mr Bourne and Mr Bregazzi. We occupied a wooden hut in a corner of what was then the playing fields of the Loughborough Colleges, in which was stored a motley collection of discarded RAF equipment. Unlike the highly structured and efficient organisation of today, the ATC in those years was more devolved, with individual squadrons being left pretty much to their own devices. There was no discernable syllabus of training, and most of the drill evenings were spent messing around under the supervision of the senior cadets with various old bits of equipment. Nevertheless, we wore our air force blue uniforms with pride, and we felt strongly the corporate link between our own modest organisation and that of our powerful but remote sponsors.

This link with our parent organisation was strengthened in several ways. There was an annual Wing Parade, usually held at a nearby RAF airfield. There were sports events organised on a Wing, Group and National basis. And, most importantly, there were Summer Camps, which were held during the school holidays at selected RAF stations. All these activities gave us a taste of military life and, for those of us already bitten by the flying bug, they provided further evidence, if any was needed, that military flying offered a viable and exciting choice of a future career.

It was at one of these annual Wing Parades that I gained what can only be described as a 'field promotion'. By this time I had been a member of the squadron for several years and was a relatively experienced cadet. I was also tall for my age and so stood out among the other cadets on parade. Passing along the ranks, the Reviewing Officer stopped in front of me and asked me how long I had been a cadet.

'Three years, Sir,' I replied.

Turning to Mr Modral, our Commanding Officer, who was accompanying him as he inspected our squadron, said, 'How about a spot of promotion?'

As far as I knew, no cadet had ever been promoted on the squadron, not because there was a lack of suitable candidates, but merely because the organisation was run in such a chaotic way that no-one had ever thought of it. Consequently, the hapless Mr Modral was completely flummoxed by the Reviewing Officer's suggestion and could only indicate a mute compliance. The upshot of this exchange was that at our next drill night I was promoted directly from Air Cadet to Cadet Sergeant, without even a cursory stop in the intervening rank of Cadet Corporal.

Field House, where the school boarders lived, was located on Ashby Road, almost opposite the extensive sports grounds of the Loughborough Colleges. Because of the long-standing association between the school and the College authorities, we were allowed unfettered use of the facilities. These included tennis courts, football and rugby pitches, a magnificent cinder athletics track and a heated indoor swimming pool, this latter facility being something of a rarity in those days. Using the sports facilities allowed us briefly to escape from the confines of the boarding house and its grounds, so during the summer months my fellow boarders and I were often to be found on the tennis courts or pounding round the track. Because of this, we not only became very fit but we also developed a high degree of proficiency at the various sports. Consequently, when it came to finding competitors to represent the Wing, those boarders who were in the ATC were always in the van for selection. It was on this basis that I came to represent the Wing in the High Jump at the Group Sports at RAF Rufforth, and went on from there to participate in the ATC National Athletics Championships at RAF Uxbridge, where I came third. These achievements were modest enough, but they were to hold me in good stead when the time came for me to apply to join the RAF.

My first summer camp took place in 1956 at RAF Thorney Island, located on the south coast of England, about mid-way between Portsmouth and Chichester. There were perhaps about 20 cadets from our squadron on the camp and we were accommodated in a long room in one of the airmen's barrack blocks. This arrangement was to give me taste for what is meant by the term 'barrack room humour', as the wits among us made jokes about every aspect of service life. ('Remember, lads, when you use the toilet, the shiny side of the paper is for the officers and the rough side for the men!' And so on, and so on.) We were fortunate to be entertained by a very well organised programme of activities, giving us exposure to the various sections of the station. Everywhere I went I found the same good-humoured and can-do attitude to work, which made a lasting expression on my mind.

One of our projects was a simulated 'Escape and Evasion' exercise, which took place across the South Downs. We were dropped off in pairs at various locations across the countryside and had to make our way to a rendezvous without being captured. I was teamed up with an older cadet and we both entered with a will into the spirit of the exercise. We sped along country lanes and across fields, carefully avoiding villages and other built-up areas. As result of our enterprise, we not only avoided capture but also arrived first at the rendezvous, well ahead of any of the other participants in the event.

Following this success, I was given a flight as a reward in a Miles Marathon, a small 4-engined aircraft used at the time for navigation training. This was my first-ever flight and, as I gazed down on the towns and harbours of the South Coast, I knew for sure that this was what I wanted to do with my life. Another bonus from my success in the escape and evasion exercise was an entry ticket to the Farnborough Air Show, together with a railway warrant for a return ticket to Farnborough station. Then as now, it was an amazing and impressive show, with some advanced aircraft of the day being displayed for the first time. Among the many highlights was a superb display of formation aerobatics by a team of Seahawks from the Royal Navy, and a loop and roll-off-the-top performed by an RAF Vulcan bomber right in front of the crowd.

Now firmly resolved on a career in the RAF, and greatly encouraged not only by my Headmaster, Mr G H F Broad, but also by the staff of the ATC Squadron, I attended the RAF Aircrew Selection Centre then located at RAF Hornchurch in Essex. I was 16 years old at the time. The first part of the selection process would determine whether I was made of the 'right stuff' for pilot training. After that, successful candidates would go on to the RAF College Cranwell to see if they were suitable for a cadetship. The initial selection process consisted of a comprehensive medical examination, which involved visiting various consultants located in different parts of the building. In full swing, the selection centre resembled the inside of a beehive, with a multitude of candidates rushing up and down the corridors from department to department, the whole process being co-ordinated by a frantically busy Flight Sergeant and a set of coloured tags. As I was fairly fit from my athletic endeavours, my medical seemed to be going quite well. My final specialist appointment, however, took me along a lengthy corridor. As I was carrying my medical report in an unsealed envelope, I decided to nip into a toilet en route and have a quick look to see how I was doing. Opening the report, I hurriedly scanned its contents. As my eye moved down the page, everything seemed to be going well, until I came to the general comments at the bottom of the page where one consultant had written 'Flat Feet!'

Having flat feet must have been no barrier to pilot selection, because the next day I went on to the second phase of the process, which involved a series of aptitude tests. These included assessments of hand-eye co-ordination, and also cognitive skills, such as determining an aircraft's attitude based on information provided by printed versions of various flight instruments. Both these aspects are particularly important elements for the successful control of an aircraft in flight. Having surmounted these early barriers to selection, I entered my third and final day of assessment. These exercises revolved around tests of initiative and leadership potential. For the most part, they involved manoeuvring large drums of 'delicate scientific instruments' over a series of obstacle courses, with each candidate being given an opportunity to lead the group in turn. Having spent my boyhood in the country, where we occupied ourselves in those far-off days of relative freedom by climbing trees, damning up streams, and generally providing our own forms of adventurous training, I did not find this kind of task too daunting.

The final phase of the assessment program, however, comprising an interview with a member of the selection board, was not such a simple proposition, being one in which I felt at a distinct disadvantage compared with some of my fellow candidates. As we sat waiting for our turn to be interviewed, I noticed that some of them were equipped with lists of the latest political appointments. I realised that, unlike me, some of the candidates had been carefully groomed for the selection process. Indeed, to say that I was as green as grass in this brave new world would have been an overstatement. Nevertheless, I duly went in for my interview, where I was greeted by a rather bored-looking Flight Lieutenant sitting behind a desk. My lack of preparation notwithstanding, the initial part of the interview went quite well, with questions about my education, sports, hobbies, etc, all of which I was able to answer in a confident and straightforward manner. I even managed to give quite a cogent response to the question 'Why do you want to join the Royal Air Force'. But then came the clincher.

‘Suppose,’ he said, ‘that we accepted you in to the RAF as a pilot, which aircraft would you most like to fly?’

For some reason, this question absolutely stumped me. Perhaps the prospect of actually being selected for pilot training was so far beyond my expectations that I had not dared to think that far ahead. Whatever the reason, I cast desperately around my mind for a convincing response, but none was forthcoming. Seeking inspiration, I raised my eyes towards heaven and, as I did so, I saw a picture of a Hawker Hunter aircraft on the wall above his head.

‘I think I’d like to fly the Hunter, Sir,’ I responded, in a confident manner.

At this moment his whole demeanour changed. He sat up in his chair, smiled, and a far-away look came into his eyes.

‘Ah, yes,’ he said, ‘I used to fly the Hunter. Splendid aircraft!’

At that moment I knew, I just somehow knew, that my application for pilot training was going to be successful.

And so it proved to be. That afternoon, along with other successful candidates, I boarded a coach to Cranwell, where the second phase of the selection process was to take place. These tests were not dissimilar with those we had taken at Hornchurch, but perhaps with rather more emphasis on the leadership and initiative aspects. One test involved a paper and pencil exercise with a map of a village. The scenario was that we were preparing for a dinner party and we had to shop for the necessary supplies. But some shops closed early, and the pub didn’t open until six o’clock, so there were various obstacles to progress. I had always enjoyed such puzzles, and I impressed my interlocutor by arriving at the optimum solution with a few moments to spare. After seeking my reasons for the various courses of action that I had proposed, he floored me completely by asking my average speed for the journey, a simple sum that I simply could not get my head around at the time.

The assessment process also involved giving a three-minute talk to a board of three officers headed by a Wing Commander. Most of the people in my group gave competent talks, but on rather predictable and prosaic topics such as ‘The Workings of the Carburettor’. The board members listened politely, but one could sense that their thoughts were elsewhere. It so happened that I had recently had a talk at school on the Dewey Decimal Classification System for Public Libraries. The ideas were fresh in my mind and seemed sufficiently far out from the usual run-of-the-mill topics that I decided to go ahead with it. In the event, my assumption proved to be correct because, as I spoke, I sensed that all three board members were taking a keen interest in what I had to say. I even slipped in a little joke about the system having been first devised by Francis Bacon, a political philosopher who lived during the 16th and 17th Centuries. He was the man who was supposed to have written the works of William Shakespeare – that is if Christopher Marlow didn't do it! After concluding the talk, I was asked a number of pertinent questions by the board members, and it was clear to me that I had really captured their interest with my topic. Overall, I must have done well enough to satisfy the board because, after a lengthy wait of some 14 weeks, I finally learned that I had been selected for a cadetship.

Selection for Cranwell brought two additional benefits in its wake. First, I was awarded an RAF Scholarship, which meant that the Air Force contributed in no small measure to the cost of my education while I was in the Sixth Form at school. With six children to feed and clothe, my parents were thankful for this windfall, which made it financially possible for me to stay on at school for two further years in order to gain the passes at A-Level GCE required for entry to the College. I should add that the RAF grant was generously supplemented by my great uncle and aunt, Mr and Mrs Jim and 'Queenie' Woodward, now long since deceased, but to whom I remain eternally grateful. The second benefit was that I was also awarded an ATC Flying Scholarship under a scheme that would allow me to learn to fly at an approved civilian flying club at the Air Force's expense.

As a prelude to my flying scholarship, I was selected to attend during the Easter Holidays in 1958 a gliding course at the Home Command Gliding Centre based at RAF Hawkinge, a famous Battle of Britain airfield located on the south Kentish coast near Folkestone. The centre was equipped with the Kirby Cadet T21 trainer, built by the Slingsby Aircraft Company, and known as 'the barge' for its stable handling characteristics. The aircraft was launched by a cable attached to winch, the pilot operating a cable-release mechanism at about 800 feet. After that, a gentle left-hand circuit brought the aircraft round on to the final approach and landing. The glider was then hauled into position and prepared for another launch. As flying goes, it was a fairly simple operation, and one with which I coped without undue difficulty. After several dual instructional flights, I was duly sent off solo, and after three such sorties I gained my 'A' and 'B' Gliding certificates, which I still have today. The certificates are signed '*Brabazon of Tara, President of the Royal Aero Club of the United Kingdom*'. It would be more than 40 years before I was to fly in a glider again, but the quiet serenity and the elemental nature of that particular type of flying are sensations that remain with me to this day. It is worth noting that gliding has continued to serve as a low-cost means of exposing ATC cadets to the thrill of flying, mainly through the Volunteer Gliding Schools (VGSs) that are today scattered around the country and manned, as the name implies, by volunteer pilots from the three services, many of them now retired. I should also mention that the airfield at Hawkinge is now covered by a housing estate.

During the Easter holidays of 1959, a year after my gliding course, I attended the Midland Aero Club at Birmingham's Elmdon Airport, for a course of basic flying instruction leading to a Private Pilot's Licence (PPL). A few weeks earlier, I had received a large official-looking parcel from the RAF containing my flying clothing. This comprised a flying suit, leather helmet and goggles, a pair of gauntlets and a pair of fur-lined flying boots. This kit was necessary because the aircraft on which I was to train, the Tiger Moth, had an open cockpit, leaving the pilot exposed to the cold breezes of the spring. There were three cadets on the course and our mentor was Mr Bradley, a veteran pilot and the Chief Instructor of the club. The other two cadets lived in the Birmingham area, but I lodged locally in the suburb of Sheldon, and took a short bus ride each morning to the airfield.

Powered by a Gipsy Major engine, the Tiger Moth was a simple, docile and rugged aircraft to fly. As the two club aircraft were not fitted with radios, flying was controlled by coloured lights from the control tower signalled by means of an Aldis Lamp. Communication between the two pilots – the instructor in the front cockpit and the student in the rear – was effected by means of a Gosport Tube. The instructor spoke into a mouthpiece in front of him and the sound was conveyed by means of the tube to the ears of the student; the reverse applying when the student spoke to the instructor. It was not a very efficient system, and it led often to misunderstandings, especially in the early stages of instruction, when the student was not entirely sure of the terminology being used. Instrumentation in the cockpit was fairly elementary, comprising an airspeed indicator, an altimeter, a turn-and-slip indicator, a rate-of-climb-and-descent indicator, and a magnetic P-type compass located between the knees of the pilot. The propeller was fixed in pitch; and power was indicated by an RPM gauge mounted on the instrument panel. The fuel tank was located in the centre section between the two upper wings and fed the engine by gravity, the amount of fuel remaining being indicated by a gauge on the tank. The was no starter motor, the engine being started by swinging the propeller, and ignition was controlled by two magneto switches mounted externally to the cockpit. The aircraft was a 'tail-dragger', fitted with a skid rather than a tail wheel, and it was not equipped with brakes.

One advantage of such a simple yet rugged construction was that there was not very much to go wrong, so the aircraft remained reasonably serviceable for the duration of our course. The weather intervened occasionally to prevent flying, but on the whole we made good progress. Mr Bradley took us through the basic exercises, and sent me off solo after some 10 hours of dual instruction, and just a few days after my 18th birthday. We then progressed through more advanced exercises such as steep turns, stalling, how to cope with an engine failure after take-off, and how to carry out a practice forced-landing in a field following a simulated engine failure. The course also included quite bit of navigation, starting with relatively short sectors, and gradually increasing in length and duration. In order to qualify for a PPL, I had to undertake a triangular cross-country flight of some length, and on a fine day in April this took me from Birmingham to a landing at Weston-super-Mare, thence to Baginton aerodrome near Coventry (now an International Airport but in those days merely a large grass airfield) and finally back to Elmdon. Having sat and passed my ground examinations in aviation law, meteorology, and various allied subjects, I completed the course with a final handling test, during which I was required to demonstrate competence in all the exercised that I had been taught. This final sortie brought me up exactly to the 30 hours flying that in those days was the minimum requirement for a PPL. My licence, which I still have, was dated 4th May 1959. In all the intervening years, I have never again had an opportunity to fly the Tiger Moth. But I still see them in the air occasionally, and when I do it never fails to remind me of those far-off days when I first enjoyed the thrill of powered flying.

My schooldays were now coming to an end, as was my time as an ATC cadet, but before they did so I was to enjoy one last privilege. At that time the ATC participated in an International Air Cadet Exchange Scheme, and I was fortunate enough to be selected for a visit to Canada. Shortly after the of the end of the summer term, a party of about 40 cadets flew in a North Star of the Royal Canadian Air Force from RAF Northolt to Montreal via the Azores and Gander in Newfoundland. In these days of mass travel by air, it is hard to believe that this was my first trip abroad, the same being true for many of the other cadets on the visit.

In the course of our travels, it became apparent that the Air Cadet League of Canada enjoyed a very high profile in the life of the country, as we were treated like royalty wherever we went. Apart from the sights we saw and the events we enjoyed, two other advantages accrued from the trip. I learned that several of the other cadets on the visit and I were due to start our training at Cranwell on the same course in September, so I would have a ready-made circle of friends and acquaintances when I arrived. I also had my first taste of long-haul flying, which was to play a major part in my life as my subsequent military flying career progressed.

Chapter 2

Basic Flying Training

On 8 September 1959 my father drove me to the station in Leicester, where I took a train to Nottingham and thence to Sleaford in Lincolnshire. Before I boarded the train, my father took the unusual step of shaking me by the hand and wishing me 'good luck'. Reflecting later on these words, I realised that the days of being supported financially by my parents were over, and from now on I was on my own. Up to that point, I had not thought to ask how much we might be paid as Flight Cadets, but it turned out to be 12/- per day (£0.60p per day in the later decimal currency.) It does not sound much today, and it was not a lot then, but with food and lodging all found, and not many other expenses, it was enough to live on at the time. At Sleaford I boarded an RAF bus for Cranwell, where I was pleased to meet up with some of my former colleagues from the recent visit to Canada.

Arriving at the RAF College we were taken to the Junior Ranks Mess, where we were divided up into three cadet squadrons and shown to our accommodation, known as the South Brick Lines. As the name suggests, the South Brick Lines were rows of huts, each building accommodating 6 cadets allocated by squadron in alphabetical order: Adcock, Annett, Bing, Coulson, etc, etc. The building comprised a small sitting room, a dormitory and ablutions. Each hut had a batman, whose job it was to keep the accommodation clean and also to provide a number of minor personal services for the cadets. We ate in the Junior Ranks Mess, where the food was wholesome and provided in more than adequate quantity. The Mess also contained a shop and a bar, known as the Fancy Goods Store (FGS), where cadets could buy personal items, cigarettes, and alcoholic drinks at specified times. In front of the Junior Ranks Mess was a large parade ground, where we were to spend much of the time under the tutelage of Sergeant Ross, our mentor and Drill Sergeant, whose job it was to turn us in the shortest possible time from a gaggle of former civilian schoolboys into a smart military unit.

On the other side of the main road that bisects the College grounds, we could see the impressive sight of the main College, a large building constructed on classical lines during the 1930s. It was made clear to us from the outset, however, that we would not take our place in the hallowed building until we had mastered the basics of military training and reached a standard high enough to satisfy the stringent requirements of the College authorities. We were the 81st cadet entry to be trained at Cranwell, and I was allocated to C Squadron, to be identified for the duration of my 3-year stay at Cranwell as 'Flight Cadet Adcock – 81C'. The entry comprised some 40 or 50 cadets, although these numbers would be whittled down over the three years as individuals either failed a phase of the training or retired voluntarily at various points of the course. Indeed, we lost one cadet on the very second day, when it was discovered that the individual was married. It transpired that married personnel were not accepted for training. There were no girls on the course, Air Force policy at the time being that there was no place for women on a front-line fighting unit. As we paraded up and down on those sunny autumn days, under the watchful eye and caustic tongue of Sergeant Ross, wearing our newly-issued uniforms, we felt a surge of hope and pride. Our schooldays were behind us and the future stretched ahead. We were at last on our way to becoming aircrew in the RAF.

For the first term we followed the traditional path of military training. We were issued with vast amounts of kit, including flying clothing, and we had to learn how to keep it all clean and tidy. We attended classes on Military Studies and various other allied subjects, including lectures on how to be an Officer and a Gentleman. Under the watchful eye of our Physical Training Instructors (PTIs) we developed our fitness, and we also did endless amounts of drill. All this activity was played out against the scream of jet engines as the senior cadets carried out their advanced flying training on the South Airfield. As we marched in a squad from one activity to another, we would watch enviously as a formation of jets tore into the circuit for a run and break, lowering their undercarriages as they turned downwind in succession and prepared for landing. At that time, ab initio pilot training was carried out on the Percival Provost, a light two-seater piston-engined aircraft, at the nearby satellite airfield of Barkston Heath. Advanced pilot training was undertaken at Cranwell on the de Havilland Vampire or, for those too big or too tall for the Vampire's small cockpit, on the twin-engined Gloster Meteor. A fleet of twin-engined Vickers Valetta aircraft, based at the western end of Cranwell's South Airfield, served as flying classrooms for navigator training. Prior to 1959, the year that we arrived at Cranwell, Fight Cadets had carried out all their flying training at the College, and had graduated as fully qualified pilots or navigators before going on an Operational Conversion Unit (OCU) to train on the aircraft type to which they had been allocated for their first operational tour. But all this was about to change, as we were soon to find out.

The reason behind the change was twofold. First, a recent study had concluded that Cranwell graduates were not faring as well in their subsequent careers as direct entry university graduates. The study had concluded that the academic training at Cranwell needed to be beefed up to the point where cadets could graduate with a degree or an equivalent academic qualification. At the same time, the Piston Provost, Vampire and Meteor were being phased out as pilot training aircraft and replaced by the new Jet Provost trainer, which had recently been introduced into service with much fanfare. Henceforth, starting with 81 Entry, the trainee pilots would undertake the first all-through jet training course to be carried out at the College. This was an ambitious enterprise, and one that could not be accommodated within the traditional 3-year syllabus of Flight Cadet training. To accommodate the additional hours of academic study required to attain a degree, it was therefore decided that only basic flying training would in future be carried out at Cranwell, with advanced flying training being conducted elsewhere after graduation. After much agonising, it was eventually agreed that, in a significant break with tradition, cadets carrying out their flying training at Cranwell would nevertheless be awarded their 'wings' at the end of the basic stage of their flying training and prior to graduation from the College.

These changes meant that instead of starting our flying training during our second term, as had hitherto been the case, we would not start flying until our fourth term, more than a year after first entering the College. Meanwhile, we were divided into three academic streams. Those with mathematical or scientific qualifications at A-Level GCE went into a science stream that was to study for an Associate Fellowship of the Royal Aeronautical Society (AFRAeS). Those with qualifications in the humanities or languages went into an arts stream that would study for a Bachelor of Arts (BA) Degree. The remainder went into a general stream that would study for internal exams set by the College. As my own qualifications were in mathematics and physics, I was allocated to the science stream. The dozen or so students in this stream were to study aerodynamics, structures and strength of materials, electronics, thermodynamics and meteorology. For those of us who joined the Air Force because we wanted to fly, this was a formidable undertaking, and one that we had not bargained for when we applied for a cadetship. Nevertheless, we bowed to the inevitable with as much grace as we could muster, and for the next twelve months we attended lectures most of the day every day during the working week. Meanwhile, our military training continued in parallel with our academic studies.

It was not, however, all work and no play. Most of the cadets were keen sportsmen of one sort or another and the College offered abundant facilities for recreation. Being tall for my age, I had played rugby at school with a fair degree of success, being captain of the First XV during my final year. But when I came to play at Cranwell, I discovered that I was not heavy enough to play as a forward and not fast enough to play in the three-quarters. So my rugby career came to an abrupt end, and I switched to basketball, a sport at which I played well enough to represent the College for most of my time as a cadet. In the summer I enjoyed athletics as a middle-distance runner, and again I was fortunate enough to represent the College in fixtures against various schools and universities. In my last year at school I had been introduced by an enterprising master to rock climbing and mountaineering, and I continued to pursue this activity during my time at Cranwell along with a group of like-minded cadets. During the breaks between terms, which were akin to school holidays, we were encouraged to undertake adventurous training activities. As a mountaineer, I was fortunate enough to take part at different times in expeditions to Norway, to the High Atlas Mountains in Morocco and to the Taurus Mountains in Turkey. In the days before the advent of mass travel, and when most people other than the very wealthy took their holidays in Britain, these were mind-broadening opportunities that were not generally available to the population at large.

The location of Cranwell in the middle of Lincolnshire made it difficult to pursue any sort of social life. When we arrived at the College, only one member of 81C had a car, a pre-war Austin Ruby, and it quickly became apparent that some form of transport was essential if we were to escape from an otherwise monastic existence. With a bit of financial help from my uncle Jim Woodward, I bought a scooter, a Lambretta, which was very much in vogue at the time. A scooter had the advantage that it could be driven solo on a provisional licence. But while scooters may have been all right for posturing around the town, they were unstable and dangerous things on the open road, as I discovered one frosty night when I fell off on the slippery railway level-crossing in Sleaford. It was not long before I traded the Lambretta up for a motorbike, a sporting 250cc P&M Panther. This fine machine provided a more rapid and safer means of transport, although it was not always reliable, and having to be rescued from breakdowns in inconvenient places became a way of life. Since I could not afford to pay for repairs on my Flight Cadet's pay, I soon learned, with aid of a workshop manual, how to dismantle and reconstruct the machine myself.

It is true to say that almost everything I know about the internal combustion engine I learned from my ownership of that motorbike. I also learned how narrow the gap can be between success and failure. One Christmas, during leave at home, I spent a frigid few hours in my father's garage repairing the machine. Soon after midnight, and by now frozen to the marrow, I managed to get all the pieces reassembled in what I thought was the right order. But when I kicked the starter, nothing happened. Cold, weary, and despondent, I made my way to bed, with the grim prospect of having to start all over again in the morning. But when I switched on the bedroom light, the first thing I saw was the motor bike's ignition key sitting on the dressing table. The next morning, with the key now inserted in the ignition, the motorbike started at the first kick, and I was back on the road again for the time being at least.

But while a motorbike provided mobility, it was not a very sociable means of transport, especially in the winter. So when the opportunity to buy a car arose, I took it, despite the fact that at that time I did not hold a full driving licence. During the winter of 1961, my Squadron Commander, Squadron Leader Petherham, had suffered an accident on the icy roads in his Riley 1.5. While the car was being repaired, he acquired an old 1936 Morris 8 as a temporary means of transport. When his first car was back on the road, he offered the Morris for sale at £10, and I bought it. With the aid of some friends who already held a driving licence, and with a knowledge of roadcraft gleaned from my motorcycling days, I took and passed my driving test in Grantham at the first attempt. Thereafter, my social life improved immeasurably. With the purchase of my Morris 8, I prided myself on having acquired a bargain, but I was soon to be disillusioned. On my way from Cranwell to my home near Leicester, I had reached the top the hill at Spitalgate, which was then an RAF Station just outside Grantham. Suddenly, there was a loud knocking sound from the engine compartment, and the vehicle ceased to function. I knew that there was a Morris garage at the bottom of the hill, just at the entrance to the town. Being by now somewhat accustomed to these situations, I took an instant decision to let the car free-wheel down the hill. Luckily, there was just enough momentum to carry me to my destination, and I came to a gentle halt on the forecourt of the garage. Having spoken to the proprietor, who agreed to have a look at the car, I continued my journey by bus. The next day I returned only to be informed that the car was a write-off. The big ends had seized and it would not be worth the cost of the repair. Seeing my crest-fallen face, the proprietor then offered the information that he had another similar car in his shed for sale, and would I be interested in that? I went with him to look at the car but when I saw it I was filled with disappointment. The bodywork was rusty, and the whole thing looked in a very sad state. However, when I opened the bonnet and looked into the engine compartment I saw that the car had, in the recent past, been fitted with a refurbished second-hand gold seal engine.

'How much,' I ventured, holding my breath, 'to take the engine from this car and replace the one in mine?'

The proprietor looked thoughtful for a moment, scratched his head, and looked at me sideways.

'Let's say £3.00 for the engine, and £3.00 for labour, shall we.'

I accepted his offer with alacrity, before he could change his mind, and within a few days I was back on the road again. I eventually did 9,000 miles in the car, and when towards the end of my time at Cranwell I upgraded to a newer car, I sold it to a fellow cadet for £20. It was the only car I ever owned on which I made a profit.

For the whole of 1960 we were fully occupied by our academic studies, and by the end of the year everyone in the science stream had passed their intermediate AFRAeS exams. Lest we should forget that we were hoping to become aircrew, we were given some occasional flying in a Chipmunk on the Cranwell North Airfield. The flying was not, however, very well organised, and there was no proper syllabus of instruction. Although I mustered some 20 hours flying, I never went solo, and in the end it was not even classed as dual instruction but merely as passenger flying.

As an Entry, we were now moving up the pecking order in the College. Since our arrival at Cranwell, Nos 76 and 77 Entries had graduated, and two new entries had started training. Rooms were now available for us in the main college building and after Christmas 1960 we moved into our new accommodation. For me, personally, it was the first time in my life that I had ever had a room of my own. The College was an impressive place in which to live. The two opposite wings on the south side of the building, in which were accommodated 'A' and 'C' Squadrons, flanked a vast parade ground, where we rehearsed and carried out ceremonial drill at regular intervals. Inside the building, long corridors joined the living accommodation to the main part of building, which housed the central rotunda, a dining hall, a lecture theatre, a bar, and, upstairs, the extensive library. The walls of this central area were lined with portraits of previous Commandants and Assistant Commandants, pictures and paintings of famous wartime aerial actions, and photographs of various College sports teams stretching back into the distant past. In the large dining hall hung portraits of Old Cranwellians who had risen to become Chief of the Air Staff. Also portrayed was Prince Charles in his flying gear, and Douglas Bader, the famous legless Second World War fighter pilot and leader, who was also an Old Cranwellian. As we went about our daily business, we soaked up the atmosphere of this iconic heritage that was soon to become our legacy.

With our move from the Junior Mess to the main College building, we said farewell to Sergeant Ross. We had by now become accustomed to his acerbic and often hilarious comments on our parade ground performance, and we were in a way sorry to move beyond his ambit. A man with many excellent qualities, he was eventually awarded a commission, and he and I met up again on equal terms later in my career. As an Entry, we kept in touch with him, and he was always a welcome guest at our many reunions. For me and my fellow cadets in C Squadron, our new drill instructor and mentor was to be Flight Sergeant Jack Holt. Known to the cadets as 'Bog-brush', owing to the nature of his bristly moustache, he was a man of powerful stature with a word of command that could rattle the windows of the College. Behind his formidable exterior he was a kindly man whose main concern was for the welfare and professional development of the cadets. At a late stage of my training he once called me into his office and spoke to me about the way in which I projected myself.

'The trouble with you, Mr Adcock,' he said, 'is that you don't bounce back!'

He meant, I suppose, that I took criticism too much to heart and, if I was to survive and prosper in the sometimes harsh environment of service life, I had to learn to shrug off adversity and maintain a positive outlook even when events did not turn out as well as I had hoped. This was good advice, and I was to recall and ponder on his words many times in my subsequent career. Flight Sergeant Holt was an outstanding personality who did a great deal to foster and develop the cadets under his supervision, and we were all delighted when he was awarded the British Empire Medal in a subsequent honours list.

At the beginning of our second year at the College, we began the ground school phase of our flying training, prior to beginning training in the air. The subjects covered included aerodynamics, meteorology, rules of the air, and various other subjects of professional concern to the aviator. We also visited the school of aviation medicine at RAF North Luffenham, where in small groups we were taken up to 30,000 feet in a pressure chamber and shown the effects of hypoxia – lack of oxygen. This was followed by a demonstration of a rapid decompression, simulating what would happen in the event of an ejection from the aircraft at high altitude. Although unnerving at the time, the exercise demonstrated clearly the enormous strides that the RAF had made in providing protective equipment and escape systems to cope with the demands of the jet age. On a less satisfactory note, it soon became apparent that the flying training syllabus was disconnected from the academic course that we were following in the science stream. One day we would be studying complex mathematical models in the academic classroom relating to aerodynamics or meteorology, and the next day in ground school we would be studying the same subjects in their most elementary form. As mere cadets, we were in no position to point out these anomalies. We merely put our heads down and made sure that we passed the inevitable exams so that we could move on to our flying training. But it did raise a question mark in our minds about the efficacy of the overall training programme, a question mark that came to determine our priorities towards the end of our training.

IN JANUARY 1961 THE great moment finally arrived and at last we student pilots began our basic flying training on the Jet Provost Mk 3. Built by the Hunting Percival Aircraft Company and powered by an Armstrong Siddeley Viper jet engine, the 'JP', as the aircraft was universally known, proved during its extensive service to be an excellent basic trainer. By the standards of today, the engine was not very powerful, producing some 2,500 lbs of static thrust; but it made a lot of noise, and this was regarded as a considerable bonus when compared with its much quieter predecessor, the propeller-driven piston Provost. Nevertheless, the JP could climb to 30,000 feet and cruise at about 160 knots, which was a step-change in performance when compared with previous RAF trainers. This performance brought an immediate advantage for flying training in the United Kingdom, where layers of low cloud often inhibited the less capable piston-engined types. The JP could easily climb to 10,000 feet or higher, where the training exercises could be carried out above cloud. The downside was that, because of its performance, the aircraft was fitted with equipment not usually found on a basic trainer. This equipment included a retractable undercarriage, together with its associated hydraulic system; an oxygen system, required by all aircraft capable of operating above 10,000 feet; and ejector seats which would operate at ground level provided the aircraft had attained a speed of 90 knots. Because the thrust that drove the aircraft forward was delivered from a jet-pipe beneath the tailplane at the rear of the aircraft, there was little or no countervailing torque on the airframe, and this made the aircraft very easy to fly; unlike the previous generation of piston-engined aircraft, where the rotating mass of air thrust rearwards by the propeller flowed over the tailplane, and the resulting torque had to be balanced out by the use of rudder. The lack of torque also obviated any tendency for the aircraft to swing on take-off or when landing. Furthermore, because the aircraft was fitted with a nose-wheel, rather than the tail-wheel that characterised many earlier types of trainer, it was much more stable when landing or manoeuvring on the ground.

To avoid congestion in the airspace around Cranwell, the nearby airfield of Barkston Heath, some five miles to the southwest, was also utilised for flying training, with pilots from A and B Squadrons flying from Cranwell, and those of C and D Squadrons flying from Barkston Heath. At Cranwell, the airfield was served by several large, permanent hangars, with an operations room and crew rooms built in as permanent structures. At Barkston Heath, however, the accommodation consisted merely of a collection of wooden huts, although the runway had been resurfaced in preparation for the arrival of the new aircraft. None of this mattered much to us at the time and there was a palpable sense of excitement as, for the first time, the pilots of C and D Squadrons boarded the bus outside the College for the short journey to Barkston Heath.

Earlier in the month there had been a considerable fall of snow, but for the moment the country was covered by a high pressure system that brought wonderfully clear, sunny weather, albeit with a bitingly cold northerly wind. It was a spectacular sight, flying over the snow-covered fields of Lincolnshire at 10,000 feet with a visibility of at least 30 miles and in these conditions our flying training got off to a good start. I progressed steadily through the initial exercises under the watchful eye of my flying instructor, Flight Lieutenant Dennis Southern, and within a month, after 12 hours of dual instruction, I flew my first solo sortie, consisting of one circuit at Barkston Heath, lasting 10 minutes.

In March, a new instructor, Flight Lieutenant Ridley Hall, arrived at Barkston Heath and I was assigned as one of his students. We got on well and under his tutelage I continued to progress. By now we had moved on to more complex exercises including, steep turns, stalling, spinning and aerobatics. We also trained in pilot navigation. The dual exercises were interspersed with solo sorties, which not only allowed a student to gain in confidence and skill but also to learn by making mistakes and correcting them himself. By now, the journeys back on the bus from Barkston Heath to Cranwell were filled with stories of derring-do, as individuals recalled their various exploits in the air, amidst great hilarity at the considerable ineptitude we all displayed from time to time. In the evening, over a pint or two of beer in the bar, these stories were polished and embellished, until they became part of the legend and folklore which bound us together into a tight-knit and cohesive group.

We moved on to instrument flying, wearing a hood attached to the visor of our flying helmets that prevented us from seeing anything other than the flight instruments. In those days, in the military aviation sphere, only operational RAF airfields were equipped with radar, so descents through cloud were made using UHF Direction Finding. Under this system, any radio transmission from an aircraft produced a directional spike on a cathode ray tube in front of the air traffic controller, who was able by this means to home the aircraft to the overhead. The aircraft was then turned onto a safe heading for a let-down and instructed to descend. After a period of time, which varied according to the wind strength and direction, the aircraft was turned inbound and redirected back to the airfield. Once the aircraft broke cloud and sighted the airfield, it then circled to line up with the runway in use and progressed to the landing phase of the flight. This procedure could also be used in the event of an engine failure above cloud. The aircraft was homed to the nearest airfield and began a steep spiral descent in the overhead. After breaking cloud, the excess speed was used to position the aircraft for a glide approach and landing on the airfield. Looking back from this more sophisticated age, it all seems to have been somewhat harum-scarum; nevertheless, after a bit of practice, the procedure worked quite well at the time. In those days, the whole of East Anglia was covered with military airfields, each with its own climb and descent lanes. The extraordinary thing was that, although aircraft regularly climbed and descended through cloud without any sort of radar cover, there were hardly ever any mid-air collisions. It was, however, due more to the vastness of the sky rather than human intervention that they so successfully managed to avoid each other.

As we entered the final and most demanding stages of our flying training, the strain of keeping up with the new Cranwell training syllabus took its toll, and our academic work began to suffer. Learning to fly to the very high standards required by the RAF was a taxing business involving both physical and mental effort. Consequently, a student who flew two sorties in a morning had very little energy or enthusiasm for academic study in the classroom in the afternoon. It was not unknown for students to fall asleep in the middle of lectures, and on one occasion when this happened we all tiptoed out of the lecture room leaving the sleeping cadet at his desk. Entering into the sprit of the joke, the next class silently entered the lecture room and took their places, so that the hapless cadet awoke in the midst of a new class with a new lecturer and an entirely different subject being taught, much to the amusement of everyone else in the room. Another downside to the new syllabus was that our flying training was inhibited by the need to continue with our academic studies right up to the end of our three-year course. One of the most important factors in a successful flying training programme is good continuity. Giving the vagaries of the weather in the United Kingdom, this is hard enough to achieve at the best of times. But when half the week is spent in the classroom rather than at the flights the problem becomes even more acute. Added to this, the final phase of our flying training coincided with our final academic exams, adding to the already severe pressures faced by the cadets. It was evident to us all that, in order to graduate from the College, a cadet had successfully to complete his flying training, and that is where we all individually decided to concentrate our efforts. As a result, the academic results were generally disappointing, with only two cadets in the science stream passing all the subjects required to achieve the AFRAeS requirements, while the remainder passed in only one or two subjects or, like me, none at all.

Another casualty of the new-look Cranwell syllabus was leadership training. The stated aim of the Cranwell Cadet scheme was to produce Junior Officers of high quality who would in time be capable of attaining the highest ranks in the Royal Air Force. However, the competing demands of the academic syllabus and flying training left little time for any formal training in leadership. Furthermore, the rigid structure of the cadet system did not provide many opportunities to learn from actual experience. Taking a few defaulters for extra drill, which was the most demanding leadership task faced by most senior cadets in the college, could hardly be considered as the best preparation for dealing with the complex issues which regularly arose on an operational squadron. In this respect I was more fortunate than most, as I was promoted to the cadet rank of Under Officer for my final two terms at Cranwell, and this gave me some additional minor administrative responsibilities in C Squadron. Even with this advantage, however, I did not feel over-prepared on graduation for the leadership challenges ahead. Some of the shortcomings in the syllabus were addressed informally by adventurous training carried out during the college vacations, and there were also lectures and group leadership exercises from time to time. We also enjoyed visits to operational stations, front-line Army units, and an exchange visit to the United States Air Force Academy in Colorado Springs. These visits served to expand our knowledge and give us a broader understanding of the purposes of the armed forces. As far as the practical aspects of leadership went, however, it appeared that these were something to be acquired by a process of osmosis as cadets went about their daily business in the august surroundings of the College. We were, of course, brought up in an age when ordinary people were used to obeying without question the word of those in a position of authority such as military officers, policemen, teachers, and others We were also at the height of the Cold War, as we were constantly reminded by the sight of Vulcan bombers circling in the sky above nearby RAF Waddington to the north. In such a climate, the prevailing orthodoxy was that Junior Officers were there not to innovate but to do as they were told. This attitude certainly coloured my own perception of what was required of a leader and probably inhibited my personal development in the early years of my subsequent career. Perhaps the main advantage of the cadet system was that, on graduation, the cadets joined an elite group of RAF officers who would provide an extremely influential network of contacts for the duration of their service careers and beyond. The limitations of the leadership training syllabus notwithstanding, many Cranwell graduates went on not only to serve with distinction but also to reach the highest ranks of the Royal Air Force. Given the rigorous selection process, however, and the fact that nearly all the cadets would have made their way successfully in any walk of life, it is hardly surprising that so many of them enjoyed successful and fulfilling careers as RAF officers.

Now in our last year at Cranwell, we progressed to the final stages of the flying training programme. Struggling to keep up with all the demands being made on me, I was allocated a new flying instructor. Flight Lieutenant John Farley was a very experienced pilot and instructor, and his relaxed and good-humoured approach to his duties was enormously helpful in ensuring that I completed the course successfully. After leaving the RAF, he went on to become a highly-regarded test pilot, who played a large part in ensuring that the vertical take-off and landing Hawker Harrier entered smoothly into squadron service. With his help, I completed the final stages of my flying training, including night flying, formation flying, high-level radio navigation and landing away at a strange airfield. Also included was the final stage of instrument flying, which involved being talked down to a landing while still under the blind-flying hood by means of Precision Approach Radar (PAR). Having completed 177 hours flying on the Jet Provost, including 22 hours on the recently-introduced and slightly more powerful JP4, I passed my Final Handling Test with the Squadron Commander, Squadron Leader Hughes. A few days afterwards, at a ceremony in the College lecture theatre, my fellow cadets and I were awarded our 'wings' by a famous wartime RAF leader and former Chief of the Air Staff, Sir John Slessor.

The next day, on 31 July 1962, a brilliant summer's day, we formed up for the last time on the parade ground in front of the College. The college band struck up and after the inspection we marched past the reviewing officer in slow time and in quick time. Our parents looked proudly on, no doubt astonished to see that their sons could march with such precision and look so smart. There was a fly-past of Jet Provosts in formation and then, as the band played Auld Lang Syne, the members of No 81 Entry marched up the steps of the College in slow time to take their place as commissioned officers in the illustrious ranks of the RAF.

After a formal lunch, and the departure of the guests, there was a lull in the proceedings before preparations began for the Graduation Ball that was to take place in the evening. I decided to use the time for a trip to the Post Office, which was located on the main road a few hundred yards from the College. I donned my new uniform jacket bearing my wings and put on my hat, on which the white band denoting a cadet had now been replaced by the black band of a commissioned officer. Carrying my gloves in my left hand, I marched smartly and proudly along the path to the Post Office. On the way, I met an airman approaching from the opposite direction and, as he neared me, he saluted smartly. I acknowledged his action, noticing with satisfaction from the corner of my eye, as I saluted in return, the thin blue ring of a Pilot Officer's braid on my sleeve.

'Good afternoon, Sir,' the airman said.

'Good afternoon,' I replied, smiling broadly, and continued on my way.

CHAPTER 3

Advanced Flying Training

At the end of our basic flying training we student pilots at Cranwell were divided into three streams. The so-called Fast-Jet stream was to go to RAF Valley in Anglesey to carry out advanced flying training on the Folland Gnat. The Multi-Engine stream was assigned to No 5 Flying Training School (5 FTS) at RAF Oakington, near Cambridge, to fly the Vickers Varsity. A small number of cadets were to go to RAF Shawbury, near Shrewsbury, for training on helicopters.

The struggle that I had encountered in completing the basic flying course, and my apparent lack of any natural flying ability, were noted in my end of course report, together with the comment that I would benefit from flying for a period under the supervision of an experienced captain before undertaking operational command of an aircraft. Accordingly, I was assigned to the Multi-Engine stream. I was not disappointed by this selection. Although I had successfully completed my basic flying training, and been awarded my wings, I recognised that flying did not come easily to me, and that I was always going to have to work hard at it if I was to succeed in my chosen career. In truth, I lacked confidence in my own ability, and it would be some years before I felt that I could consistently deliver an assured performance in the air. These reservations notwithstanding, I noted that many of my particular friends at the College were also assigned to the Multi-Engine stream, and I looked forward to enjoying their company on the next stage of our training.

After a spell of leave, I arrived by train at Oakington station on 19 August 1962, where I was picked up in an RAF vehicle and delivered to the Student Officers Mess. I had hoped to travel by road, but my car had been damaged in an accident and was temporarily off the road. Reaching my 21st birthday in April that year, I had inherited a small sum of money from my now deceased uncle and benefactor, Jim Woodward. The sum was not large, but it was just enough to enable me to sell my old Morris 8 and purchase a second-hand 1947 MG-TC sports car in British racing green. To own one of these cars was a young man's dream. Not only were they a delight to drive but they also brought the owner enormous kudos and status. To complete the image, I had bought myself a flat cap and a pair of string gloves. I had also grown a moustache.

Owing to my inexperience of the motoring scene, I did not at first realise that the drum brakes on the car were badly worn. During my leave I was absent from the country for several weeks participating in a climbing expedition in Turkey and, while I was away, I lent the car to my elder brother. The brakes failed as he was descending a hill and the car was involved in a collision with another vehicle. Fortunately, no-one was seriously hurt; nor was the car a complete write-off. It was, nevertheless, to languish in a garage near Leicester for several months awaiting the arrival of spare parts so that the necessary repairs could be put in hand.

The arrival of the first-ever course of Cranwell graduates to be trained at 5 FTS was not an unmitigated success. Up to that point, all the pilots under training at 5 FTS had joined the RAF as direct entrants, many of them after graduating from a university. Their lack of previous service experience meant that their officer training was undertaken in parallel with their flying training, initially at one of the Basic Flying Training Schools, and subsequently at an Advanced Flying Training School. It was put to us that we were to follow the same programme, but when we discovered that the training involved a considerable amount of drill, there was a violent outcry of protest. We argued that we had already spent three years at Cranwell, a course of training that enabled us to perform drill up to the very highest standards, and we did not see the need to carry out further training at Oakington. Nor did we see the need for any more training as officers. Graduating from Cranwell, we had already been commissioned, and all we wanted to do now was to complete our advanced flying training and move on to our Operational Conversion Units.

Surprisingly, the authorities at Oakington accepted our arguments, and from then on we were able to concentrate exclusively on our advanced flying training.

THE VICKERS VARSITY TMk1, on which we were to carry out our advanced flying training, had been introduced into the RAF in 1951 as a crew trainer. The Varsity differed from its sister aircraft, the Vickers Valetta, in that it was configured with a nose-wheel rather than a tail-wheel, and it had a bomb-aimer's compartment situated underneath the fuselage. In the parlance common at the time, the Valetta was known as 'The Pig' while the Varsity was referred to as 'The Super Pig'. Both aircraft had been designed as crew trainers, with the Varsity being used for instruction in air navigation, bomb aiming, and air signals. In our case, the aircraft was also used for pilot training. Having been designed as an aircraft that would fly sorties of several hours duration, a necessary requirement for rear crew training, the Varsity did not take kindly to being pounded round the circuit by student pilots, with the undercarriage being raised and lowered after each take-off and before each landing. These greater demands on the airframe resulted in a relatively high degree of unserviceability, which in turn delayed the flying programme. Consequently, when we started our flying training, the courses ahead of us were already behind schedule and, once again, when they were given priority, our continuity suffered.

The Varsity was powered by two Bristol Hercules 264 14-cylinder radial engines of complex design, each delivering some 2,000 horsepower. Paradoxically, before the advent of the Jet Provost, the RAF had always carried out its basic flying training on propeller driven aircraft, and its advanced flying training on jets. Now here we were having completed our basic flying training on jets and carrying our advanced flying training on a propeller-driven aircraft!

Contrary to popular belief, however, jet powered aircraft are much simpler to operate than those that are propeller-driven, particularly those with propellers that are variable in pitch. In a jet, the pilot simply moves the throttle forwards, the fuel flow is increased and, as the engine rotates faster, it develops more thrust. Apart from the fact that the aircraft accelerates, there are virtually no other complications to be taken into account.

In a piston-engined aircraft, however, moving the throttle forward opens a butterfly valve in the carburettor or supercharger, allowing more air into the cylinders and increasing the boost or manifold pressure. Extra fuel is drawn in, and the power output increases. This extra power is felt by the propeller, which automatically varies the angle or pitch of the blade, allowing it to bite off a larger chunk of air with each rotation, thereby increasing the speed of the aircraft. The extra flow of air over the control surfaces increases the torque on the airframe, and this has to be balanced out in turn by the application of rudder. To provide for maximum efficiency, the RPM of the propellers can also be varied by means of pitch control levers, adding a further complication to what is already a fairly complex process.

Before we could begin flying, we had to spend some time in the classroom learning about the engines and the airframe of the Varsity, together with other supplementary but important subjects such as propeller theory, weight and balance, air traffic control, and survival. Fortunately, the ground school was staffed by some highly capable and articulate NCOs, who were able to explain these mysteries to us in an interesting way by interspersing their lectures with stories and anecdotes drawn from their own extensive operational experience.

WE DID EVENTUALLY MAKE a start on our flying training, but progress was slow, and we suffered once again from a lack of continuity. After some 16 hours of dual instruction, I eventually went solo, although 'solo' in this instance meant flying with another student acting as co-pilot instead of an instructor. The Varsity was not a difficult aircraft to fly, and the only real hurdle was learning to cope with an engine failure on take-off. The sudden loss of power on one side of the aircraft produced a yawing moment that had to be countered by the use of rudder. At the same time, the rate of climb had to be reduced to prevent the aircraft from stalling. Finally, to reduce drag, the failed engine had to be shut down and the propeller feathered.

In those days there were no simulators in which to gain experience before trying out the manoeuvre in the air, so the first attempts were quite exciting, especially for the instructor. The really important thing was to identify correctly which engine had failed, since inadvertently to shut down the good engine would have been fatal. A boot-full of rudder was required to prevent the aircraft from yawing towards the failed engine, so the expression 'left leg is dead; left engine has failed', and vice-versa, was a good mantra to remember.

Our operating area was to the north east of Oakington, towards Ely and March, although we had to avoid the nearby airfield of RAF Waterbeach, which hosted a Hunter squadron at the time, and also RAF Wyton, to the north of us, from which operated Victor and Canberra reconnaissance aircraft. Fortunately, the Bedford Levels (or 'twin canals', as they are sometimes known) were a significant geographical feature, so it was very easy to keep track of the aircraft's position.

Unlike Cranwell, which was located in the middle of nowhere, Oakington was only a few miles from Cambridge, so we were within easy reach of civilisation. By this time, many of the students had acquired a car of sorts, so we were able to take advantage of the many delights that Cambridge had to offer, both cultural and social. There were also many good pubs in the area, providing excellent places in which to unwind after a hard days flying. With the encouragement of a fellow student, I took up golf, using an old set of clubs that had once belonged to my father, and was soon hooked on a game that I would still be playing some 50 years later. We also started a Bridge School in the Mess, and this was another game that I have continued to play right up to the present day.

During November and December of 1962 we made steady progress with our flying, but then the weather intervened. Shortly after Christmas Day there was a heavy fall of snow which blanketed almost the entire country. Returning from leave in my MG, which had finally been repaired, I travelled with difficulty by road to Oakington. The next day, at our morning briefing, we discovered that the entire airfield was covered in six inches of snow, and there was no immediate prospect of a thaw. Using snowplough blades attached to the front of fuel bowsers, an attempt was made to remove the snow from the runway and the taxiways, but the only outcome was to create an inch-thick layer of ice on all the surfaces.

Then as now, airfield operators faced the dilemma that the very high cost of efficient snow-clearing equipment could not be justified by the modest snowfall that only occasionally affected the country, so we were left waiting for nature to take a hand. In fact, it was to remain perishing cold for the next few weeks, with severe disruption affecting the entire country, and little or no prospect of any flying. We filled in the time as best we could, playing endless hands of Bridge in the crewroom, and with various other indoor activities, but January was a frustrating and depressing month.

Eventually, the thaw came, and training resumed once more. By now we were the senior course and so for once had priority. As result, we achieved some solid flying during February and March and I made good progress. By this time I had learned that I was to be posted onto the Hastings aircraft, and that my course would begin in early April. Other students, allocated to different aircraft types, found themselves in a similar situation, and the decision was taken that we would complete our so-called advanced flying training at the end of March, notwithstanding the fact that we were someway short of the number of flying hours officially prescribed by the syllabus. Having previously spent three years at Cranwell, where we had enjoyed the best that the RAF had to offer, it was perhaps inevitable that the next stage of training would come as something of an anticlimax. All told, however, the course at Oakington was a dispiriting experience, and we were all glad to be moving on to the next stage of our training.

After a week's leave, I set off in my MG to RAF Thorney Island, located on the South Coast mid-way between Portsmouth and Chichester. I had happy memories of the station from my first camp as an ATC cadet, and I was looking forward to my return visit. I was not to be disappointed, as my short stay led to some important turning points in my life. At that time Thorney Island was the home of the Operational Conversion Units for the RAF's three tactical transport aircraft: the Hastings, the Beverley and the Argosy. Unlike the Argosy, which had only recently been introduced into service, the Hastings and the Beverley had both been around for many years. The conversion course was, in consequence, well-established, and within a few days of arrival our training was well underway. As newly-trained pilots, my ex-Cranwell colleagues and I comprised only part of the course, the other pilots being older and more experienced aircrew, men who were either transferring from other aircraft types or refreshing their skills after a period on the ground.

The rest of the course comprised navigators, flight engineers and air signallers who were also converting to type. There was, therefore, a nice mixture of operational experience and youthful exuberance amongst the students, ensuring that the training was always lively and entertaining. Flight Lieutenant 'Nick' Nicholls, one of the experienced navigators refreshing his skills on the Hastings after a period spent flying other types, kept us all entertained with a series of stories, jokes and anecdotes that had us all in stitches. The various instructors took it all in good part, but payback time came with the final ground school exams. When the papers were handed out, we were looking over the questions prior to starting the exam, when there was a howl of consternation from the back of the class.

'What the bloody hell is this?' cried Nicholls, as we all turned to stare.

It transpired that the ground school instructors had banded together to prepare for him, and him alone, a special paper consisting of fiendishly difficult questions from the most arcane and obscure sections of the various training manuals. The first question, for example, posed the following problem:

"You are the captain of a transport aircraft operating more than five nautical miles from the coast at high tide, when you discover that one of your passengers has forgotten his life jacket. List your actions in order of priority." And so on...

After the dust had settled and order had been restored, he was eventually given the same paper as the rest of us; one that we all passed without difficulty. We then moved on to the flying stage of our training.

The Handley Page Hastings had entered into RAF service in 1948 as a long-range general purpose transport aircraft, just in time to play a significant part in the Berlin Airlift. A derivative of the wartime Halifax bomber, the Hastings was powered by four Bristol Hercules 101 sleeve-valve radial engines, each developing some 2,000 horsepower. Fully laden, the aircraft could carry 50 fully-equipped troops, 30 paratroops or 32 stretchers. The commercial variant of the aircraft, the Hermes, had been designed with a conventional nose-wheel, but the Hastings was equipped with a tail-wheel. Folklore had it that the purpose of this design was so that a heavy beam could be fitted underneath the fuselage, thereby allowing bulky items of equipment, such as a vehicle or a piece of artillery, to be carried externally. At some point in the life of the aircraft the RAF must have considered this arrangement to be too dangerous, because I never heard of it being used in practice. The tail-wheel configuration did, however, leave a significant legacy for the pilots, as the aircraft was inherently unstable on the ground. What this meant in practice was that once the aircraft departed from the direction in which it was travelling while taxying, taking-off or landing, it would continue to turn at an ever-increasing rate until corrective action was taken by the pilot. Because of this, taxying the aircraft was not easy. To inaugurate a turn, the pilot had to apply a bit of outboard throttle, accompanied by a dab of inboard brake. After a few moments, allowing for inertia, the aircraft would begin to respond to these inputs and start to turn. To prevent the turn from speeding up, it was then necessary to close the outboard throttle and apply a bit of inboard throttle instead. With just the right application of power, the aircraft would then turn at a constant rate until it was time to straighten up, when the whole process had to be reversed. Needless to say, we ex-Cranwell students, who had been trained almost entirely on nose-wheeled aircraft, took some time to adjust to this new set of circumstances.

The problems encountered when taxying were even more acute during the take-off and landing phases of flight, because at higher speeds the aircraft had considerable inertia, so it took longer for any corrective action to take effect. Thus any tendency for the aircraft to swing could be countered by the application of rudder, but it took a moment or two for the control input to take effect, for which due allowance had to be made. In the pregnant pause between the application of rudder and the aircraft's response to the controls, it was easy to over-correct and hence induce a more violent swing in the opposite direction. In extreme cases, this could result in the aircraft leaving the runway, and this what happened to me on my third attempt at a take-off. I pushed the four throttles forward and the engines opened up with a mighty roar; as we gathered speed, I pushed the stick forward to raise the tail-wheel off the ground. Then, without any apparent warning, the aircraft suddenly swung abruptly to the right. By the time I recovered from my surprise, and began tentatively to apply corrective rudder, it was far too late.

'Don't try and straighten it,' my instructor called, grabbing the controls, 'take it across the grass.'

And to the amazement of everyone on the airfield, the huge aircraft lumbered across the grass, miraculously avoiding all obstacles, and eventually gained sufficient speed to get airborne. Astonishingly, a subsequent check by Air Traffic Control revealed that no damage had been done to the runway lights or any other equipment on the airfield.

LIKE MANY RAF STATIONS, where the old wartime runway had been extended to accommodate larger, faster and heavier post-war aircraft, Thorney Island had a public road that ran across the airfield to the Officers Mess and Married Quarters. The crossing was controlled by traffic lights operated by Air Traffic Control, who allowed vehicles across when there was a sufficient gap between the landing aircraft. Sometimes, when the circuit was busy, which it often was, and this coincided with a lot of vehicular movement, such as happened at lunchtime, long queues would build up at the lights. And so it was that one of my fellow students, who had departed the runway after a violent swing on landing, was heard to remark that 'he didn't so much mind going off the runway, but what really upset him was waiting in the line of traffic for the lights to turn green so that he could taxi back on again!' After this incident he was transferred to the Blackburn Beverley, which was far less prone to such erratic behaviour.

Not only was the Hastings unstable on the ground but it was also difficult to land. The aircraft had been designed long before the advent of powered flying controls, so a considerable amount of manual effort was required to manoeuvre the aircraft in the air. Furthermore, when the throttles were closed prior to touchdown on landing, there was a significant tendency for the nose of the aircraft to pitch down. This change of pitch could be anticipated by trimming the aircraft nose up in the final stages of the approach, so that the pilot had to push hard on the control column to keep the descent going. Then, as the aircraft crossed the threshold of the runway, and the flight engineer closed the throttles, the pilot went from pushing forward to pulling back the control column with as much force as he could muster. Providing this manoeuvre was carried out with exemplary timing, the aircraft would transition from a nose-down to a nose-up attitude, and land gently on the main-wheels. Inevitably, it took the students some time to acquire the necessary judgement and skill to consistently accomplish this manoeuvre. In the interim, there were some spectacular results. To cushion the shock of landing, the huge undercarriage had been designed on the principle of rapid hydraulic compression and slow pneumatic expansion. When a heavy landing occurred, as it often did in training, this resulted in a kind of kangaroo hop, as the shock of the landing was absorbed by the rapid compression of the hydraulic fluid in the undercarriage legs, and then slowly released by compressed air. After a really solid landing, the aircraft might perform four or five of these hops before all the energy in the system was dissipated, much to the general amusement of the rear crew and any interested outside observers.

With aircrew training being carried out concurrently on the Hastings, the Beverley and the Argosy, the Mess was full to bursting, and some lively evenings were spent in the bar exchanging stories about our various escapades in the air. The Mess also had a block membership at two golf clubs in the area, where officers were entitled to play through a monthly subscription to a sports fund. On neighbouring Hayling Island there was a delightful and challenging 18-hole course where one could play at any time for a modest fee of 2/6d (12.5p in today's money). Further to the east it was possible to play Goodwood Golf Course without a fee merely on production of an RAF officer's identity card. I also joined the station Dramatic Society and took part in a performance of the farce 'Reluctant Heroes'. During mid-course leave, I drove to Newhaven, crossed the Channel by ferry to Dieppe, and spent a few days in Paris sightseeing in the delightful company of a young Frenchwoman whom I had met in Cambridge during my sojourn at Oakington.

AS SPRING MERGED SEAMLESSLY into summer, there was a vibrant and active social life to be found along the south coast. One of our favourite spots was an establishment in Portsmouth called the Pomme d'Or, where there was a bar, music and dancing. It was here that I met a young Irish woman, a nurse who was qualifying as a midwife at St Mary's hospital in the town. She told me that her name was Breda, an anglicised version of her Gaelic name in Ireland. We arranged to meet again, and soon afterwards I invited her to the Officers Mess Summer Ball. I still have a photograph taken at the event, in which we look youthful and innocent; me in my mess kit, Breda in her first ball-gown, and both of us holding cigarettes, as was the fashion in those days. On another occasion, she agreed to walk with me while I played a round of golf at Hayling Island. It was a beautiful summer afternoon as we left Portsmouth in my open sports car, but the traffic was dense and we crawled along the coast road towards Havant. Then, as we turned onto the long causeway that links Hayling Island with the mainland, the traffic cleared, and I was able to put my foot down. I roared past a Jaguar that appeared to be idling along the road. As I did so, however, a motorcycle overtook me and a long black arm motioned for me to pull over.

'Did you realise, Sir, that when you overtook that Jaguar you were doing 42 miles per hour in a 30 miles per hour zone?' asked the policeman.

'Oh goodness me, no,' I replied, trying to sound as innocent and guilt-free as I could manage,

'Can I see your driving licence, Sir?'

I duly handed over the document, which he studied for a moment. He looked at my companion, sitting serene and lovely in a blue and white spotted summer dress, with her hair tousled by the wind, and then his gaze turned back to me.

'You wouldn't want the other officers in the Mess to know that you had been stopped for speeding, would you?'

Realising that he had deduced my status from the address on the licence, I answered as innocently as I could, 'Oh no, officer.' 'Certainly not.' My mouth was so full of humble pie that I could hardly speak.

'Well, just watch your speed in future, then, and be on your way.'

'Right, officer! Thank you, officer!'

I drove on carefully, observing every speed limit that we came to on the way. After the golf, sitting in the Art Deco club house overlooking the golf course and the sea, I realised that I had succumbed to the beauty and Irish charm of my companion. I also knew by then, however, that she had already been accepted for a nursing job in New York, while I was to be posted to Cyprus.

So our lives were heading in different directions, and it appeared that it would be some time, if ever, before we were to meet again.

CHAPTER 4

With 70 Squadron in Cyprus

Having completed the Hastings OCU and successfully passed my final handling test, I was detached to RAF Abingdon, near Oxford, for a few weeks, where we underwent a short course in dropping parachutists and supplies from the Hastings. After that I enjoyed a several days of pleasant summer leave at my home before taking up my posting to Cyprus. I had previously stayed a couple of nights in the Officers Mess at RAF Nicosia when, at the end of my Cranwell training, I took part in an expedition to the Taurus Mountains in southern Turkey. Our small group had been made very welcome by the permanent residents of the Mess, who went out of their way to offer us hospitality, and I was looking forward to renewing the acquaintance. I was also excited and not a little apprehensive about taking up my first operational appointment. The only downside to the posting was that I had to sell my MG, which was eventually snapped up for song by a dealer in Nottingham.

At the beginning of October, 1963, I travelled to RAF Lyneham in Wiltshire, where I boarded a Comet of 216 Squadron for a flight to RAF Akrotiri, a large airfield on the south coast of the island of Cyprus. The final stage of my journey from Akrotiri to Nicosia was made in an RAF bus. My tour of duty took place in the days before the advent of mass tourism, and Cyprus was not at that time regarded as a holiday destination. Indeed, the EOKA[1] troubles had only recently come to an end. Consequently, in political terms, Cyprus was still feeling its way as a newly-independent state.

There being no charter flights, the island was served only by a daily schedule from Greece and from Turkey. Unless a ride could be hitched on a military aircraft, the cost of returning to the UK was beyond the pocket of most servicemen. Once posted to Cyprus, you could, therefore, expect to remain on the island for the duration of your tour of duty lasting some

[1] EOKA was a Greek Cypriot nationalist paramilitary organisation that fought a campaign for the end of British rule in Cyprus, as well as for self-determination and for union with Greece. The insurgency lasted from 1955 to 1960, when Cyprus achieved independence.

2½ to 3 years. As a pilot on an air transport squadron, I was to be, in this respect, more fortunate than most.

No 70 Squadron, also known as LXX Squadron, was formed at Farnborough in 1916 and during the First World War took part in operations on the Western Front. In 1920 the squadron reformed at Heliopolis in Egypt and, since then, had operated continuously in the bomber and air transport roles from various locations in the Middle East. In 1955 it re-equipped with the Hastings and moved to RAF Nicosia in Cyprus. As part of the Near East Air Force (NEAF), the squadron's role included air transport operations, parachute dropping, and search and rescue. At the time when I joined the squadron, it had perhaps a dozen aircraft and there were about eighteen six-man crews. The only other operational squadron on the base at that time was 29 Squadron (XXIX Squadron), which operated the Javelin all-weather fighter in the air defence role.

70 Squadron's motto was *Usquam* (everywhere) and that is where our operations took us. A regular weekly task for the squadron was to fly fresh fruit and vegetables, obtained from the market in Nicosia, to the staging post at RAF El Adem near Tobruk in Libya. Other tasks took us further west to RAF Luqa in Malta, to RAF Idris, near Tripoli in Western Libya, and to RAF Gibraltar. In the east we carried oxygen bottles and other aircraft support equipment to various airfields in Turkey and Iran. Further south and east our tasks took us to the Persian Gulf and round the coast of the Arabian Peninsula, calling at Bahrain, Masirah, Sharjah and Aden.

During the summer it was fearfully hot, with the temperature often exceeding 40°C (104°F),[1] while in the winter it could be bitterly cold. On one occasion, during a night stop in Ankara, the temperature dropped to -32°C (-27°F), which was technically outside the limit for starting the engines. Our highly experienced flight engineer said that it would probably be all right to give it a go, and the engines started without difficulty. To provide warm air for the cockpit and the cabin, heat-exchangers drew hot air from the engine exhausts. Because the aircraft were old, however, the seals around the large freight doors at the rear of the cabin leaked like a sieve, so it was always boiling hot at the front of the aircraft and freezing cold at the back. Furthermore, the aircraft was not equipped with weather radar, and once in cloud it was difficult to know what lay ahead.

On one trip, from Aden to Nicosia, we took off at midnight and followed a course northwards over the Red Sea. Our route took us over the Sinai

[1] At the time, Fahrenheit was used as the normal scale for temperature, and only later was the change made to the Celsius scale.

Peninsula, and here we ran into some particularly severe thunderstorms. Having lumped and bumped our way in the dark for about 30 minutes, with ice covering the windscreen, and the engines coughing and spluttering in an effort to keep the fuel flowing, we turned sharp left following the airway towards Cairo. Within a few minutes we emerged from the clouds into clear air, just as dawn was breaking. Looking back, we could see a long line of thunderstorms, through which we had just flown, flashing and banging over the hills of the peninsula. It was now obvious to us that, if only we had known to route over the sea, just a few miles further west, we could have avoided the storms altogether.

Like many piston-engined aircraft of the day, the Hastings suffered its fair share of technical problems, to the extent that when we set off on a trip we were never quite sure when we would return. My very first route trip after joining the squadron was from Nicosia to Çigli, a Turkish Air Force Base near Izmir in western Turkey. I was acting as copilot for the Squadron Commander, Squadron Leader Johnny Grobler, and after dropping off our cargo we were delayed on the return journey by a 'mag drop'. When the engines were run up prior to take-off, and each of the two magnetos on each engine switched off in turn, an excessive drop in rpm on one of the engines indicated a fault, possibly brought about by excessive engine oil fouling one of the spark plugs. The aircraft was shut down and various attempts at rectification ensued, but all to no avail. It was decided that spare parts were needed; the problem was how to get hold of them.

There were no mobile phones in those far off days, and even the fixed telecommunications systems were hard to access in a foreign country, and not always reliable. Fortunately, the RAF operated a Flight Watch system on its routes to the East, where a series of powerful High Frequency (HF) radio transmitters enabled communications to be maintained between aircraft en route and their various operating authorities. By means of the aircraft's HF radio and the use of Morse code, the signaller was able to pass a message back to the NEAF Operations Centre requesting help. Given the remoteness of our location, it was clear that help would be some time arriving, so we decamped to a hotel in the town and prepared ourselves for a long wait. Having reconsidered the problem overnight, the flight engineer suggested that he might be able to fix the problem himself, so in the morning we returned to the airfield, where we enjoyed a substantial breakfast at a United States Air Force detachment located on the base. Suitably fortified, and with some borrowed tools, the engineer removed the ignition harness from the affected engine and, with the help of our new-found American friends, he sand-blasted each of the 28 spark plugs to ensure that all the contacts were clean and bright. Then he reassembled the engine and, with the assistance of the rest of the crew, gave it a ground run which showed that it was now working satisfactorily. By now it was too late to go anywhere so, having cancelled the earlier request for assistance, we returned to the hotel for another night. The next day we completed the return trip to Nicosia without further incident. We were three days late on our original schedule.

On another occasion I was a member of a crew tasked to fly the Cyprus Go-Cart Team and their supporters to RAF Idris. The championships took place over a week-end, and our instructions were to carry out some training during our stay. In the course of a highly challenging low-level cross-country over the vast reaches of the Libyan desert, the engineer reported that an oil slick could be seen coming from a spinner on the hub of one of the propellers. The Captain decided to shut the engine down and return to base. Inspection on the ground revealed that an oil seal in the propeller mechanism was leaking and a replacement part would be needed in order to rectify the problem. Once again, various messages were sent requesting assistance. The next day a signal arrived from HQ NEAF saying that all service personnel were to return to Cyprus on the Monday 'MEDAIR', a charter flight that linked the various RAF bases in the Mediterranean. The go-karts and the supporters were to return on the Hastings when it had been rectified. As the supporters comprised about a dozen wives of the participants, this led to some merry parties in the Transit Mess before we eventually returned on the Wednesday.

Not all engine failures were so benign. On a trip from Nicosia to Teheran, carrying a hefty load of oxygen cylinders, we lost an engine over the mountains of eastern Turkey. Unable to maintain our cruising height of 18,000 feet, we drifted down and eventually stabilised at some 14,000 feet with maximum continuous power applied to the remaining three engines. Fortunately, it was mid-summer, without a cloud in the sky, and we were able to see clearly the peaks of the mountains sliding by on either side. Had it been winter, with the possibility of thunderstorms and cloud covering the mountain ranges, our plight would have been perilous indeed. Luckily, with the prevailing conditions as favourable as they were, and due to the airmanship and skill of the captain, Flight Lieutenant Geoff Norton, we landed safely at Teheran International Airport without further ado.

Another incident occurred when I was returning from a trip to Aden and the Persian Gulf with the Station Commander at Nicosia, Group Captain Campbell. It was the final trip of his tour of duty in Cyprus and, during our stay in Aden, he had taken the opportunity to stock up with some high-value duty-free goods. The final leg of the trip was to take us from Bahrain to Nicosia, and hardly had we settled into the cruise when one of the engines developed a fault and had to be shut down. At this point we still had about a thousand miles of the barren Iraqi desert to transit, followed by a sea crossing to Cyprus. The prudent course of action would clearly have been to return to Bahrain and have the engine repaired. However, the Group Captain, who was a highly-experienced Hastings captain, ruminated on the problem for a few moments, and then he said, 'I think we'll press on.' Not long afterwards the cylinder head temperature gauge on one of the other engines decided to stop working. Despite these difficulties, we limped on, and eventually landed safely at Nicosia.

Minor servicing of the aircraft was carried out on the flight-line at Nicosia, but for major servicing they were flown back to RAF Colerne, a Hastings base in the UK. As my first Christmas on the squadron approached, I was offered the opportunity, along with some of the other bachelor crew members, to fly one of aircraft back to the UK for a major service. We would then be able to spend Christmas at home and return on a passenger flight a few days later. As a seasonal gift, I bought a large wicker basket filled with oranges and lemons in the market at Nicosia, and took it with me on the aircraft. After a night-stop in Malta, we duly arrived at Lyneham, where we cleared customs and left the aircraft to be collected by a crew from Colerne. An RAF bus took the navigator and me to Swindon station, where we were to catch a train to London. As we reached the bottom of the steps leading up to the platform we heard the train approaching. Carrying the basket of fruit between us, we attempted to rush up the steps, but in our haste the basket caught the very top step and tipped over. To the amazement of the waiting passengers, dozens of oranges and lemons rolled along the platform. Willing hands helped us to recover all the fruit in record time and we boarded the train with only seconds to spare before it departed.

Arriving home a few days before Christmas, and tired after my long journey, I went to bed early and slept soundly. The next morning I was astonished to pick up the morning paper and see from the headlines that a serious outbreak of violence had occurred between the Greek and the Turkish communities in Cyprus. As far as I knew, the British military organisations in Cyprus had had no warning that serious trouble was about to erupt, and now here was the island in flames all around. Concerned as I was for my colleagues at RAF Nicosia, I have to admit that my first thought was for the second-hand Sunbeam Rapier that I had recently purchased from a dealer in the town, which was even then parked outside my billet behind the Mess! My return to the island by air was delayed by several days, as all available aircraft were being used to airlift troops, whose role for some time to come would be to keep the warring parties apart along a cordon known as the 'green line'. When I did eventually manage to return, it was to find that most of the aircraft and crews from Nicosia had been detached to the more secure base of Akrotiri. After several weeks of detached operations, we eventually returned to Nicosia, where I was mightily relieved to find that all my possessions and my precious car were still intact.

For some months the political situation on the island remained extremely tense. In a strange reversal of recent history, British service personnel were held in high regard by the local population, as they kept the two warring factions apart. Off base, we had to travel in uniform, but that apart there were no other restrictions on our movement, and we received a friendly welcome as we made our way through the various temporary check-points that had sprung up to restrict access between the Greek and Turkish communities. Meanwhile, back at the Squadron, life went on much as normal. To maintain proficiency, each captain was required to carry out monthly continuation training by day and night, and on these exercises a full crew was always carried. The training would involve climbing out to the east or the west before returning for a let-down using a Non-Directional Beacon (NDB) located in the vicinity of the airfield, and then circling from the approach for a visual circuit and what was termed in those days a 'roller' landing.[1] After touchdown, once the aircraft had settled firmly on the runway, the throttles were opened to full power and a further take-off initiated. Other exercises followed, with the final one usually involving an approach and landing with one engine shut down. From a copilot's perspective, these sorties were an opportunity to watch and learn while the captain worked his way through the mandatory exercises. Occasionally, however, the captain would hand over control so that the copilot could have a go at a let-down or a circuit, and in this way we gradually gained experience. There was an allocation of hours specifically for copilot training, which was carried out under the supervision of one of the squadron instructors. The aircraft, however, were often unserviceable and, because copilot training had the lowest priority, it didn't come round very often. Nevertheless, as the months passed, I slowly became more proficient as I gained in experience and skill.

As is the way in learning new skills, however, it is often a matter of one step forward and two steps back. Every six months I had to undertake a proficiency check with the Wing Pilot, the designated Hastings examiner at RAF Nicosia. In the course of my first such check, the examiner and I worked our way through the various exercises required by the test schedule and all went well until we came to the final asymmetric landing. My approach was reasonably accurate and the touchdown was smooth. No sooner had we landed, however, when the aircraft decided to take a sudden

[1] In modern aviation terminology, these are now known as 'touch and go' landings.

swing to the right. I corrected with left rudder, but the inertia of the aircraft was such that it failed to respond and continued instead towards the edge of the runway. In desperation I now applied full rudder together with a generous helping of left brake, just at the moment when the aircraft overcame its inertia and began to respond to my initial input to the controls. The result was that the aircraft reversed its course and took a violent swing to the left, so that we now came perilously close to the left-hand edge of the runway before I finally managed to bring it under control. Having encroached upon the soft area at the edge of the concrete runway, the aircraft threw up a huge pall of dust and sand which could be seen without difficulty by everyone on the station. As a result of this incident I was given some additional training and also assigned to one of the most experienced captains on the squadron, but it was some time before I was able to live the incident down.

As well as flying duties, officers on the squadron also had what were termed 'secondary duties'. These were routine tasks on the station of an administrative nature. I was 'volunteered' by my colleagues to become the Mess Entertainments Officer. On overseas units the Officers Mess, the Sergeants Mess and the Airmen's Mess were the focus of social life for everyone on the station, and RAF Nicosia was no exception. As a member of the Mess Committee, my job was to organise and deliver a series of social events. We had regular dances, for which I booked and paid the bands, and in the summer we had Sunday Night Films on the patio under the stars. There were visiting shows, to raise the morale of the troops, and there were more formal events, such as the annual Battle of Britain Cocktail Party, at which we hosted civic dignitaries from the local community. There were also formal Dining-in Nights. In the summer we had 'shipwreck' parties at the station swimming pool (come as you were when the ship went down). The great event of the year in the Mess was the annual New Year's Eve Fancy Dress Ball, to which almost everyone came. With few other distractions to occupy their time, people put an inordinate amount of effort into making their costumes, and these parties really went with a swing. The festive atmosphere was helped along by the fact that all drinks were duty free and a brandy sour cost 6d (2½p in today's money). My responsibilities for organising many of these events were made considerably easier by the Mess staff, local employees who were not only very well-versed in the traditions of Mess life but also ensured that the events themselves ran smoothly and efficiently.

I was also responsible for the condition of the squadron mascot, a Shetland pony named 'Bruneval'. Prior too my arrival on the unit, the mascot had been presented to the squadron by the Second Battalion of the Parachute Regiment to mark the close co-operation between the two units in the Middle East over many years. Bruneval was the name of a small village near the coast in Normandy from which the Paras had, in one of their most daring raids of the Second World War, snatched a top secret radar installation from under the noses of the Germans. The presentation of the mascot was, therefore, an event of considerable magnitude. At a big parade attended by various high-ranking officers, the little pony had been transferred to the squadron with due pomp and ceremony. Unlike the Army, however, the RAF was not geared-up to look after horses, and the presence of Bruneval on the station posed some almost insuperable administrative problems. At first he was housed in the stables of the riding club but, being a stallion of diminutive stature, he created mayhem among the mares. Furthermore, when he did appear on parade, he disgraced himself by showing his sexual longings in a most obvious and physical way. After various other shenanigans, the exasperated Wing Commander in charge of Administration on the station was forced to conclude that 'the only way to keep this horse quiet is to keep him in a constant state of post-erotic lassitude.' All this I learned from Bruneval's file; because, when I became responsible for his well -being, he had already been found a new and permanent home in Limassol Zoo. Consequently, my duty consisted merely of driving down to Limassol once a month, inspecting the horse, and reporting on his condition when I returned to Nicosia. Whenever I saw him, however, he always looked very contented in his little compound, which he shared with a camel. The camel, too, always had a very supercilious and self-satisfied look on its face.

Apart from social activities on the Station, there were also many off-base activities to be pursued. During the hot summer months there were picnics and barbecues on the almost deserted beaches of the north coast to the east of Kyrenia. I joined the Mountain Rescue Team, a small RAF cadre based at Nicosia, and spent many an enjoyable week-end climbing and camping with the hardy bunch of NCOs who comprised the professional element of the unit. I also played golf at a 9-hole course owned by the Cyprus Mining Corporation. The course was located at Morphou Bay on the north west coast of the island where, in the extreme heat of the summer, a cooling breeze blew in off the sea. There was grass on the fairways, but the 'greens' were constructed from rolled sand mixed with oil, and were known locally as 'browns'. There was also a 9-hole golf course in Nicosia, but it fell right in the middle of the Green Line. After the outbreak of inter-communal hostilities, it gradually fell into disrepair, as no-one would take responsibility for looking after it. Rumour had it that the day after the troubles started four English ladies came out to play. Approached by an armed faction of one of the warring parties and told that they could not play there any more, one of the ladies is reported to have said in a cut-glass accent, 'I say, are you members?' In the winter I played basketball for the station in a sports hall on the outskirts of Nicosia. So although we were inhibited to some extent by the political and military situation on the island, we were still able to maintain a full, active and highly enjoyable lifestyle.

After I had been on the squadron for some nine months, an opportunity came up to fill temporarily the post of Flying Wing Adjutant while the permanent incumbent was on leave. I hesitated and, before I could make up my mind, the job went to another junior officer on the squadron. My hesitation occurred partly because I was scheduled to go on an interesting trip to Aden and the Gulf, and I didn't want to miss it. But I also hesitated because, like everyone else on the squadron, I was in awe of the Wing Commander Flying, who had a fearsome reputation, and I was nervous about working in close proximity to him. It was several years before I realised that junior officers in the RAF have only limited opportunities in which to shine, and that they should therefore endeavour to take every advantage of them when they do come up.

Wing Commander Peter Bairsto, aka 'The Bear', was a forceful character with a background in fighters. He flew the Hastings occasionally, but he was probably more at home in the Javelin. Shortly before he was due to move on to another assignment he decided to make one last sortie in the Hastings, and I was assigned as his copilot. We went through the usual upper air exercises and then returned to Nicosia for some circuits and landings. The Wing Commander made a steady first approach, but when we arrived at the threshold he flared about five feet above the ground and, as the speed decayed, the aircraft touched down with an almighty crash, followed immediately by a series of kangaroo hops down the runway. He opened the throttles and we took off again for another circuit. Once more we approached, and again he flared too high, with the same shattering result. As we took off for another circuit I could sense the rear crew exchanging glances between each other, although they were too polite to make the usual raucous comments over the intercom that normally accompanied such occasional disasters. The third and final attempt produced and equally catastrophic result, after which he handed over the controls to me saying gruffly, 'I think you'd better have a go.' By now I had mastered the art of landing the Hastings, and on my first attempt the wheels kissed the ground smoothly as we touched down. Round we went again and once more I managed the smoothest of smooth landings. My third and final attempt was even better, with a landing so smooth that you could hardly tell that we were on the ground – 'like a gnat peeing on velvet' - as one of the rear crew was to describe it later when recounting the story. As we left the aircraft, and walked back to the squadron building, the Wing Commander was gracious enough to say to me, 'Well, you seem to have overcome your earlier problems.' Many years later I was to fly with him again under very different circumstances and when we met I felt honoured by the fact that he remembered me at once.

Other skills that had to be mastered on the aircraft were those of low flying and dropping parachutists and supplies. For training purposes, these were normally combined together into one exercise, with a low-level navigation route followed by a delivery onto a dropping zone (DZ) near the airfield. Usually, we dropped what were known as SEAC packs. These were wicker containers loaded with supplies of one sort or another which could be delivered by air to troops on the ground. They were first used during the Second World War in what was then known as South East Asia Command, where they proved to be a very useful means of re-supply. The Hastings was fitted with a pair of large freight doors opening at the rear of the fuselage on the port side. A carpet of roller-conveyer was laid over the floor of the aircraft on which were mounted the SEAC containers, each with its own parachute attached. As the aircraft approached the DZ, speed was reduced and the freight doors opened. At the calculated release point, a green light in the cabin was switched on by the pilot and the Air Load-master released the brake holding the SEAC packs in place. With aircraft now in a relatively high nose-up attitude, the packs hurtled down the roller conveyer, turned through 90 degrees by means of a protective metal screen at the rear of the freight doors, and shot out of the opening like an express train. Provided everything went according to plan, the packs floated gently down on their parachutes and landed in a line right across the centre of the DZ, where a ground party was waiting to recover them.

Of course, not everything went according to plan. Because of the relatively small land mass of Cyprus, much of the low flying was carried out over the sea. As the aircraft was not fitted with a radar altimeter, height over the water had to be assessed visually. Under calm conditions, and with a glassy surface, this was not easily done, especially when flying into the sun. On one occasion, when such conditions prevailed, the pilot in command flew so low that the inboard propellers touched the water, resulting in the instant failure of the number 2 and 3 engines. Fortunately, because of the dihedral of the wings, the outboard engines were few inches higher above the surface than those inboard, otherwise disaster would surely have followed. In the event, with full power applied to the outboard engines, the aircraft was climbed to sufficient height above the sea to allow a recovery to Akrotiri. There the aircraft remained for several weeks, looking sad and lonely, with the propellers of the two inboard engines twisted out of all recognition. After all four engines had been replaced, and numerous checks carried out for signs of overstress, the aircraft was returned to service with the squadron. Following the incident, the Captain was Court Martialled and charged with 'negligently damaging one of Her Majesty's aircraft'. Although he was found guilty, the Board must have had some sympathy with his predicament because, as far as I can recall, he was given a severe reprimand and a modest fine. In the circumstances, he escaped lightly.

On 6 July 1965, towards the end of my second year on the squadron, a Hastings aircraft from RAF Colerne was involved in a fatal accident in the course of taking off from RAF Abingdon with a load of paratroops on board. Forty-one military personnel lost their lives. As a result of the crash, all the Hastings aircraft were grounded pending the results of an inquiry into the cause of the accident. It soon became obvious that the aeroplanes would not be back in action for some considerable time, so I took advantage of the hiatus to return to the UK on what was known as 'Luck-Free Leave'. Under this scheme, single personnel serving in Cyprus were given the opportunity once during their tour to take home leave with a guaranteed passage in each direction on a military aircraft. Shortly before my flight home on a Comet from Akrotiri, I had a letter from my Irish girl-friend, with whom I had kept in touch, saying that she was returning from America and would be at her home in Ireland for a few months until she had decided what she wanted to do next. I decide there and then that a short holiday in Ireland would be in order once I had concluded my filial responsibilities at home. Breda arranged for me to lodge with one of her married sisters, and we met up when I arrived at Dublin airport, having flown by Aer Lingus from Birmingham. It soon became apparent to us both that our feelings towards each other were unchanged, and at the end of the week, while walking by the lake in Killarney, I asked her if she would marry me. This she agreed to do, although quite how we were going to accomplish the marriage was not yet clear to either of us, as I still had some nine months to serve overseas in order to complete my tour of duty. At the end of the week she returned with me to England to meet my parents and other members of my family. We did not mention our intention to marry at the time because of the uncertainty of our future plans. In the event, however, we decided that on my return to 70 Squadron I would put an advertisement in the Cyprus Mail and see if a job for her could be found locally.

At the end of August I returned to duty only to find that all the Hastings were still grounded. The accident inspectors had quickly discovered that the crash occurred because of a fatigue fracture of the hinge-bolt bracket that connected the elevator to the tail plane, and now a programme was in hand to modify all the aircraft with a view to preventing any further occurrence. In fact, none of the squadron's aircraft came back on line until the middle of October. Meanwhile, to carry out some of the essential services, the squadron had acquired a Valetta, the two-engined aircraft also known as 'the Pig'. The task of flying this aircraft was assigned to Flight Lieutenant Peter Crampton, a very experienced captain, who normally carried out the squadron's VIP tasks. I was nominated as his copilot. The cockpit layout of the Valetta was similar to that of the Varsity, on which I had not so long ago carried out my advanced flying training, so the transition to the new aircraft was fairly straightforward. We carried out a local training sortie and, a few days later, an air test. Then we were ready to take the aircraft en route.

Our task was to fly a load of fresh fruit and vegetables from Nicosia to RAF El Adem; so, with the petrol tanks filled to the brim, we were at our absolute maximum all-up weight. It was about noon when we took off on the last day of September, and still very hot, with the temperature well above 38°C (100°F). We rumbled down the runway, slowly gathering speed, and lurched into the air. We had barely reached 300 feet when there was an urgent call on the intercom from the Air Loadmaster who said, 'Captain! There's oil pouring from the starboard engine.' 'I'll come back and have a look,' he replied, and without further ado he handed over control of the aircraft to me, climbed out of his seat, removed his headset, and started back towards the cabin. While he was doing this I noticed the oil pressure on the starboard engine gauge suddenly drop to zero. Turning in my seat, I just managed to grab the sleeve of the captain's flying suit, and pointed urgently at the gauge with my finger. Without hesitation, he reached over my shoulder and pulled the starboard throttle to idle. Then he pulled the RPM lever back through the feathering gate and pressed the button that operated the feathering pump. At the same time he motioned me to start turning back towards the airfield. This was easier said than done as the starboard engine came to a sudden stop with the propeller in the feathered position, and I was left trying to hold off the yaw with a boot-full of left rudder, while at the same time keeping the aircraft in a shallow climb without letting the airspeed decay. Even then the drama was not over, because the aircraft was equipped with lightweight headsets, which were different in design from those we normally used in the Hastings. In his haste to return to his seat, the captain grabbed his headset and rammed it onto his head, but with the microphone boom round the back of his neck instead of in front of his lips. Eventually communication was restored and with it some sort of order in the cockpit. The captain took control and, without further ado, carried out a visual circuit followed by a successful asymmetric landing. The entire flight was over in less than ten minutes, although at the time it seemed like a week. It also turned out to be my last ever flight in a Valetta.

In the meant time, on the domestic front, the advertisement for a nursing post was answered by a Greek-Cypriot doctor who ran a clinic in Nicosia. In due course Breda took the job, travelling out to Cyprus via Athens on a commercial flight, and taking up residence in the clinic where she was to work. After nearly two years of separation, we were now able to see each other almost on a daily basis. Later in the year we became officially engaged, and in February 1966 we were married in the Roman Catholic Church at RAF Nicosia in the presence of all the squadron officers and their ladies. After a formal reception in the Mess, we flew by Cedar Airlines to Beirut, where we spent our honeymoon. It was a very romantic affair, the only downside being that, because of the high cost of travel, none of our respective family members was able to attend the wedding. We rented a small house in the suburbs of Nicosia, not far from Breda's place of work, and there we lived until the time came for me to return home at the end of my tour. I had learned by now that I was to become a flying instructor, and I was looking forward to my new responsibilities.

Looking back on those amazing years at Nicosia, I realise that I was fortunate to experience life overseas as it must have been almost since RAF aircraft were deployed to the Middle East in the early 1920s. The limitations on travel and the lack of instant communication with the outside world led to a closeness and camaraderie on the squadron that could never be replicated today. Hardy and self-sufficient, we went about our daily tasks in a determined and pragmatic way, taking pride in our ability to get the job done notwithstanding the often hostile and rugged environment in which we had to work. But even as I winged my way back to England with my new wife, things were already changing. A decision was taken to relocate the units from Nicosia to the more secure location of Akrotiri, and within a few months my former Station was to close. Then the Hastings aircraft were withdrawn from service and 70 Squadron re-equipped with the Argosy. Not long afterwards, the unit underwent another drastic change, when after almost half a century of service in the Middle East, it returned home to the UK and relocated to RAF Lyneham where it re-equipped with the RAF's new tactical transport, the C-130 Hercules. This re-organisation was a portent of the many changes that the Service was to undergo as Great Britain struggled to come to terms with the post-war world.

CHAPTER 5

Flying Instructor

On returning to the UK I enjoyed a period of disembarkation leave, which my new wife and I spent visiting some of my relatives and showing them photographs of the wedding that they had so unfortunately missed. We also had to find somewhere to live in the vicinity of RAF Little Rissington, near Bourton-on-the-Water in the Cotswolds. Luckily, this was in the days before the gentrification of the Cotswolds had taken place, and there were still properties to rent at a reasonable price. We managed to put down a marker on a converted school house in the village of Church Westcote, just east of the main road that runs southwards from Stow-on-the-Wold to Burford, and about two miles from the base. The property was occupied by a student who was already on the instructor's course, and we arranged to take it over when he vacated it. Meanwhile, I was to undertake a short jet-refresher course at RAF Manby near Louth in Lincolnshire.

While I was still on leave, however, I received instructions to report for an interview with the Air Secretary's Department at the Ministry of Defence in London. Although I did not know it at the time, this Department was responsible for personnel matters; including, of particular concern to me, officers' careers and postings. A year after graduating from Cranwell I had been promoted automatically from the rank of Pilot Officer to that of Flying Officer, and eighteen months into my tour in Cyprus I had advanced further to the rank of Flight Lieutenant. That, however, was the end of my automatic advancement, and from then on promotion was to be in competition with my peers. Here I was at something of a disadvantage, because careers and promotion were subjects that had not been much discussed on 70 Squadron. This lack of interest in advancement was because most of the aircraft captains and the rear crew members were getting on in years, many of them having joined the RAF during the war. The only other officers of a similar age to me were the other copilots and one or two first-tour navigators, most of whom were serving on short-service commissions. By and large, therefore, they were content to take life as it came, and were not much interested in personal development or in seeking promotion. On the other hand, I had been granted a permanent commission in the General Duties (Pilot) branch of the RAF on graduating from Cranwell, and I had the opportunity to serve until the age of 55; but, if I were to forge a worthwhile career, I needed to broaden my experience. I had rather naively thought that selection as a trainee instructor had put me on the right career path, so I was completely taken aback when I reported for my interview in London to be told that I was being considered for a post as an Aide-de-Camp (ADC).

To the best of my limited knowledge at the time, an assignment as an ADC meant being taken off flying duties and filling a ground post acting as a flunkey for a high-ranking senior officer. Frankly, the prospect filled me with horror, and I fought strongly against it. The desk-officer conducting the interview did his best to convince me that the job was in my own best interest. My counter-argument was that during my first tour I had flown just 11 hours as Captain, and that only on 'copilot solo' training flights at base. I needed, therefore, to build up some Captain time in order to gain in skill and confidence. Furthermore, I already had a posting to train as a flying instructor, a job ideally suited to provide the experience I lacked, and to take me away from this and put me in a ground post at this stage of my career would be a travesty.

In the end the desk officer gave in and conceded my position. He could see that my heart was not in the job I was being offered, and somewhat reluctantly he agreed that I should continue with my instructor's course. The interview presented me with one of those strange 'fork in the road' situations that sometimes occur in life. Had I become an ADC, my career would undoubtedly have taken a different path, but whether it would have been more or less successful, and against what criteria, I was never to know. What I did learn later in life was that that a spell as an ADC would have allowed me an insight at an early age into the workings of higher command in the RAF, an insight that would have been invaluable to me when I came later to fill more senior appointments. I might also have gained a powerful sponsor who could have continued to watch over me during my subsequent career. Looking back on the incident, I have always thought it as a poor example of man-management. Had I been given earlier notice of the interview and the reason for it, I could have sought advice from a Flight Commander or my Squadron Commander, and I might have approached the interview in a different frame of mind. But to spring it on me out of the blue and ask for an instant decision was, I thought, a rather cavalier way to manage an officer's career. The most likely explanation, however -

as is often the way in life - is that a requirement for an ADC came up at short notice and I just happened to be available at the time.

I completed my refresher course at Manby on the Jet Provost without undue difficulty, although after flying for so long with a crew it felt strange at first to be alone again in the cockpit during my solo flights. Then, in August 1966, I reported to the Central Flying School (CFS) at Little Rissington to train as a flying instructor. The course began with an intensive ground school phase intended to bring us up to speed on various professional subjects including aerodynamics, meteorology, navigation, the flight instruments, the engine and systems of the Jet Provost, and instructional technique. Quite soon we were introduced to the various flying exercises designed to take a student from his first flight up to the standard required to be a pilot in the RAF. These exercises were broken down into various elements such as the effects of the controls, straight and level flight, turning, climbing, descending and, most importantly, how to fly a circuit and execute a successful approach and landing. Each element was written up in an instructor's handbook, together with suggestions as to how best to teach it.

A flying exercise would start with a staff instructor teaching you one of the elements as if you were a basic student. The next flight would be flown with a fellow student on the course, when you would teach him as if he were a basic student. The fellow student would then reciprocate. On the third flight you would give the exercise back to your staff instructor, and he would then deliver the next element of the course. In this way, we worked our way gradually through the syllabus. Each flight required a full briefing using a whiteboard and various coloured pens on which the key points of the exercise were summarised, and every flight was followed by a comprehensive debriefing. There was a lot of information to absorb and we worked hard not only at taking it all in but also trying to remember it. Once we had completed the basic exercises we went on to the more advanced phases of flying training: stalling, spinning, aerobatics, forced landings, instrument flying, high and low-level navigation, and formation flying.

It was often difficult to pretend that the experienced and often elderly instructor sitting beside you in the cockpit was a basic student, although the staff pilots were good at simulating the sort of mistakes that a student might make. One day, however, a group of young student officers came over from nearby RAF South Cerney, where they were doing a basic officer training course before starting their flying training. Our Flight Commander asked us to take them up for a flight and teach them the effect of the controls. I was allocated a Malaysian student and together we strapped in and set off on our flight. Once we were established in the cruise, I started in on the lesson, noting with interest how tentative he was when it was his turn to fly the aircraft and I said to him 'You have control.' About twenty minutes into the exercise he said he felt sick and I could see that behind his oxygen mask he did look rather pallid. Consequently, I cut the sortie short and made my way back to base as smoothly and expeditiously as I could. All went well until we came to climb out of the cockpit, when I realised that he had not released his leg-restraint garters and was therefore still attached to the ejector seat. 'There's a little yellow knob on the right-hand side of the ejector seat', I said. 'Just push that forward and the restraints will release.' The next thing I knew was that he had pulled the black and yellow knob at the rear of the seat which operated the emergency oxygen bottle, and I was left trying to explain to an irate Chief Technician how this had come about. Nevertheless, the experience not only gave me an insight into what it might be like to fly with a real student but also taught me the importance of being very precise when issuing instructions in the cockpit.

DURING OUR STAY AT Little Rissington, my wife and I had settled comfortably into our delightful cottage in the heart of the Cotswolds. She had taken a job nursing in the hospital at nearby Chipping Norton and every working day the local bus driver would stop outside the house and toot his horn to signify his presence. On Saturdays we went into Cheltenham or Oxford to browse around the shops and have lunch. We did not make many purchases, however, because in those days servicemen were still relatively poorly paid and money was tight, especially as we had between us only recently borne the cost of our own wedding. I had sold my Sunbeam Rapier when we left Cyprus and now could only manage an Austin A40, which was a most unimpressive car. I did not feel deprived, however, partly because all my colleagues were in the same boat, but also because I was buoyed up by the tremendous pride and camaraderie that came from being a pilot in the RAF.

As the end of the course approached we were asked to indicate our preferences for posting, there being at that time five Basic Flying Training Schools (BFTSs) operating the Jet Provost. Cranwell and RAF Syerston were close together, bracketing the town of Newark. The other locations were RAF Linton-on-Ouse, near York; RAF Leeming, in North Yorkshire; and RAF Acklington, on the coast of Northumberland near Alnmouth, some 30 miles north of Newcastle Upon Tyne. I asked my wife where she would like to go and she said that she didn't much mind except that she didn't want to go to Acklington as it was too far north. Having already spent three years at Cranwell I wanted somewhere different, and Syerston was too near to my home, so I opted for Linton, Leeming and Acklington in that order. Inevitably, when the postings were announced, I found that I was posted to Acklington. When I asked the desk officer why this was so, he replied that I was the only student on the course who had so much as even mentioned Acklington, and I had therefore been allocated to the one available post. Never having lived in that part of the country I thought it might be rather interesting; the problem was how to break the news to my wife. By now, autumn was merging into winter, and a few days later she returned home from work and said to me 'I had a piece of good fortune today as I managed to buy a pair of new boots for half price in a sale in Chipping Norton market.' 'Oh, that's good,' I replied, as you are going to need them for our next posting.' Her face fell as the penny dropped, but she soon saw the funny side of it, and before long we were making plans to move to a new home. With the instructor's course almost complete, I flew an aircraft on a 'navigation exercise' up to Acklington, where I took over a married quarter before flying back to Little Rissington the same day. We were almost ready to move on.

AFTER PASSING MY FINAL Handling Test, I was formally designated a 'Qualified Flying Instructor' (QFI), and the course came to an end. We still had a few days to go before the Christmas break, so three fellow students and I decided to play a round of golf at Burford Golf Club. After the game I invited them back to my home for some refreshment. It was late afternoon and the evening was drawing in when I heard the bus pull up in the road outside. After a few moments my wife came into the room followed by the bus driver who was carrying a large Christmas tree. Thanking him for helping my wife, I asked him if he would like a drink. He said that as he had no more passengers to deliver he would be delighted to join us. So the seven of us sat around the fire and chatted like old friends until the driver said he must be going. And without further ado away he went, leaving us all rather bemused by his rather nonchalant approach to his duties. The incident summed up the relaxed and pleasant way of life that existed at that time in the Cotswolds – a time that my wife and I still remember fondly as an ideal start to our married life together.

Shortly after Christmas we set off in our modest little car to drive the 300 miles to our new home in the north of England. Much of our journey was along the old A1, which in those days, before the construction of the M1, was the main route to the North East. It rained steadily for most of the day and we were constantly sprayed with muddy water by the many heavy trucks that clogged the road. At Leeming Bar we stopped overnight, continuing our journey the next day in conditions that were, if anything, slightly worse. The road wound its way through narrow village streets and was mostly single track, making overtaking difficult if not impossible, and all the while we travelled in a relentless stream of heavy trucks. Eventually we made our way over the Tyne Bridge and through the centre of Newcastle, finally emerging into the more open countryside of Northumberland. But it seemed as if the further north we went the darker and more threatening the clouds became. Finally, just after passing through Morpeth, we turned off the A1 and made our way along an endless country lane until, in the gathering late-afternoon gloom, we finally reached the airfield at Acklington.

Our married quarter had been unoccupied for several weeks and it was absolutely freezing cold. The only sources of heating appeared to be an open fireplace in the lounge and a coke stove in the kitchen. When I looked in the shed outside there was neither coal nor coke. Enquires revealed that the nearest source of supply was the town of Ashington, about ten miles to the south. So off we went again in the pouring rain, with the light rapidly fading, until we came to the mining town of Ashington, which in the near-darkness seemed to consist of one enormous slag-heap. The feeling of depression that had been hovering about us all day now almost overwhelmed us. Having loaded the car with bags of coal and coke and some provisions, we set off back to Acklington. I lit the fire and the stove in the kitchen while my wife prepared a simple meal, after which our spirits revived. The house was comfortably furnished and it was not long before we were sound asleep in bed. The next day the sun was shining and everything looked decidedly better.

THERE WERE TWO SQUADRONS at Acklington, comprising about 50 instructors in all. Each squadron consisted of two flights, and I was assigned to B Flight of No 1 Squadron. After several introductory familiarisation sorties to accustom me to local flying procedures, I was allocated three students and set to work in my new role as a flying instructor. Two of my students were university graduates and they were both mature and pleasant individuals. We got on well, and they made good progress with their flying. Both students graduated successfully from the basic flying course and went on to their advanced flying training. The third student was a direct entrant, and therefore younger than the other two. He lacked the interpersonal skills and the self-confidence of the older students, and this impaired both his ability to learn and his progress. After about three months he was embroiled in a personal domestic problem and eventually withdrew himself from training. Meanwhile, I too was on a steep learning curve as I sought to master the skills required of an instructor. The thing that struck me most, however, in those early days, was the sheer hard work of flying two or three sorties a day, day in and day out, for weeks on end. It was physically and mentally draining, and the weekends provided a welcome respite in which to rest and recuperate.

I was perhaps unfortunate in that I joined my squadron at a time when a new batch of students were beginning their training, a phase of the course that required a lot of time in the circuit while they mastered the skills needed to make a successful approach and landing. To relieve the inevitable congestion in the circuit, we made use of a satellite airfield at RAF Ouston, some 20 miles south west of Acklington. This arrangement required and early start, with a met briefing at 07.30 hours. Depending on the programme for the day, half the Flight took off from Acklington for the first sortie of the day and then landed at Ouston to refuel. Meanwhile, the other half of the Flight and the remaining students went by bus to Ouston, a journey of about 45 minutes, arriving in time to take the aircraft for the second sortie of the day. We then spend the rest of the day pounding the circuit with our students until the time came to return to base. Then those pilots who had flown the aircraft out to Ouston in the morning returned to Acklington by bus, while those who had made the journey by bus in the morning flew the aircraft back to their home base. The next day the roles were reversed, and so on throughout the week. It was not unusual for an instructor to fly four sorties a day with different students, often amounting to more than 20 circuits. Each sortie required a high degree of concentration, not only to ensure that the student made a safe approach and landing but also to maintain safe separation and spacing from the three or four other aircraft that were in the circuit at the same time. This phase of the course lasted for some two months and we were all mightily relieved when it came to an end.

Of the five BFTSs, Acklington enjoyed by far the best location for flying, with a vast area of open country to the north-west of the airfield. Of all the features that are visible from the air, coastlines are the most easily observable; and with the airfield being located some two miles inland, even the students said that it was almost impossible to become lost. To the extreme north of our local flying area were Berwick and the River Tweed, while just off the coast and a little further south were the distinctive shapes of Holy Island and the Farne Islands. Further south still were the little harbours at Alnmouth and Amble, with Coquet Island conveniently situated just abeam the airfield. Inland to the west, our area was bounded by the impressive bulk of the Cheviot Hills. On a clear day in the summer it was a truly magnificent spectacle; while in the winter, with the hills covered in snow, it was breathtaking. There was, however, a downside to a coastal location, because in the winter the airfield was subject to a local effect known by its Scottish name of the 'Haar'. The Haar was a north easterly wind that blew in off the sea bringing with it low-lying fog and mist. In the winter, especially, it could spring up quite suddenly, and in a very short space of time visibility at the airfield would go from being perfectly satisfactory to almost zero. It was left to the hapless Duty Instructor in the control tower to monitor the situation and recall all the aircraft if and when conditions started to deteriorate, and this sometimes led to some close shaves. On one such occasion, I was some distance away from the airfield when a recall came. I set course immediately for base but, by the time I arrived overhead, the threshold and half the runway were already covered in fog. Fortunately, the other end of the runway was still visible and I was just able to land downwind before flying operations came to an abrupt end for the day.

In our leisure time there were plenty of things to do, especially during the summer. I joined the golf club at Foxton Hall, near Alnmouth, where I played at the weekends with some of my colleagues. Foxton Hall was one of several magnificent courses along the coast between Alnmouth and Berwick, with those at Dunstanburgh Castle and Bamburgh being the most picturesque. I took over as Officer i/c Golf, organising and playing in matches against nearby clubs. The local people that we played against were always warm, friendly and very generous with their hospitality. Meanwhile, my wife had taken a job at Ashington Hospital and now, with two salaries coming in each month, we were able to enjoy a slightly higher standard of living. We bought a black and white television and during the winter months we were, like much of the rest of the nation, enthralled by weekly instalments of The Forsyte Saga. I traded in my Austin A40 for a Ford Cortina, the first of several Cortinas that I was to own over the next few years. It was not a new car, but it represented a considerable step up in motoring terms. At the garage in Gosport near Newcastle, where I made the trade, I enjoyed nearly two-hours of cut and thrust with the salesman, David Hopper. By the time we had concluded the deal it was near to closing time, and he suggested that we went for a drink at the local Conservative Club. It transpired that he ran a local football team that played Sunday morning matches, and we arranged that he would bring his team to Acklington for a game against a scratch team of QFIs. After the match we all retired to the Officers Mess for some refreshment, where the visitors were mightily impressed by the pictures of aircraft and the various bits of memorabilia that adorned the walls of the bar. At a later date, David and I went to a football match at St James's Park, where we stood on the terraces surrounded by hundreds of men in flat caps shouting 'Away the lads.'

Newcastle beat Arsenal 3-0, making it a good day all round for the Geordies, who took their football very seriously. Not long afterwards, David invited Breda and me to his home, where we met his wife, Eileen, an Irish girl and a former air hostess with Aer Lingus. We became firm friends and often socialised together, keeping in touch for many years after we had left the district.

In addition to the two flying squadrons at Acklington there was also a small unit known as 'Standards Squadron', staffed by experienced QFIs. Their job was to improve the flying skills and instructional standards of the QFIs on the line. Periodically, each QFI spent a week in 'Standards', where he flew all the basic instructional sorties with a supervising pilot, who also role-played as a 'student'. In between the flying exercises, time was spent in the classroom, brushing up on professional knowledge and answering questions posed by the 'students'. Flying Training Command, as it then was, graded its instructors through a series of 'Categories'. A newly-qualified instructor emerged from the CFS course with a B2 Category, which equated to being 'proficient'. After a few months gaining experience, and subject to a satisfactory week in Standards, an instructor would be upgraded to a B1, or 'average', category. The next step, and a much greater challenge, was to upgrade to an A2, or 'above-the-average', category. This category could be awarded only by a CFS examiner, and the test, which involved both air and ground exercises, was carried out at Little Rissington. The final accolade was to achieve an A1, or 'exceptional', category, but in my experience only a handful of instructors ever achieved this distinction.

After 15 months on the squadron, and following a successful week in Standards, I was put forward as an A2 candidate and I flew down to Little Rissington to take the test. I had worked hard to prepare myself for this opportunity, spending many evening hours studying the various books and publications covering the likely exam questions. Consequently, the ground school phase of the test went well and I was complimented by the examiner on my level of knowledge. Unfortunately, the flying test, which I took the following morning, was less successful. The exercise was simple enough, with the CFS examiner playing the role of a student who had been taught to fly straight and level flight on a previous sortie but had experienced some difficulty in applying the principles when he came to put them into practice. As I realised later, the best way to approach the problem would have been as a fault-finding exercise, giving the aircraft to the student in various different attitudes and asking him to return it to straight and level flight. In doing so, I could have reinforced the key points of the exercise until we reached a situation where the student had fully grasped the fundamentals and could repeat them without the intervention of the instructor. Being nervous and a little apprehensive, and anxious to do everything by the book, I went back to basics and taught the straight and level exercise all over again from scratch. While this was a perfectly satisfactory approach, it lacked the insight and flair that would have lifted my performance from merely ordinary to above the average. Furthermore, during the remainder of the sortie, when I was asked to teach some aerobatics and various circuits, I made one or two minor errors. In themselves, these were of little consequence, but in the context of the exam, they again failed to lift my performance to the level required for an A2 category. Thus my first attempt to upgrade ended in failure.

The main consequence of this set-back was that it precluded me from taking up one of the supervisory positions that might have become available in the normal course of events. As it happened, however, the normal course of events did not take place, because changes were afoot that were to have a significant bearing on my tour as an instructor. It had been rumoured for some time that one of the five BFTSs was to close as a 'cost-saving measure'. (And how many times was I to hear that phrase repeated in the course of my years of service!) Another rumour held that even if all the other BFTSs were to close down, Acklington would remain open as the best possible location for a flying training station. On the strength of this assertion, a new hanger was constructed on the station at huge expense. In the final analysis, however, it was decided that Acklington would close in the summer of 1968, and the training task would be dispersed among the other four BFTSs, all of which were to remain open. I was to be posted to Cranwell to complete the balance of my tour.

Before this move took place however, another event occurred that was to profoundly affect our domestic circumstances, and that was the birth of our first child, James. One evening in early January my wife announced that the birth was imminent and I drove her to Ashington Hospital. I escorted her to the maternity ward and there I left her. Husbands were not encouraged to hang around in those days and it was almost unknown for a father to be present at the birth, so I made my way home and drank a large brandy before retiring alone to my bed.

Early next morning I rang the hospital to be told that the baby had arrived and that both mother and child were doing well. I arranged to visit them later in the morning. Meanwhile, I attended the morning met briefing and afterwards approached my Flight Commander to ask him if I could have some time off for my visit to the hospital.

'What are the visiting hours?' he asked.

'I can visit at 11.30 this morning,' I replied.

'Oh good,' he said, 'then you can fly a sortie before you go.'

And fly I did, although it's fair to say that my mind was not really on the job. The baby was a boy and we called him James.

One of the perks of being an officer was that we enjoyed 'batting'. In recognition of the fact that most officers were now married, the former concept of a 'batman' to look after an officer's uniform and personal effects while he was living in the Mess or under field conditions had been modified, and batting now meant the services of a cleaning lady a couple of days a week. Our batting was provided by a very pleasant local lady who readily agreed to keep an eye on the baby while my wife went to the nearby house of a friend where she was learning to play bridge.

Meanwhile, I was on one of my periodic visits to Standards Squadron, where I just happened to be flying with my next door neighbour, who was one of the staff instructors. As we returned from our sortie to the airfield, I noticed that there was smoke pouring from the chimney of one of our houses.

'Alan,' I said, 'I think your house is on fire.'

He took control and banked the aircraft for a better look.

'It's not mine, it's yours,' he said, with an air of finality.

We called the tower and informed the controller of the situation, and a fire vehicle was dispatched to the scene. It transpired that my wife had lit a fire in the lounge to keep the baby warm in his crib, and the chimney had caught fire, producing a vast quantity of smoke but, fortunately causing very little damage. Luckily, smelling the smoke, our cleaning lady had rescued the baby, and also called the emergency services, so no-one was harmed, although my wife had a nasty shock when she arrived home.

It was not too long after that that batting services were withdrawn as another 'cost-saving measure'.

One of the drawbacks of being a flying instructor was that the job was fairly mundane. No matter what great events occurred in the world you knew that, come the morning, you would be up there boring holes in the same patch of sky. Furthermore, a lot of an instructor's time was spent acting as a safety pilot and lookout, while the student flew the aircraft and developed his skills. After months of flying from the same airfield, I would often look back with nostalgia to those days when we took off in our Hastings and headed for distant and unknown exotic places.

We instructors were, therefore, excited by the news that we were to take part in a fly-past at RAF Abingdon to mark the 15th anniversary of the Queen's accession to the throne. The formation was to be in the form of the royal cipher – EIIR – with four of the BFTSs each flying one element of the symbol. Acklington was allocated the 'R'. Altogether, the formation involved 36 Jet Provosts. I managed to scramble a place as one of two airborne spares. Amidst great anticipation we were detached to RAF Gaydon in Warwickshire for a couple of weeks to prepare for the event. During rehearsals, all 38 aircraft line up on the runway with my aircraft and the other spare right at the back. Then each element of the royal cipher took of in pairs and orbited around until a long line of aircraft filled the sky. Once the formation had organised itself into four parallel lines of pairs of aircraft the whole ensemble set course for Abingdon, some 20 miles to the south. Shortly afterwards the command was given, 'Royal Cipher, go!' And after a flurry of movement within the formation the letters appeared as if by magic in the sky. Above the formation flew a lone aircraft known as the 'whipper-in'. His job was to observe the formation from above and ensure that its shape was perfect by calling minute adjustments to any aircraft that was slightly out of position. 'Romeo Six, move forward slightly.' 'Echo Three, close in a bit.' And so on. Then, with about three miles to run, the whipper-in and the two spares broke away and returned to Gaydon, leaving the main body of aircraft to complete their journey in perfect formation past the royal dais.

During the practice runs the formation was observed by Gaydon radar and on one occasion during the run in the controller advised that there was a light aircraft showing dead ahead at a range of about two miles. Back came a laconic response from the lead aircraft, operated by the Wing Commander Flying from Syerston, 'Well, we are 36 aircraft and he is but one, so I suggest that you tell him to get out of the way'. Whether or not the pilot of the light aircraft ever received the warning is not on record, but it must have been a nasty shock for him when a vast formation of jet aircraft suddenly appeared out of a bright blue sky and swept past him. The formation was a challenging and most enjoyable enterprise, my only regret being that all the aircraft worked perfectly both during the rehearsals and on the day, so I never had an opportunity, even on a temporary basis, to fill in as one of the aircraft in the main formation.

Rather strangely, during the detachment, I had a telephone call asking me to attend for an interview as an ADC. I explained that I was involved in rehearsals for a royal flypast and that I could not be spared at that particular time. I never heard any more about it.

In the summer of 1968 I travelled southwards to take up my new post at Cranwell. Acklington was closed down and the land sold off. The last I heard the site had become an open-cast coal mine. I found the facilities at Cranwell much better than those at Acklington, as might be expected of the RAF's showpiece training venue. In time-honoured style, we operated from permanent offices built onto the sides of the hangars, rather than from the wooden huts that had been our home at Acklington. We also had the use of the York House Officers Mess, a building in traditional style that was surrounded by well-kept lawns and carefully-tended rose gardens. After flying had ended for the week, the QFIs would meet in the bar for the ritual TGIF – Thank God It's Friday – where the excitement and adventure of the week's flying would be relived all over again in the course of downing a few pints of ale. After a short period of temporary accommodation, my wife and I took over a married quarter on the domestic site, where we settled quickly into our new surroundings.

I WAS ASSIGNED TO A Flight of No 1 Squadron, where I soon acquired some new students and my tour as a flying instructor continued much as before. Having carried out my own flying training in the Cranwell area, and being by now a relatively experienced QFI, I adapted easily to my new surroundings. I was also a much more skilful and confident pilot and instructor, so at the end of the year, when I again flew with a CFS examiner, I successfully upgraded to an A2 Category. With my new status as an 'above-the-average' instructor, I now found myself flying more often with students who were having difficulty in making the grade. In this capacity I had some success.

The ghost that haunted every student pilot was fear of suspension from training through lack of progress, known colloquially as 'the chop'. Having been a Flight Cadet myself, and having also struggled to make the grade as an RAF pilot, I had a good insight into the stresses that could affect a student's performance, and I could empathise with the predicament of those who stared suspension in the face. Once a student failed to reach the required standard on one of the assessment check-points built into the course, he was put under review. This process invariably involved a change of instructor, in case there was some incompatibility or personality clash between the pairing. The student was given an additional 10 hours of instruction in which to achieve the required standard. If successful, he was allowed to continue with the course, but if he failed he was suspended from further training.

On several occasions I was obliged to break the news to a student who had failed to make the grade and it was always a doleful experience to dash such high expectations so early in a young man's career. I usually put it to the unfortunate individual that it was better to discover early on that he lacked the aptitude for the career to which he aspired, rather than struggle on year after year in a job for which, through no fault of his own, he was not entirely suited. While nothing I said at the time could dispel the disappointment of the moment, I hoped that my homily might resonate at some point in the future, once the individual had found his niche in a different walk of life.

RAF flying training was, however, a well-honed operation, with most students graduating successfully and going on to advanced flying training. Just occasionally, in the hazardous world of military aviation, this success could be short-lived. With one particular student, a very personable young man, but one who was in danger of failing to make the grade, I spent a considerable amount of time getting to know him and working with him to help him overcome his difficulties. He responded well to my approach and within the space of a few sorties he suddenly saw the light and began to progress. In due course he graduated with his fellow cadets. Prior to the end of the course I asked him what aircraft he would like to fly and he said that he was very keen to fly helicopters. I recommended that he should carry out his advanced flying on helicopters and my recommendation was accepted. He passed his advanced flying course and was undergoing further training at an OCU when he was unfortunately killed in a mid-air collision between two helicopters.

Flying with less able students also brought its own hazards. In order to maintain currency, one such cadet needed to carry out a spin under supervision. As we had a number of other exercises to accomplish during the sortie, I decided that we would do the spin first and then move on to the main exercise of the day. One of the checks prior to spinning in the Jet Provost was to ensure that there was no fuel in the tip tanks, as the extra weight at the extremities had an adverse effect on the stability of the aircraft during this particular manoeuvre. We took off as usual with half full tip tanks and, as we were the first aircraft of the day to get airborne, I decided that a beat-up of the airfield would be in order. Having first cleared the manoeuvre with Air Traffic Control, we shot across the airfield at low level and high speed, followed by an upward vertical roll. As the speed decreased we settled into a normal climb and it was not long before we reached the 18,000 feet, the minimum height for commencing a spin. I handed over control to the student who went through the customary checks and clearing turns. We had spent so little time climbing to height that the tip tanks were barely empty and may indeed have had some fuel in them still. This oversight was then compounded by the student, who failed to apply full pro-spin controls.

A spin was normally accomplished by allowing the speed to decay almost to the stall, then applying full rudder in the direction of the intended spin and pulling the control column right back. With one wing now stalled and the other still producing lift, the aircraft would settle into a steady spin with high rate of descent and the airspeed low and stable at around 80 knots. Recovery was achieved by applying full rudder to oppose the spin and, after a pause to allow the rudder to take effect, moving the control column progressively forward until the spin stopped. The aircraft then had to be recovered from the ensuing dive. On this particular occasion, the student applied only half rudder and moved the control column only half way to the rear. Before I could correct him, the aircraft rolled violently to the left and entered a rapid descent with the airspeed reading somewhere between 140 and 150 knots. The horizon was now spinning round at such a rate that for a moment I was completely disorientated and could not quite grasp what was happening. It was not a spin of the type that I had known and practised with perfect safety on dozens of occasions in the past. I thought fleetingly that the aircraft might be autorotating in the pre-spinning stage of the manoeuvre, and I centralised the controls in the approved manner and waited for the rotation to stop. For what seemed like an eternity, the aircraft continued to rotate at high speed, all the while maintaining its rapid rate of descent. I saw the altimeter pass 14,000 feet, and I realised that if we had not recovered by 10,000 feet we would have to eject. And then, as suddenly as it had started, the rotation stooped, and I was able to recover from the ensuing dive by about 12,000 feet. At the end of the sortie I retired to a quiet corner of the crew room with a cup of coffee and thumbed through the Pilot's Notes for the Jet Provost. And there, towards the end of a lengthy chapter on aircraft handling, I came to a small paragraph about high rotational spinning that described exactly the symptoms I had experienced, together with a warning about the dangers of allowing such a situation to develop. I filed the experience away in the back of my mind, along with many other things that I learned about flying during my time as an instructor. They were to hold me in good stead during the rest of my flying career in the RAF.

In addition to my normal duties as a flying instructor, I took on the job of Air Cadet Liaison Officer (ACLO). Part of my role was to maintain contact between the local ATC squadrons that were parented by Cranwell, but my main task was to organize a series of week-long camps lasting for the duration of the school summer holidays. The cadet units came from all over the country and were housed in an airmen's barrack block in part of the Cranwell estate known as East Camp. With the assistance of two colleagues from the ground instructional staff, I put together and published a programme of activities for the cadets. Taking time out from instructing, I set up a small headquarters in the barrack block where I was supported not only by my two colleagues but also by a small administrative element that had been drafted in for the duration of the camps. One of our most important tasks was to ensure that the cadets had the opportunity to fly during their camp, and to this end we were able to utilise the small flight of Chipmunks that operated from the grass North Airfield at Cranwell.

Having flown the Chipmunk previously during my time as a cadet, I needed only one sortie to re-qualify on type. I was then able to join the other Chipmunk operators for half a day on most days of the week giving the cadets air experience. Although I could not know it at the time, cadet flying was to be one of the main preoccupations of my life when I came towards the end of my RAF career. After a few initial teething problems, which were quickly resolved, the camps ran smoothly throughout the school holiday period. At the end of each week my team and I received some well-earned praise from the ATC Officers and their staff who accompanied the cadets during their stay. Running the camps was hard work but, for me personally, it provided an excellent opportunity to exercise and develop some leadership skills.

I WAS BY NOW coming to the end of my tour as a QFI and beginning to think about what the future might hold for me. Unlike my time on 70 Squadron, where I had worked with men in the sunset of their careers, the instructional world was full of eager young men, many of whom were anxious to make their mark on the world. Under this influence, I had taken and passed the exam for promotion to the rank of Squadron Leader, and further advancement now rested on earning the necessary recommendation in the course of my annual appraisals. There was, however, a significant domestic problem bearing on my next move, as my wife was now expecting our second child, whose anticipated arrival coincided almost exactly with my end-of-tour date. Accordingly, I approached my Squadron Commander to see if there was any news of a posting, and he set the appropriate wheels in motion. About a week later, late on a Friday afternoon, I received a telephone call from my desk officer who said he understood that there was a problem and that I wanted to be screened from my posting. Anxious as I was to escape from the limited existence of instructional flying and return to operations, I quickly explained to him that I merely wanted to know when and where I would be going so that I could make the arrangements for my wife's confinement. 'How would you like to fly the VC10?' he said. My heart leapt. The VC10 was the latest and most magnificent aircraft to join the air transport force, and I thought that it would suit me very nicely. 'There is a conversion course starting at RAF Brize Norton in mid-January,' he said, and I could put you on it. Would you like the weekend to think about it?'

I was afraid that by Monday he might have changed his mind, so I said, "No thank you. I'll take your offer now." And with that, the deal was done.

Not long after I left Cranwell, the college training programme was subjected to another sweeping change even greater than the introduction of the academic course that had borne so heavily on 81 Entry and on subsequent cadets. I was not privy to the study that brought about the transformation, but I gathered that it was partly the result of financial pressures and partly because the new training syllabus was manifestly not working. So the 3-year cadet system that had survived almost since the college was opened in the 1930s was swept away and replaced instead by the recruitment of entrants who had already acquired a university degree. The course was drastically reduced from three years to a matter of months, while the syllabus was restricted to basic military training and the development of leadership skills. Pilot training and the skills and knowledge required for other branches of the RAF were in future to be taught in other locations after graduation. Over the years, the 3-year cadet system had served the RAF well, producing many great leaders who had distinguished themselves in the higher ranks of the service. But the world was changing rapidly and, to accommodate these new developments, the traditional forms of military training were being forced to change as well.

CHAPTER 6

FLYING THE VC10

JUST THREE DAYS before Christmas, our second child, another boy, whom we named Brian, was born at RAF Nocton Hall, a military hospital near Lincoln. Three weeks after his birth, I took my place on No 11 VC10 Conversion Course, run by No 241 OCU at RAF Brize Norton. The year was 1970, and it was a time when the post-war surge in house prices had just begun; a surge that was to continue to the present day. Prior to that time, most officers had been content to live on base in Married Quarters, secure in the knowledge that the gratuity they would receive at the end of their service would be sufficient for them to buy a decent house in a location of their choosing. Even by 1970, however, it was becoming apparent that this arrangement was no longer viable, as any potential increase in the gratuity was highly unlikely to keep pace with the steeply rising cost of housing. Some our contemporaries had already bought their own homes and, as it seemed likely that we would be based at Brize Norton for some considerable time, we decided this was the moment to take the plunge. Given our limited financial resources, finding the money for a deposit was a considerable challenge, and I was eventually forced to cash-in a life insurance policy that I had taken out as a cadet at Cranwell, much against the advice of my broker. Before Christmas, we had spent several weekends viewing properties in the Brize Norton area, and we eventually agreed on the purchase of a three-bedroom semi-detached house in Carterton, a village immediately adjacent to the airfield. The agreed price was £4,650. I managed to arrange a mortgage through a broker in the locality, and my very last flight on the Jet Provost was a 'navigation exercise' from Cranwell to RAF Lyneham, where I met with my broker in the Officers Mess and signed the necessary papers. The mortgage repayments amounted to what was then the staggering sum of £32 a month. Fortunately, under a Conservative government led by Margaret Thatcher, a new military salary was introduced in 1970, bringing with it a welcome rise in rates of pay for service men and women. This rise was a great help in off-setting the extra financial burden of repaying a mortgage.

The introduction of the VC10 into service with the RAF brought a step change in air transport operations. Compared with the Hastings, for example, it could carry nearly three times as many passengers, at more than twice the speed. Whereas it took some 8½ hours in a Hastings to fly from the UK to Cyprus at 10,000 feet, the VC10 could do the same journey in less than half the time while cruising above all the weather at 35,000 feet. Two versions of the aircraft had been produced for the commercial market, known respectively as the Standard and the Super models. The latter type had a longer fuselage, more sophisticated wings and uprated Rolls Royce Conway engines. The RAF VC10s retained the Standard fuselage but were fitted with the Super wings and the uprated Conways, giving the aircraft the most awesome performance. To allow the aircraft the better to fulfil its military role, it was also fitted with a large freight door on the front left-side of the fuselage, and a strengthened cabin floor. As a result, the aircraft could be operated either in the full passenger role, or as a freighter using palletised loads of cargo. It could also be operated in the passenger-cum-freight (PCF) role, depending on the task in hand. Its flexibility as a military aircraft was further enhanced by the facility to fit stretchers in the cabin so that it could be used in the medical evacuation role.

In sum, the new aircraft incorporated all the latest features of design technology, combining superb performance with a high degree of flexibility and safety. There were, however, two distinctive features of the military VC10s that separated them from their civilian counterparts. In the cabin, the passenger seats faced rearwards, in the long-held belief that this configuration provided for much greater passenger protection in the event of a crash. In addition, each aircraft was named after an RAF holder of the Victoria Cross, the name being emblazoned on the fuselage near the front passenger door. With its graceful lines and RAF markings, the VC10 was the epitome of a modern airliner and, in the early days of its introduction into service, the aircraft always aroused enormous interest and comment wherever it went.

The ground school phase of our conversion course involved a number of visits to the huge maintenance hangar at Brize Norton, where the VC10s underwent periodic deep servicing. To facilitate access, scaffolding was erected around the aircraft, and it was possible to climb to the top of the T-tail and look down on the vast planform of the wings and fuselage from a position some 40 feet above the ground. Similarly, to stand on the ground beside the aircraft and look up was also to be presented with a thrilling sight. The prospect of flying such a magnificent machine filled us with anticipation but also with a certain amount of awe at the challenge ahead.

In the meantime, however, there were numerous lectures to be attended on the aircraft's systems, on its performance, on climatology, on communications, and on various other aspects of world-wide operations. To facilitate the learning process, the OCU was equipped with a fully functioning flight simulator, which replicated exactly the cockpit of the actual aircraft. At the back of the simulator was a seat for the instructor and a control panel by means of which he could programme the exercise for the day. Outside the machine sat the console operator, a man of many voices, who played the part of the navigator, the air loadmaster, air traffic control, and any other party whose presence was required only briefly for the purpose of the flight. The simulator itself was mounted on a moveable platform that responded to inputs to the controls.

This facility was connected to a visual display system, so that any apparent motion of the aircraft such climbing, descending or banking was replicated by the attitude of the aircraft relative to the horizon. Unlike modern flight simulators, in which the visual display is produced by computer-generated imagery (CGI), the first-generation VC10 simulator relied for its information on a huge scale model of the local area, with the airfield in the centre.

The model, which was some 20 feet high and 60 feet long, was mounted vertically, and the aircraft's track over the ground was followed over the model by a moving camera from which the visual display was derived. This dynamic arrangement was also linked electronically to the aircraft's navigation system so that, as the simulated flight traversed the local area, the navigation instruments responded accordingly. Using this system, it was possible to carry out simulated instrument approaches to the airfield at Brize Norton, or to any other major airfield that was stored in the database. Because of the limitations of the visual display, however, an instrument approach at, say, Dulles Airport in Washington DC, always ended up at an airfield that bore a remarkable visual similarity to RAF Brize Norton.

There was in addition a second visual display model, replicating the conditions to be found on an approach to Kai Tak airport at Hong Kong. At this airfield, landing in a north-easterly direction involved a last-minute turn over the high-rise flats of Kowloon, before lining up with the runway at about 400 feet on the approach. All this was faithfully replicated on the scale model of Hong Kong, except that at some point in the past someone had descended too soon causing the mobile camera to strike one of the model blocks of flats, so that for ever afterwards on each simulated approach to the airport the tower block leaned over alarmingly at an angle of about 45°. Another limitation of the visual system in the simulator was its tendency to exaggerate small movements of the aircraft in the final stages of the approach. This made landings in the simulator very challenging, as the slightest movement of the controls would cause the runway to float about in a most disconcerting way. Judgement of height near the ground was also difficult, as the system lacked the sophistication to project those vital visual clues that pilots use to flare the aircraft at the right moment and so execute a smooth landing. As a result, approaches in the simulator, particularly in the early stages of training, often led to a crash landing, whereupon the visual shut itself down and the crew were left sitting rather sheepishly in a darkened cockpit.

These limitations notwithstanding, the simulator was a remarkably useful training tool. All the aircraft systems, together with their associated instrumentation, were represented in the cockpit. This was particularly handy when it came to learning about the various complex systems in the aircraft, such as those that controlled the fuel, the hydraulics and the electrics. For example, the simulator could be used to replicate the procedure for transferring fuel from one tank to another, or even to jettison fuel rapidly down to landing weight, so that the aircraft could return back to the departure airfield without delay in the event of a major emergency immediately after take-off.

Other aircraft systems could be replicated in a similar way, allowing the trainees to learn not only the normal modes of operation but also emergency procedures as well. Many of these procedures, such as an aborted take-off, or a double engine failure immediately after lift off, could not be practised in the aircraft for obvious safety reasons.

Having worked our way through all these various systems and procedures one by one, without ever leaving the ground, it was a great day when we finally went through the whole start-up procedure, taxied out to the end of the simulated runway, took-off, and flew one circuit before coming in to land. After that, we taxied back to dispersal, and completed the exercise by shutting down the aircraft successfully. We were at last ready to begin flying training on the aircraft itself.

Unlike earlier transport aircraft in the RAF's inventory, the VC10 was equipped with powered flying controls, and this made it relatively easy to fly. The design incorporated an all-moving tailplane that allowed for very precise trimming of the aircraft so that it was very stable when configured for the final approach. The elevators, too, were very responsive, even at the relatively low speeds required for landing; and the flare could be precisely controlled, allowing for consistently smooth landings after a bit of practice.

The conversion sorties were conducted by an OCU instructor who occupied the left-hand seat, with the trainee pilot in the right hand seat. The flight engineer sat sideways on the right-hand side of the cockpit, while on the left-hand side sat the navigator facing aft.[1] In the centre of the cockpit was a jump-seat that was usually occupied by another trainee pilot. A typical sortie would consist of a climb to high level with a demonstration of different features of high speed flight, a return to base with a couple of turns round the holding pattern, and then some instrument approaches followed by several visual circuits. After a couple hours, the aircraft was landed and allowed to sit on the ground for about 20 minutes while the brakes cooled down. Then the other student pilot would occupy the right-hand seat, and off we would go again for another two hours.

None of the aircraft that I had flown previously had offered much in the way of pilot-interpreted navigation aids. By comparison, the VC10 was equipped not only with twin Automatic Direction Finding (ADF) receivers but also with TACAN, which gave both range and bearing from a beacon. In addition, it provided further navigation information to the pilot from twin VHF Omni-Radial (VOR) receivers. These fed a flight director system that could be used for tracking along the world's airways. Learning how to interpret and process all this information, especially when flying in cloud, presented a significant challenge to any pilot coming on to the aircraft for the first time, and in this respect I was no exception. By selecting an appropriate frequency, the VOR receivers could also supply information to the aircraft's Instrument Landing System (ILS), thereby allowing approaches to be made in cloud down to a decision height of 200 feet above the threshold.

Another approach practised on a regular basis utilised Precision Approach Radar (PAR), whereby the pilot was talked down by a controller who could see on his radar screen the aircraft's position in relation to the ideal approach path and issue adjustments accordingly. Much of our training was spent practising these different approaches, both on four engines and on three. With the four Conway engines mounted in pairs at either side of the rear fuselage, asymmetric flight presented very few problems. In the event of an engine failure, either simulated or for real, there was very little yaw, and what there was could easily be corrected by a small application of rudder. So powerful were the engines that there was hardly any loss of momentum, especially at the relatively light aircraft all-up weights used for training, so a slight reduction in the rate of climb was the only noticeable effect. For an asymmetric approach, the power on the live

[1] In all modern airliners, the old nautical terms of 'port' and 'starboard' have been superseded by 'left' and 'right', as viewed facing forward.

engines was increased by about 3%; that apart, everything else remained the same as for a normal approach.

Having completed our conversion to the aircraft both by day and by night, we then undertook a global training flight as an introduction to future world-wide operations. Our route took us eastward via a short stop in Cyprus to Bahrain, where we enjoyed a night's rest. This was followed by an overnight leg via the Maldive Islands to Singapore, which we reached at dawn. After a further period of rest our next stop was Hong Kong, where we stayed a day for a training flight to familiarise ourselves with the local procedures. Then it was on across the Pacific to the island of Guam.

It was during the departure from Hong Kong that I fell foul of the confusion that can sometimes occur on long-haul flights that involve crossing several time zones. Improvements in HF communications meant that there was no longer any need to carry an air signaller as a member of the crew, since all long-range radio transmissions could now be made by voice, thereby obviating the need for Morse code. The normal operating procedure was for one pilot to fly the sector while the other manned the radios. On this particular flight it was my responsibility to operate the radios, and all went well until Air Traffic asked us for an estimated time of arrival (ETA) at a distant boundary of their Flight Information Region. In the world of aviation, all flights are conducted in Greenwich Mean Time (GMT), usually referred to as 'Zulu' Time.[1] With Hong Kong local time being 8 hours ahead of GMT, I became confused about where we were on the 24 hour clock, and I when I passed the estimate it was 12 hours out. The controller came back, 'Check your estimate!' Had he left it at that, I would have quickly realised my error, but then he added for good measure, 'Check your estimate. You are giving me local time!' By now the whole crew was listening in to the conversation, and for a few minutes mayhem ensued while the training captain, the navigator, the screen navigator, the screen signaller and almost everyone else on the flight deck tried to right my error with helpful suggestions as to what the correct estimate should be. Eventually order was restored and I passed a revised estimate to the controller. Feeling humiliated, and much chastened, I learned a valuable lesson about international time-keeping; one that was to hold me in good stead during my lengthy future association with world-wide aircraft operations.

After a night stop at Andersen Air Force Base (AFB) in Guam we continued our journey eastwards across the vast blue reaches of the Pacific Ocean. We stopped briefly at Wake Island and then continued on to Hickam AFB in Honolulu, crossing the International Date Line as we did so. So having

[1] Now superseded by Universal Co-ordinated Time, designated internationally as UTC.

taken off from Wake Island on Thursday evening, local time, and flown overnight, we landed in Honolulu on Thursday morning. It was all very confusing, and accounts for the fact that crew members on long-haul flights keep their watches on GMT, adding or subtracting the time difference as appropriate in order to ascertain the local time. It was in Honolulu where I first experienced another feature of long-haul operations, and that was the scourge of 'jet-lag'. By this stage of our journey, all the crew were suffering to a greater or lesser degree from fatigue, induced not only by the tempo of operations but also by the cumulative effects of disruption to our normal sleep pattern.

As far as possible, we adjusted to local times, going to bed at night and rising in the morning. But the further local time became removed from GMT, the less our disturbed and confused metabolisms co-operated. So it was that in Honolulu I went to bed in my hotel as midnight approached, only to find that at 2am I was wide awake again. And not just wide awake, but absolutely-bright-as-a-button awake and simply raring to go. Unfortunately, we were not scheduled to leave until about mid-day and, try as I might, I could not get back to sleep again. By the time we reached our next staging post at McClellan AFB, near Sacramento in California, I was so tired that I could hardly keep my eyes open.

We were by now coming towards the final stages of our journey. The next day, after a very welcome good night's sleep, we took off from McClellan in a temperature of 46°C (115°F) and made our way across the northern states of America to Offutt AFB in Nebraska, Headquarters of the Strategic Air Command of the United States Air Force. After a brief stop to refuel we continued on our way, heading north-eastwards across the Great Lakes and on into Canada, where we landed at Gander Airport in Newfoundland. Another period of rest and we were ready for the final leg of our journey across the Atlantic Ocean and back to Brize Norton.

To allow for navigator training in the northern latitudes, however, we returned not by the direct route but by a lengthy semi-circular track that took us almost to the North Pole before turning south-eastwards to cross Greenland and Iceland. Having taken off from Gander in the evening and flown overnight, dawn was breaking as we coasted in over the West Coast of Scotland and made our way southwards along the spine of England to our base at Brize Norton. As it happened, it was my turn among the four pilots on board to fly the last leg, so after an extremely long and tiring journey I found myself under radar control flying a precision approach into our destination.. It took an immense effort of will to overcome the fatigue I felt and summon up the concentration required for the approach, but somehow I managed it, and followed a credible approach with a smooth and successful landing.

Compared with the relatively modest route trips that we had carried out on the Hastings, flying right round the world in a single mission had been an enormous enterprise. The aircraft, however, had performed magnificently, and we had maintained our planned route on time chock-to-chock for almost the entire journey, even down to arriving back at Brize Norton within minutes of our scheduled time of arrival. After such a long flight, there was hardly a single technical snag on the aircraft, which was soon back on the line for another mission after replenishment and cleaning. As we headed to our respective homes for a few days well-earned rest and recuperation, I reflected that the trip augured well for my forthcoming tour on No 10 Squadron.

10 Squadron's main peacetime role was supporting the extensive British military establishments in the Far East, and to this end it operated what was known as the 'Changi Slip'. The 'slip' was a route between Brize Norton in the UK and RAF Changi in Singapore. Crews were positioned at intermediate refuelling stops along the way, so that the aircraft could operate continuously from one end of the route to the other, each crew handing over to the next one at each stage of the journey. Leaving Brize Norton at 3.00 o'clock in the afternoon, a crew would operate the first leg direct to Bahrain in the Persian Gulf, before handing over to the a slip crew who would take the aircraft on its next stage. Twenty four hours later, the first crew would meet the next day's schedule at Bahrain at around midnight, and take it on to Singapore with an intermediate refuelling stop at RAF Gan, a staging post at the southernmost tip of the Maldive Islands in the Indian Ocean.

A night stop at RAF Changi was followed by a 7.30 pm departure for Gan, arriving at about midnight and handing on to the crew ahead. The next leg involved another middle-of-the-night departure for the long flight to Akrotiri in Cyprus, with the final leg, 24 hours later, direct from Akrotiri to Brize Norton. Once a week the schedule was extended from Singapore to Hong Kong and back, and a slip crew from Changi would operate the flight. Depending on the various schedules, it would a take a crew some 10 to 13 days to complete the 'slip'. Then, after a period of stand-down, the whole process would begin all over again. The composition of the crews was not fixed, with the leader of each aircrew section allocating a crew member in accordance with his own priorities. A basic crew would consist of two pilots, one of which would be the designated the aircraft captain and the other the copilot. Also on the flight deck were the navigator and the flight engineer. The cabin crew comprised an air loadmaster and three air stewards. In the full seat fit, the aircraft would normally carry about 130 passengers. These would be military personnel and accompanying wives and children. The crew for the mission circulated round the slip like a group of nomads, moving from one staging post to another in accordance with the dictates of the schedule. At each resting place we would invariably have a wind-down drink together before fatigue overcame us and we made our way to bed. Thereafter, depending on the length of our stay and the predilection of the various crew members, we might arrange to socialise again if there was a convenient opportunity before departure. In the main, the rule of no alcohol in the 10 hours prior to departure was regularly observed.

Because the slip pattern involved such long absences from home, there was no requirement to be present at the squadron in between flights. Each Monday morning, however, there was an obligatory aircrew briefing for all squadron members not away en route. The minutes of each meeting were placed in the Captain's Diary, which also contained the aircraft itinerary, copies of the various diplomatic clearances for each country to be transited during the flight, and various other items of information pertinent to the mission. By reading the minutes of the Monday meetings, all crew members could keep up to date with day-to-day changes affecting the squadron. That apart, crew members were free to follow their own devices when they were stood down. There was an occasional commitment to the daily stand-by crew. For the pilots, there was also a monthly slot in the simulator to practise emergency procedures and brush up on any changes to normal operating techniques. In the welcome period of stand-down at home, I was able to catch up with the normal administration of domestic affairs, try my hand at the numerous maintenance tasks that came with being a householder, and assist my wife with the demanding task of bringing up two small but energetic boys. For relaxation, I joined the nearby Burford Golf Club.

For the next three years the Changi slip regulated my life to the point where I knew the routes like the back of my hand. Operating every other leg, I also became more proficient at handling the aircraft, and more knowledgeable about its performance. I flew with many different Captains, and I was able to observe at first hand how they handled the responsibility and conducted the flight. The initial batch of pilots to be trained on the VC10 had been drawn from the ranks of highly experienced aircraft captains, some from the V-force and others with many years in the air transport role. Being not yet 30 years old when I joined the unit, I became one of a younger group of pilots who were to follow in their footsteps. In my early days as a copilot, I was somewhat overawed by the distinguished company I was keeping, and kept a low profile; but as I gained experience on the aircraft my confidence grew, and I began to play a wider role in the life of the Squadron. Because of the demands of the slip, however, there were 36 crews established on the Squadron, and with so many people involved in the operation it was not easy to make your mark. For my part, I was still keen to pursue my career as far as possible, so I enrolled in the Individual Staff Studies Course, a correspondence course designed to prepare Junior Officers for staff appointments. At first I studied this course at home in between periods en route, but I soon realised that I had a lot of spare time on my hands at the various staging posts while waiting for the next aircraft movement, and the days would pass more quickly if I spent some of the time working on my course. So began a habit of study that was to continue for the remainder of my time on 10 Squadron and to hold me in good stead for the rest of my life. I discovered that I had an aptitude for staff work and I did well on my correspondence course. Next, I decided to fill in some of the gaps in my education, which at school and at Cranwell had been largely science-based. Accordingly, I began to study the arts. Starting with a correspondence course in A-Level History, which I enjoyed enormously, I subsequently went on to study for many years with the Open University. Having undertaken numerous courses in the arts faculty, I was eventually awarded a Bachelor of Arts Degree with Honours in 1989.

After a year on the Squadron spent almost entirely flying the Changi slip, I went on a training flight across the United States, and after that my horizons expanded considerably, with flights to many different parts of the world. The RAF VC10s were often involved in contingency operations, and about half-way through my tour as a copilot I was called out unexpectedly for just such event. It transpired that an East African Airways VC10 had crashed while attempting to take off from Addis Ababa airport, and there were many casualties urgently requiring intensive and specialised care that the local hospitals were unable to provide. The UK government offered to assist and an aeromedical evacuation flight was mounted at very short notice. We took off from Brize Norton at 8.00 o'clock in the evening and flew overnight, arriving at Addis Ababa at dawn. The plan was that we would then have 12 hours rest before flying the return leg with a full load of patients. Because the airfield at Addis Ababa is some 7,500 feet above sea level, and it is also very hot, it was not possible with a full payload to put on sufficient fuel for a direct flight to Brize Norton. The return itinerary therefore included a refuelling stop at Akrotiri. When we disembarked at Addis Ababa, however, we discovered that there had been some confusion locally about the arrangements, and all the patients had been brought to the airport ready for an immediate departure. There was chaos everywhere, but one thing was clear; we would have to forego our rest and take off as soon as we reasonably could. The aeromedical team, who had had some rest on the overnight outbound journey, set to work with a will loading the patients onto the VC10. Many of the patients were badly burned and injured, some to such an extent that they were not to survive the journey back to the UK.

Using facilities provided by one of the handling agents at Addis Ababa, I attempted to send a message back to our Operations Centre at RAF Upavon, informing them of our earlier-than-planned departure and the pressing need for a relief crew to take over the aircraft at Akrotiri. The message, however, must have gone astray in the melee at the airport, because there is no record that it was ever received. We eventually took off at about 10.00 am local time and set course for Akrotiri, some four hours flying distant. As soon as we were safely established in the cruise I attempted to raise one of our Flight Watch stations on HF. Under normal circumstances I should have been able to contact any one of these stations without difficulty, but conditions for the propagation of radio waves must have been unusually bad on that particular morning, as after nearly an hour of trying I had been unable to raise anyone.

Finally, in desperation, I succeeded in contacting the British Airways station in London. I impressed upon them the urgency of the situation, and they agreed to pass on the message to Upavon without delay I learned later that the message had indeed been received at Upavon and forwarded on immediately to Akrotiri. With less than three hours to go before the aircraft was due to arrive in Cyprus, the Operations Staff at Akrotiri sprang into action. As was often the case, the slip crews were being accommodated in hotels in Limassol, a town about 20 miles from Akrotiri, so a vehicle was dispatched to the town, where the seafront cafés were scoured for itinerant crew members, and a scratch crew hastily assembled. All went well, and when we eventually landed at Akrotiri after an exhausting 20 hours or so of continuous operations, and more than 24 hours without sleep, a full crew was ready to fly the aircraft back to the UK.

On another occasion I was again called out at short notice, this time as part of a scratch crew that was to fly a VIP to Washington DC for the funeral of President Lyndon Johnson, who had died suddenly of a heart attack shortly after leaving office. It was January, and although the runway and taxiways at Heathrow had been cleared of snow, it was still quite slippery around the area of the hard standing where we parked the aircraft nose-in to one of the terminals. It was customary on these VIP flights to fly a standard above the cockpit roof, erecting it through a small port that was normally used by the navigator for the telescopic sextant. So with our flag flying, and our VIP safely on board, we attempted to push back from the terminal. Because of the slippery conditions, however, the tug that was attempting to push the aircraft back could not get sufficient purchase, and, try as we might, the aircraft would not move. After various remedies had been unsuccessfully attempted, and in some desperation, the Captain eventually selected reverse thrust on both outboard engines and, with a great roar of escaping jet exhaust gases, combined with a mighty heave from the tug, we eventually emerged onto the taxiway. We were by now some 20 minutes late on our scheduled departure time.

The Heathrow air traffic controllers were aware of our VIP status and gave us priority over all other aircraft as we sped along the taxiway towards the runway in use. As was normal, we carried out the pre-take off checks on the roll and as we approached the runway we were given clearance for an immediate take-off. As soon as we had we lifted off and retracted the undercarriage, we became aware of an unusual noise on the flight deck like the sound of escaping air. With a growing sense of disbelief and dismay we realised that we had taken off without retracting the VIP's standard, which was now flying bravely at about 250 knots immediately above our heads. The navigator left his station and attempted to retract the flagpole, but it was held firmly in place by the suction applied by the airstream passing over the roof of flight deck, and it refused to budge.

Having depressurised the aircraft, the flight engineer left his station and joined the navigator pulling on the handle of the flagpole. Still it refused to budge. The Captain handed over control to me and I was left carrying out the Heathrow departure procedure on my own while he joined the navigator and the engineer in what appeared to be a frantic tug-of-war. I reduced speed as far as could without actually stalling the aircraft and the slight drop in suction over the roof of the flight deck coupled with the combined efforts of the three men suddenly allowed the flagpole to retract. The proper seal was inserted into the roof aperture, everyone resumed their seats, and with a huge sigh of relief order was restored and the departure continued. There was not, however, much left of the standard other than a few strips of torn cloth, and when we arrived at Andrews AFB in Washington we decided that it would probably be best not to fly it.

Reviewing the incident in the post-flight debrief, we realised that there was an item in the pre-flight check-list that called for the flag-mast to be lowered but, as it was rarely used on normal route operations, some navigators habitually omitted the check. In this instance, the navigator, as was his custom, omitted the check, and the two pilots, preoccupied with the rushed departure procedures at a busy airport, failed to notice. It is on such small matters that the success or failure of an operational mission can sometimes hang.

In the summer of 1973, after three years as a copilot on the squadron, I went back to 241 OCU for a Captain's Conversion Course, which I completed successfully. In addition to several sorties at Brize Norton, during which I converted to the left-hand seat in the cockpit, I also carried out a route trip to Akrotiri and back under the supervision of an OCU instructor. All went well with the outbound leg. Then, following a night's sleep and an early morning call, we were scheduled to take over an aircraft inbound from the Far East. We were in the flight planning section preparing for the leg home when we heard the roar of the reverse thrust as the inbound aircraft landed. The passengers had disembarked and were stretching their legs in the transit lounge when I received a telephone call from the engineers. There was a problem with the 'honey truck', and the aircraft toilets could not be emptied. What was I going to do? In my capacity as a Captain under training, I faced up to my new responsibilities, watched with interest by my instructor. Would it be possible to fly the five hours back to Brize Norton without the toilets being emptied? Probably not, seeing as how the aircraft had just completed an eight-hour leg with 130 passengers on board! What other options were available? Delay the aircraft and its passengers until the honey truck could be repaired. Not a very promising course of action. Empty the toilets onto the dispersal and have the fire section wash away the waste with their hoses. Good idea! And everyone on-board with the plan! So we went out to the aircraft and prepared for the flight. The passengers re-boarded, the doors were closed and the toilets were emptied onto the dispersal. Just at that moment there was a call from a visiting Victor aircraft that was returning to base with one of his refuelling hoses still extended, and all the fire engines rushed off to the end of the runway to deal with the emergency. There was now nothing for it but to start the engines and taxi slowly out to the end of the runway leaving behind a steaming pile of effluent. It was a somewhat inglorious start to a new chapter of my life.

Having spent more that five years of my life as a copilot in one capacity or another, I was more that ready to take my turn as a Captain, and I greatly enjoyed the responsibility and prestige that came with my new status. An added bonus was that I was automatically promoted to the rank of Acting Squadron Leader, an advancement that brought with it a welcome increase in my salary. When the VC10s came in to service, the RAF was faced for the first time with an aircraft that was directly comparable with those being flown by the civilian airlines. Given the huge disparity in the rates of pay, there was an understandable fear that the RAF-trained VC10 pilots might depart in droves for the more lucrative world of commercial aviation, so automatic promotion to Squadron Leader was offered as an inducement to stay. While this policy met with some success, its downside was that it alienated all those RAF aircrew who flew as captains on aircraft other than the VC10. At that time there were three other air transport squadrons based at Brize Norton, two of Britannias and one of Belfasts, whose captains did not benefit from this arrangement, and there was some understandable rancour towards those who did. After many years, and constant representation from 10 Squadron, the policy was eventually rescinded, but it took the personal involvement of the then Commander-in-Chief to bring about the change.

My time as a Captain on 10 Squadron coincided with the withdrawal of British forces from Singapore and this brought about a significant change in our route structure. After the run-down had been completed, the RAF staging facilities at Bahrain and Gan were closed down. There was still a large garrison in Hong Kong, however, so the slip pattern was altered with crews now staging through Bahrain and Colombo, and night-stopping in Hong Kong. We were also accommodated in hotels rather than RAF transit messes, so the change brought with it a welcome increase in our allowances. Additionally, we undertook more flights across the Atlantic to North America, with a regular weekly schedule via Ottawa to Dulles Airport in Washington DC. Another new venture found the squadron involved operations from Germany to Calgary, in western Canada, in support of the British Army Training Unit at Suffield (BATUS), where a large-scale tank training area had been set up.

It was on a direct flight from Brize Norton to Calgary that I met an RAF Flight Lieutenant Engineering Officer in his late 30s, who came on to the flight deck during the long transit over the polar regions and sat on the jump seat. He told us that he was leaving the RAF and emigrating to Canada with his family. He had written to several companies in the Vancouver area and been invited for job interviews. His plan was to travel to Calgary by means of an indulgence flight and then take a train to Vancouver, returning by the same means a week later. We were impressed by his initiative and enterprise. When we reached Calgary in mid-afternoon we offered him a lift from the airport into the town on our crew transport, and he arranged to stay for the night at our hotel. At that time the crews were accommodated in the Palliser Hotel, which was located right in the centre of downtown Calgary and next door to the railway station. In the basement of the hotel was a bar where they served cold beer and excellent beef sandwiches; and there, joined by our new-found colleague, we retired for a post-flight drink and a snack. We stayed rather longer than originally intended, but when it came to our cut-off time for the consumption of alcohol we made our excuses and went to bed in anticipation of an early start the next day. When I came down into the hotel lobby in the small hours of the morning I was surprised to find the Flight Lieutenant, still in uniform, talking to members of my crew. As I came up to the group he approached me and asked me if he could fly back with us to Brize Norton, a request to which I readily agreed, as we had a virtually empty aircraft on the return leg. I didn't like to press him too hard on his reasons, but it transpired in conversation during the return flight that he had tried Canada and found the country wanting!

Despite these changes to our route structure, a lot of our time was still spent in the Far East. On one such trip my crew and I had travelled as far as Hong Kong. We were expecting to return by our normal route to Brize Norton, but our itinerary was changed and we were directed to fly on to Fiji and Australia instead. Departing Hong Kong in the late afternoon, we flew overnight to Fiji with a refuelling stop in Guam. Dawn was breaking when we landed at Nandi airport, the latitude of which is 180° E/W, exactly on the other side of the world from the Greenwich meridian, and almost as far from the UK as it is possible to travel. We put the aircraft to bed and made our way wearily to a nearby hotel where, in lieu of breakfast, we ordered wind-down drinks from the bar instead. There was a young Corporal Air Stewardess on the crew who was making her first route trip with the squadron. On the way out to Hong Kong she had been full of beans, excited by all the exotic sights and sounds of the East, and enjoying every minute of the experience. As we sat sipping our drinks in the early morning, I noticed that she had tears streaming down her face.

'Whatever's the matter?' I asked her, in as kindly voice as I could muster.

'I'm homesick,' she said, through her tears.

Fortunately, we had an experienced female Air Loadmaster on the crew, and I asked her if she would see the young girl safely into bed, which she did. Later that day, fully rested, the stewardess had fortunately recovered most of her former bounce and zest. The next day we resumed our trip across Australia and then rejoined the slip once more at Gan before returning to the UK some five days later than originally scheduled.

I HAD VISITED AUSTRALIA once before when we operated in support of exercise Northern Star/Southern Cross. This was an exchange between Army personnel from the UK and Australian soldiers from Townsville on the coast of Queensland near the Great Barrier Reef. Picking up the aircraft in Gan, we had flown some eight hours across the Indian Ocean to Perth in Western Australia. A refuelling stop, and another five hours across the vast empty centre of Australia, brought us to Townsville, where we were due on the chocks at 10.00 am local time. We landed exactly on the dot and taxied slowly round the perimeter to the dispersal where the Mayor, a band, and a Guard of Honour were waiting to greet the British contingent. On the aircraft's HF radio, we had tuned in the BBC World Service, and as we approached the dispersal we could hear the introductory music to the news being played. As we turned onto the dispersal the pips started 'pip... pip... pip... pip... pip...' and a longer 'peep' as we stopped precisely in front of the dais. 'That should impress the Australians,' I thought to myself with some satisfaction. 'We bring the contingent 12,000 miles and they arrive at their destination exactly to the second.'

Some two years into my tour as a VC10 captain, 10 Squadron was involved in an international airlift set up under the auspices of the United Nations to bring refugees from Angola to Portugal. Angola, a former Portuguese colony, had gained its independence in 1975 following a war of liberation, but independence was followed almost immediately by a vicious civil war as various factions sought to gain control of the country. Almost half a million of the Portuguese settlers in Angola sought to flee the fighting, most of them hoping to resettle back in their native land, and it was in response to this crisis that the airlift had been initiated. For six weeks my crew and I were detached to Lisbon, from where we flew regular flights to Angola and back, each leg being some seven hours in length. On the way down to Luanda, the capital of Angola, we were empty, and on the return leg to Lisbon we were full.

Leaving Lisbon at 10.00 am, we arrived in Luanda in the late afternoon, where we handed over to a second crew who were to fly the return leg. We then spent the night in a hotel in the centre of the town before returning to the airport in mid-afternoon to pick up the next days schedule for the return flight. Arriving in Lisbon at midnight, we then had a day off before repeating the schedule all over again. Once we adapted to the routine, it became quite a pleasant life-style. Although at that time subject to considerable political unrest, Lisbon was still a very attractive town, and we were able to enjoy its many delights without let or hindrance. In Luanda there was considerably more tension, but by exercising due caution it was possible to move freely about the town during daylight hours. Because of the war, however, food was in short supply. The hotel was supposed to provide breakfast but, on inquiring, we discovered that there was no food. Consequently before our next trip, we went shopping in Lisbon and took with us a few basic provisions such as bread, bacon and eggs. When at breakfast time we were once again informed that there was no food, we offered up our own provisions, which were then cooked in the kitchen and served up to us. I expect, however, that the hotel still charged us for breakfast.

Not only was there no food in Luanda, but there was hardly anything else in the shops. Oddly enough, however, not far from the hotel there was an ironmonger who still had plenty of stock. As our allowances were paid in US dollars, we were able to purchase various tools and implements at knock down prices and these were then shipped back to Lisbon in the forward belly-hold of the aircraft. Amongst other items, I bought a spirit level and a mole wrench which I still have to this day. On another occasion I decided to have a haircut in the hotel barbers shop. It was obvious that the barber did not have many customers as he spent an inordinate amount of time washing, drying and cutting my hair. As he spoke no English and I no Portuguese, conversation was a bit limited, but at the end of this elaborate process I held out a note for 1,000 Portuguese escudos. The barber shook his head. I added a second note. Again he shook his head. A third, and still there was no reaction. Finally, and now in some desperation, I offered him 4,000 escudos, at which he smiled and pocketed the cash. We shook hands and I left the salon. I cannot now remember what the exchange rate was between Portuguese escudos and English pounds, but I reckoned afterwards that it was probably the most expensive haircut I had ever had, either then or since.

Our route from Lisbon to Luanda took us southward across the Sahara Desert, where we came under Algiers Control. Our operations were almost invariably carried out under what are known as Instrument Meteorological Conditions (IMC), meaning that the world-wide network of Air Traffic Control Centres were responsible for the safe separation of aircraft within their Flight Information Regions (FIRs). However, most of the air-to-ground communications in these remote parts were by less-than-reliable HF radio. Accordingly, it was also common practice amongst all airlines operating in Africa to listen out on 126.7 KHz, a VHF frequency providing a sort of self-separating air traffic control in a continent where communications were always difficult and often lacking altogether. Listening out on VHF, I heard a blind transmission passed by an airliner that was en route from South America to Rome. He was at the same flight level as we were and it seemed as if we were also in close proximity and possibly converging rapidly. I called him on VHF and he acknowledged my call. I told him that we were close together, at the same height, and possibly converging. If he would climb 500 feet, I would descend by the same amount. Hardly had we levelled off at our new temporary height than I saw him approaching from our one-o'clock position. Our closing speed was close on 1,000 mph and he passed almost right overhead, so close that I could see clearly the rivets on the underside of his fuselage. It was obvious to everyone on the flight deck that, had we not taken action, we would surely have collided in mid-air. We should have reported the incident to Algiers Control, but HF communications were poor to non-existent, as indeed was the possibility of sending any sort of ground communication after landing in Luanda. Consequently, we shrugged our shoulders, putting the incident down to one of those extraordinary mishaps that sometimes occur even in the highly safety-conscious world of global aviation.

One member of my crew during the detachment was a young man who was on his first tour as a navigator, and on one of our early sorties we had a discussion on the nature of time. For obvious reasons, it was important that each member of the crew recorded the same time for take-off and landing so that all the various logs agreed. Times were logged in intervals of five minutes and normally this was not a problem. Occasionally, however, the take-off or the landing would take place between two five-minute intervals, such as 7½ minutes past the hour. On these occasions, it was my invariable practice to agree the time with the navigator. On this particular occasion, however, we disagreed, with me saying that we should call it 5 minutes past the hour and the navigator saying that it should be 10 past. He insisted that as the navigator he was the arbiter of time and, as I was older and more experienced, I kept my counsel and let him have his way. It so happened that on our final leg from Luanda to Lisbon, we needed 7 hours flight time to complete 100 hours of flying during the detachment. We were supposed to land just after midnight, but we actually touched down a couple of minutes prior to the hour. 'Shall we call that 5-past?' I asked the navigator, thus bringing our flight time on the detachment to exactly 100 hours. 'Roger, Captain,' he said, without argument, thereby proving conclusively that the Captain has the final say on everything that happens on an aircraft.

The following year the squadron was involved once again with detached operations, this time with two crews being based in Hong Kong. The task arose because of cuts to the RAF's air transport force that had taken place earlier in the year. The two Britannia squadrons based at Brize Norton had been axed, together with the Belfast Fleet, leaving the VC10 as the only remaining strategic airlifter in the RAF's inventory. Tactical airlift continued to be provided by four squadrons of Hercules based at RAF Lyneham in Wiltshire. The Hong Kong detachment, which 10 Squadron had picked up from the now defunct Britannia squadrons, was set up to fly Gurkha troops and their families from Kathmandu in Nepal to Hong Kong. At that time the useable runway at Kathmandu was only 6,600 feet in length. As the airfield was also some 4,000 feet above sea-level, it was not possible to take off with a full load of passengers and enough fuel to reach Hong Kong. Accordingly, Calcutta airport was used as an intermediate refuelling stop. The normal pattern of operations was to take off from Hong Kong in the morning and fly to Calcutta. Enough fuel was then uplifted to fly to Kathmandu and back. From Calcutta we undertook the short but exacting route to Kathmandu, with just enough room to circle between the hills surrounding the airport before landing on the relatively short runway. A night stop in Kathmandu was followed by a return flight via Calcutta to a late-evening arrival at Hong Kong. A second crew took the next day's schedule, while the first crew had a day off in which to rest and recuperate.

From a pilot's perspective, one of the most spectacular sights of this operation was the departure from Kathmandu. As the surface wind was nearly always light and variable, we invariably took off in a northerly direction to avoid damage to the control tower from our jet blast. Usually the airfield was covered in a blanket of thick haze with visibility restricted to a couple of miles. As the aircraft climbed above the haze layer and emerged into the clear air, we were treated to the magnificent sight of Mount Everest right ahead of us and seemingly so close that you could reach out and touch it, with its banner cloud streaming out like a long white scarf from the summit. Then the spectacle was lost to view as we turned south and set course for Calcutta. If the departure from Kathmandu was spectacular, the night approach into Kai Tak airport at Hong Kong was equally impressive, particularly when landing on the north-easterly runway, involving as it did a last-minute turn over the high-rise apartments of Kowloon.

To help the pilots with this turn, a chequerboard had been mounted on a high hillside behind the town and the initial approach was made towards this using a modified Instrument Landing System (ILS) for guidance. At 600 feet on the descent, by which time the chequerboard would be in view, a right-hand turn was made to line up with the runway at about 300 feet. The runway itself projected out into the harbour, with high ground all round, and in any sort of wind it took a considerable degree of skill to accomplish a smooth landing in the dark. In later years, a new Hong Kong airport was constructed on an island further away from the mainland, so the pilots of today are no longer treated to that hair-raising thrill of manoeuvring a large aircraft near to the ground over a densely-populated area.

While refuelling was being carried out at Calcutta, where the outside air temperature often exceeded 38°C (100°F), we normally sat in the cockpit, which remained relatively cool. The passengers, too, were kept on the aircraft. On one such occasion I was approached by the Air Loadmaster who informed me that there was a young Gurkha boy on board who appeared to be seriously ill. I went down to the back of the aircraft and there was the child who did indeed seem to be at his last gasp. His face was a pale grey and he had hardly any pulse. I pondered on what to do. It would obviously be risky to fly him for five or six hours on the next leg, yet I was reluctant to leave him in Calcutta, where we had no staff who might take responsibility for his well-being.

After some deliberation, and after consulting with the Air Loadmaster, I decided that his best chance of survival would be to get him to Hong Kong. We had some portable oxygen sets on board the aircraft and I arranged for him to be put on oxygen and his condition to be carefully monitored during the next leg. We had taken off and climbed to altitude when a note was handed to me by a member of the cabin crew. Typed in English, the note was from a doctor in Kathmandu, stating that the boy was suffering from a hole-in-the-heart and was urgently in need of an operation. It went on to provide more details of the boy's condition and of the procedures required for its treatment. We contacted our operations in Hong Kong by HF radio, explaining the circumstances and passing on the contents of the note. We also asked for an ambulance to meet the aircraft on arrival. To our immense relief, the boy survived the journey.

No sooner had we landed in Hong Kong and opened the doors of the aircraft, than the boy and his parents were whisked away to the British Military Hospital. We heard later that the boy had been operated on that very night and was expected to make a satisfactory recovery. Reflecting later on the incident, I surmised that the boy's parents had been told that the only hope for the boy had been to get him to a hospital for an operation as soon as possible. The movement of the family to Hong Kong had presented an unprecedented opportunity and the parents had said nothing of the boy's condition in case he was refused a passage. Once on board, the flight from Kathmandu to Calcutta had exacerbated his condition, not only putting his life in danger, but also presenting me as Captain of the aircraft with a challenging dilemma.

After nearly three years as a VC Captain, and some six years on 10 Squadron altogether, I was concerned about what the future might hold for me. I had held the acting rank of Squadron Leader for almost three years, yet there was still no sign of promotion to substantive rank. This lack of progress was despite the fact that I was by now a senior member of the squadron and regularly assessed as an above-the-average pilot and aircraft captain. Over the preceding 12 months I had also held a non-established Flight Commander's post in charge of the Air Loadmasters and Air Stewards on the squadron. Furthermore, many of my contemporaries had been already been promoted, and it was clear to me that in career terms I was being left behind. Fortunately, my efforts had not gone entirely unnoticed and in the middle of 1976 I was informed by my desk officer that I was to be promoted to the substantive rank of Squadron Leader and re-toured on 10 Squadron as the Flight Commander Training. It was with some relief that I took up my new appointed and looked forward to the challenges ahead.

132 Squadron at camp

Thorney Island, 1956. The author, in flying kit, is in the third row, second from the left
[Courtesy of John Cope]

A Midland Aero Club Tiger Moth at Birmingham Elmdon Airport, 1959

Advanced Flying Training on the Vickers Varsity at RAF Oakington, January 1963.
(From left to right) Back row: Ross, McCarthy, Balquez, Adcock, Rolfe
Front row: Annett, Cane, Cross, Sawyer [Courtesy Barry Priest]

Flight Cadet with Morris 8.

Jet Provosts in Formation over the RAF College Cranwell
Courtesy RAF Air Historical Branch (AHB)

Vickers Varsity T Mk 1 [Courtesy AHB]

Handley Page Hastings C Mk I [Courtesy of AHB]

Handley Page Hastings [Courtesy of AHB]

Breda Allen, 1964

A Cyprus Wedding – Guard of Honour at the Officers Mess RAF Nicosia

The Vickers VC10 [Courtesy AHB]

RAF VC10 in Australia [Courtesy AHB]

BAe Jetstream [Courtesy AHB]

RAF Andover [Courtesy AHB]

The Mississippi and the St Louis Arch

E Street, Scott AFB, Illinois with Plymouth Fury and Chevrolet Caprice Classic

Lockheed C141B of the Military Airlift Command [Courtesy Bob Harrington]

Colonel John J Vilensons
Chief of MAC DOV

A C-141 approaching a KC-135 tanker
[Courtesy Richard Seaman]

The IALCE at Bandfoss

The IALCE at Corlu

BAe Bulldog flight trainer [Courtesy AHB]

Taking Command of RAF Newton – 2 April 1993

A Chipmunk over the River Trent. [Courtesy of the artist, Tim O'Brien]

Vigilant Powered Glider [Courtesy AHB]

RAF Newton Air Day, 1995

The Grob Tutor [Courtesy AHB]

The Wedding of James & Sarah Adcock, September 1994
[Courtesy Shaun D. Smith, Kamara Photographs]

The Marriage of Brian Adcock and Caroline Southern, February 1999
[Courtesy Bill Mutler Studio]

Flying Officer Brian Adcock RAFVR(T)

The Grandchildren – Florence, Chloe, Esther, Niamh & Arthur – 2011

Steve Jarmain - OC 2 AEF

The author and his wife, Breda, being dined-out at the 2 AEF Annual Dinner 2010 in the Officers Mess, Boscombe Down

CHAPTER 7

Flight Commander

NOW THAT I was assured of at least two more years of service at RAF Brize Norton, my wife and I decided to invest in a new home. Our two boys had reached the ages of eight and six and as a family we needed more space. Some new larger homes were at the time being constructed in Faringdon, a pleasant market town located some 10 miles to the south of Brize Norton, and we eventually purchased one of these. In the six years that we had lived in Carterton our small 3-bedroomed house had increased almost threefold in value, so we considered ourselves fortunate to have entered the property market when we did. The increased mortgage that we took on with the new house was more than off-set by my pay as a Squadron Leader, particularly as this had recently benefited from the introduction of the Military Salary under Mrs Thatcher's Conservative Government. The only downside to the move was that I now had to buy a second car in which to commute daily to Brize Norton, and to this end I bought a second-hand Fiat 500, which admirably served the purpose.

My new duties as the Flight Commander Training on 10 Squadron consisted not only of looking after all matters relating to pilot training on the squadron but also responsibility for the 36 Acting Squadron Leader Captains. My main function was the allocation of individuals to the various tasks that arose each month. As an operational squadron, not only were we heavily tasked but the tasking itself was subject to constant changes. Consequently, the programme had to be continually updated. Desktop computers had yet to be introduced into the workplace, so all the planning was done with a chinagraph pencil on large Perspex boards. Unlike many other squadrons in the RAF, where proficiency was based on a monthly continuation training (MCT) commitment, VC10 training for 10 Squadron crew members was carried out by 241 OCU on a 6-monthly cycle known as periodic refresher training (PRT). A lot of this training was carried out in the VC10 simulator, which came under the auspices of 241 OCU, and it made eminent sense for the flying element of PRT to be carried out by the same organisation. From my perspective as the Flight Commander, therefore, it was merely a matter of assigning captains to the OCU shortly before their categories became due for renewal. When they returned to the squadron at the end of the week, having been retrained and re-categorised, they were then ready for another six months of squadron operations before the whole cycle began all over again. Under normal RAF operations, aircraft captains would be briefed by a Flight Commander or an Authorising Officer prior to a sortie, and it would be the responsibility of those officers to ensure that the captain had considered all the factors that might affect the flight. Captains of air transport aircraft, however, who operated for long periods away from their home base, were merely authorised for the task before leaving base, and then it was up to them to get on with it. Periodic refresher training, with its associated categorisation system, was designed to ensure that they were fully capable of doing so.

Most of the captains were highly professional in their approach to their duties, and it was a pleasure and a privilege to work with them. There were, however, one or two who fell slightly short of the mark. It was not that they could not fly the aircraft to an acceptable standard, nor that they were in any way dangerous, but they could not always be relied upon to make the optimum decision when faced with situations that fell outside the scope of normal operations. In aviation terms, what they lacked was 'airmanship', a quality that might be defined as being constantly aware of the multitude of factors affecting a flight and adjusting their decision-making accordingly. 'Airmanship' is to the pilot what 'roadcraft' is to the motorist; that is the ability to assess what is going to happen in a dynamic situation and take timely and appropriate action. Most people acquire this ability through experience, but there are a few who never fully develop the skill.

On the squadron this lack of awareness sometimes manifested itself in small ways, but on other occasions it could have more significant consequences. For example, on one of my trips to the Far East I took over the aircraft from one such captain, who briefed me that our Air Officer Commanding (AOC) and his lady were travelling out to Hong Kong on the flight as indulgence passengers. When I boarded the aircraft I found them seated right at the back of the cabin next to the toilets. It so happened that the aircraft was carrying two VIPs on the return flight and there were two up-graded empty seats protected by dust covers at the front of the passenger compartment. I immediately arranged for the air loadmaster to remove the dust covers and then I offered the seats to a grateful AOC. I found it hard to understand why the captain on the first leg could not have performed the same service to the man who was, after all, the supreme head of our transport operations.

On another occasion I was dead-heading back from Hong Kong after screening a newly-qualified captain on the outbound sectors of his first flight in command. I spoke briefly to the captain of the inbound flight and then I took my seat in the cabin and left the crew to it. In effect, I was merely a passenger on the aircraft but, as a Flight Commander on the squadron, I took more than a passing interest in the way that the aircraft was being operated. As the flight approached Bahrain it was brought to my attention in an informal chat with the flight engineer that there was a problem with one of the engines, although it was not entirely clear whether the fault lay with the engine or with the instruments that were monitoring it and supplying information to the cockpit. If the fault was with the instrumentation, the snag could be carried back to base, but a faulty engine would ground the aircraft and all its passengers causing enormous disruption and delay. Both the captain operating the flight and the one taking over the next leg were two of our weaker brethren, and during the handover at Bahrain they managed to turn a drama into a crisis.

As the oncoming captain dithered over what to do, the hours crept by towards midnight, and it seemed that we might soon run out of crew duty time. Eventually I felt compelled to intervene and ask what the problem was. It transpired that what was needed was an engine run to determine whether or not it was developing full power. It was the captain's intention to taxi the aircraft out to the end of the runway and carry out the engine-run. Then, if everything was satisfactory, the aircraft would return to the terminal, board the passengers and proceed. The airport authority in Bahrain was, however, reluctant to authorise an engine run in the middle of the night. I put it to the hapless captain that the solution to his problem was simple. Board the passengers and taxi out as normal. When cleared for take-off, enter the runway and run the engine up to full power. If everything worked normally, continue the take-off. If the engine was faulty, abort the take-off and return to the passenger terminal.

Following this plan, we departed without incident, arriving at Brize Norton several hours late on schedule. Some days later I took the captain to task for unnecessarily delaying the flight, and I went over with him in detail the circumstances affecting his decision. He was duly contrite, but I doubted his ability to rise to the occasion if other untoward circumstances were to arise on his future flights. Nevertheless, I felt also that there was a shortfall in our methods of training. As an organisation, we had a good system for teaching pilots the skills necessary to fly the aircraft, but we lacked the ability to address the problem of poor airmanship. At the time I was only dimly aware of the problem, and it was not until much later in my flying career that I began to develop some ideas about how we might address it.

A lot of flying, especially in the air transport role, is fairly repetitive and routine, but the air is a dangerous element, and problems can develop into a full-blown crisis with unexpected speed. No matter how experienced they may be, aircrew are particularly vulnerable when they are distracted by an unusual development or their critical faculties are dulled by fatigue. In 1976 I was tasked to fly a VC10 back from London Heathrow Airport to Brize Norton. We had positioned at Heathrow in the morning, but various technical and operational complications had delayed our departure until the early evening. It was an extraordinarily hot summer summer's day, with the temperature well into the nineties - conditions usually encountered only in the Mediterranean or the Tropics. By the time we eventually took off from Heathrow and set course for the short flight to Brize Norton, all the crew members, myself included, were exhausted from the heat and stresses of the day. Within a matter of minutes after taking off from Heathrow we were lined up with the westerly runway at Brize Norton and cleared by Air Traffic Control to land. It was still very hot and, furthermore, there was no headwind to help us slow down during the landing run. Meanwhile, the aircraft was at its maximum weight for landing, so we were approaching the runway at a much higher speed than normal. We landed smoothly, but well into the runway.

In other circumstances, a light touch of the brakes would have been sufficient to bring the aircraft down to taxying speed with plenty of room to spare. But on this occasion the large distance-to-go marker boards were flashing by at an alarming speed. I began to apply the brakes, gently at first, but then harder and harder as the end of the runway loomed ahead. Perspiration poured from my brow as I now braked as hard as I could in a desperate attempt to stop in time. At last, with just a few feet of concrete remaining, the huge aircraft came to a halt, allowing us to turn safely off the runway and on to the taxiway. As we made our way slowly back to a safe parking area, with our wheels glowing like red-hot coals from the severe application of the brakes, we were followed by a lengthy procession of fire trucks, police vehicles, ambulances and sundry other vehicles. To make matters worse, our route took us close to the Officers Mess, where a party was in full swing. Adding to our embarrassment, everyone came out to view the spectacle and raise a glass to the hapless crew at the controls. Our journey over, we arrived safely in dispersal and parked the aircraft. Then, with an immense sense of relief, we made our various ways home in the gathering darkness.

Being by now one of the most experienced captains on the squadron, I was selected by the Squadron Commander in the autumn of 1976 to carry James Callaghan, then the UK Prime Minister, on an official visit to Canada. The trip got off to a bad start. We had positioned the aircraft at Heathrow ready for an early take-off the following morning. Accommodated for the night in an airport hotel, we were just enjoying a post-flight beer in the bar when I was called to the telephone. I was informed by the Group Operations Officer that the departure had been delayed; we were to return to Brize Norton and await further instructions. It transpired that a political crisis had arisen that had necessitated the presence of the Prime Minister in the country, so his departure had been postponed. I explained that we had already had a drink in the bar, and our return to base was deferred to the following morning. Another day passed without any further developments except, rather disappointingly, that our itinerary was no longer to include Vancouver but would instead involve a direct flight to Calgary. Departure would now be on the Saturday evening at a time to be notified in due course. On Saturday afternoon I was about to leave my home in Faringdon and set off to Brize Norton when the doorbell rang. To my amazement, it was my elderly aunt and benefactor, Mrs Queenie Woodward. It transpired that she had been staying on the south coast with one of her relatives. Having been out for a drive with a couple of their friends, they had decided on a spur-of-the-moment visit. My wife and the two boys were out for the day, so I invited them in and offered them a cup of tea. Being elderly, they were all rather deaf.

'I have to leave in a few minutes,' I said to my aunt, 'I am going to London to fly the Prime Minister to Canada.'

'What did he say?' said another, who must have thought that she had misheard what I had said.

'He said he's going to fly the Prime Minister to Canada,' relayed my aunt to the astonished group.

This information ricocheted round the group for a few minutes while they drank their tea, then I ushered them out of the door and made a dash for my car.

Once again we positioned the aircraft at Heathrow, this time with a scheduled departure time of eight o'clock at night. When we began our flight planning, however, we discovered that we had 100 knots of wind on the nose for the entire flight, which was now going to take 30 minutes longer than scheduled. I relayed this information back to my Group Operations and asked them to inform the Canadian authorities of our later-than-scheduled arrival. Our departure from Heathrow was to take us northwards towards the Scottish Isles where we would coast out over the Atlantic. Although I had never before flown this particular departure, it was not unduly complicated, even thought it involved routing over two consecutive VOR beacons. An additional factor, however, was the requirement to comply with Heathrow's noise-abatement procedures. Listening posts were located beneath the departure path and there was a limit on the number of decibels that could be emitted by an aircraft at these points. The technique used by all aircraft was to climb at full power initially, so that the worst noise was confined within the airfield boundary, and then throttle back sharply just before the listening post, accepting a lower rate of climb, and reducing the noise footprint over the built-up areas close to the airport. Full power was restored once the aircraft had climbed above 3,000 feet. On the VC10, the point at which the power had to be reduced was calculated by the navigator by means of a graph that took account of the runway in use, the wind speed and direction, the ambient temperature and the all-up weight of the aircraft. After the appropriate interval at full power, the navigator would call 'throttles', and the flight engineer would bring the power smartly back to 90%. It was a procedure that we had used on numerous occasions and one that normally went without a hitch. We had discussed all these requirements at our pre-flight briefing and none of them seemed to pose any particular problem.

As we sat in the darkened cockpit, awaiting the arrival of our distinguished passenger and his accompanying staff, the tension mounted. In due course, a motor cavalcade arrived at the foot of the steps and our passengers boarded the aircraft. We started the engines and taxied out to the runway, carefully remembering to lower the flag-mast before we reached the take-off point. Air Traffic Control cleared us for an immediate take-off and the engineer opened the throttles to full power. We thundered down the runway and launched into the night sky. Holding the aircraft in a steep climb, I scanned the navigation instruments for indications from the first VOR beacon ahead of us and to the right. As I started the turn and headed towards the beacon I sensed that something was amiss, because the needle that should have been pointing towards the second VOR beacon on our departure path was wandering aimlessly around. I quickly asked the navigator for a heading for the second beacon, a request that caught him slightly unawares, and he was forced to peruse his charts for a moment before coming up with the answer. As he did so, he realised that, in the course of this momentary distraction, we had passed the point where he should have called for a reduction in power. Although action was taken immediately to rectify the situation, there was a distinct possibility that we might have exceeded the noise limits in the course of our departure. It had been an exciting few moments, and my heart was still thumping in my chest when reached the top of the climb and settled down in the cruise for the long night-flight to Calgary overflying Iceland, Greenland and northern Canada.

About three weeks after our return from the trip I was acting as the CO of the squadron while the Wing Commander was on leave, when a letter arrived from the Civil Aviation Authority (CAA). It indicated that our flight had indeed exceeded the statutory noise level on that particular departure and asked if we would care to offer an explanation. I wrote a polite reply, citing as a cause the failure of a navigation instrument at a critical moment on the departure and the urgent and overriding need to rectify the situation. I signed the letter as the acting CO of the squadron and sent it off. Not long afterwards I received a second letter from the CAA. This letter not only thanked me for the fullness and frankness of my reply but expressed the wish that all aircraft captains who found themselves in my situation would be as straight-forward and honest. The letter went on to say that no further action would be taken and that the matter was now closed. I filed both letters in the waste paper basket, and nothing more was ever heard about the incident.

During his visit to various ports of call in Canada, the Prime Minister was transported by Air Canada. All we had to do was to stay in reasonable proximity to his location in case of an urgent requirement to return home for political reasons. Accordingly, we spend four nights in Calgary and two in Ottawa, before positioning at the Canadian Air Force base of Shearwater, near Halifax on the north east coast of Nova Scotia, in preparation for the return flight to the UK. Meanwhile, the Prime Minister was spending the final days of his tour at the small town of Sidney, also in Nova Scotia, but on the north coast of the peninsular. The plan was that Air Canada would fly him from Sidney to Shearwater, an airfield with a longer runway, where he would immediately board the VC10 for an overnight return flight to Heathrow. The take-off was scheduled for the evening on the day after our arrival. On the day of our departure I was having a nap in my hotel room during the afternoon when the telephone rang.

'Is that Squadron Leader Adcock, the captain of the VC10?'

'Speaking.'

'Oh. This is Air Canada Operations from Halifax International Airport. We have a flash message for you from your Group Headquarters. They say that it is forecast to be foggy at Heathrow tomorrow morning, and they want to know what you intend to do about it.'

For a few moments I weighed up various possibilities in my mind.

'Tell them that I will check on the weather when I report for briefing at 8.00 o'clock tonight, and I will let them know then.'

I turned out the light and dozed again for perhaps another 20 minutes. Then the telephone rang once more.

'This is the Air Attaché's office from Ottawa. We have received a flash message from your Group Operations. They say that it is forecast to be foggy at Heathrow tomorrow morning, and they want to know what you are intending to do about it.'

I repeated the information that I had already given to Air Canada, then I tried once again to get back to sleep. After about 15 minutes, the telephone rang.

'This is the personal secretary to the Prime Minister, calling from Sidney, Nova Scotia. We hear that it is forecast to be foggy at Heathrow tomorrow morning, and we would like to know what you intend to do about it.'

Having repeated my earlier statement, I decided that further sleep was impossible, so I would get up and dress. Hardly had I sat up in bed than the telephone rang again.

'This is 10 Downing Street...'

WHEN WE ARRIVED AT Shearwater and I checked the weather for various UK airports the forecast did not seem too bad. The minimum visibility for our planned arrival time at Heathrow was 1,500 metres, which was well within our capabilities, so I decided we would proceed as scheduled, and I sent a message to our Group Operations to this effect. There was, however, another problem yet to be overcome, as fog was now swirling about the base at Shearwater. We were in the flight planning section preparing for the flight home when I was called to the telephone in operations.

'This is the captain of the Air Canada flight that is bringing the Prime Minister from Sidney to Shearwater. I hear it's a bit foggy at the base, and I wondered whether or not we would be able to land there.'

'Hang on a minute,' I said, 'I'll step outside and have a look.'

From the steps of the operations building I could see that the airfield was now enveloped in thick fog.

'The prospects of a successful landing don't look too good,' I said, returning to the telephone. 'What are you going to do about it?'

He thought about the situation for a moment. Then he said that he would attempt to land at Shearwater but, if the weather was not suitable, then he would divert to Halifax International Airport, where the forecast was better. I passed this information on to the Shearwater Operations Officer, together with the suggestion that he might want to arrange for a police escort if the Prime Minister was forced to change airports by road. Arrangements were duly put in hand. After a while I was informed that the Air Canada flight was about to make its approach. I heard the sound of engines as the aircraft neared the airfield and then a sudden increase in engine noise as the pilot carried out a missed approach. About 20 minutes later, I heard that he had landed at Greenwood Air Force Base, about 20 miles inland. After a lengthy wait, the Prime Minister and his party arrived and boarded the VC10. For the moment, the fog had lifted slightly, and there was now sufficient visibility for us to depart. We carried out an uneventful night crossing of the Atlantic and landed safely at Heathrow. A few days later I had a letter from the Prime Minister's Personal Secretary passing on the Prime Minister's thanks for the excellent service provided by all the crew during the flight. The letter went on to say that "The Prime Minister realised that the very short notice given for postponed departure must have caused considerable inconvenience to all of you, and he was most appreciative of the way in which you all responded."

How little did he know!

In April the following year I undertook another lengthy and demanding VIP flight when I took Dr David Owen,[1] the then Foreign Secretary, on a tour of what were known as the 'front-line states' in southern Africa. The ostensible purpose of the trip was an attempt by the Foreign Secretary to resolve the long-standing dispute arising from a unilateral declaration of independence (UDI) by Southern Rhodesia in 1965. We took- off on time for the first leg from London to Cairo, where we refuelled, before continuing on to Dar es Salaam in Tanzania, arriving just in time for breakfast. After a day off and a night's rest, we rose the next morning for the trip to Maputo in Mozambique, which was the next stop on the itinerary. We travelled as a crew from our hotel to the airport in several taxis but, when we arrived at the aircraft, I discovered that my suitcase was missing. Apart from the uniform I stood up in, everything else I needed for the seven-day trip was in my suitcase, so this presented me with a dilemma. I could not delay the flight because of its high profile, nor had I the time to look for the missing case myself. On the other hand, my clean uniform shirts, and all my other personal accoutrements were in the case, and I could not really afford to leave them behind. Unusually, we were carrying a staff officer from Group Operations on the trip as a supernumerary crew member, and he volunteered to return to the hotel and there resume the search. We were within a few minutes of the engine-start time when he returned to the aircraft carrying the missing suitcase. Apparently, the luggage had been loaded into five taxis but only four had made the journey to the

[1] Now Lord Owen.

airport. Luckily, the fifth taxi had remained sitting outside the hotel with my suitcase still in the boot.

We were on the ground for three hours in Maputo, while the Foreign Secretary conducted more talks, after which we continued our journey to Cape Town. Following two days of negotiations with the South African government, the decision was made that the Foreign Secretary would proceed to Salisbury, the then capital of Southern Rhodesia,[1] for direct talks with the regime in power. We routed first to Johannesburg, from where the Foreign Secretary and some of his party flew to Botswana in a smaller aircraft, while we continued on to Salisbury. As the first RAF aircraft to land in Rhodesia in the 12 years since UDI, we caused something of a stir when we landed in Salisbury to drop off an advance-party that was to prepare for the subsequent talks. On this occasion, however, our visit was short-lived, as we had to return to Johannesburg to collect the Foreign Secretary and his party, now returned from Botswana, and deliver them to Lusaka for talks with the government of Zambia. Arriving at Lusaka in the dark, dead on time, as always, and at the end of a long and tiring day, we were glad of a good night's rest in a comfortable and well-appointed hotel.

The morning's talks completed, we set off again in the late afternoon for a short and uneventful flight from Lusaka to Salisbury. The next scheduled stop on our itinerary was Luanda in Angola, and then on to Lagos in Nigeria. As our stop in Luanda was to be fairly brief, I agreed with the navigator and the flight engineer that we would put on sufficient fuel for the round trip, thereby eliminating the need to refuel in Luanda. Consequently, when we landed in Salisbury, and I was approached with a slightly conspiratorial air by a representative of the Shell Oil Company and asked how much fuel I would like, I asked for 100,000 lbs. At the time, it seemed like perfectly routine aviation transaction, and I thought no more about it. When I awoke in my hotel room the next morning, however, I found that a local newspaper had been pushed under the door of my room, and I read it while I was eating my breakfast. On the front page was a splendid photograph of the VC10 arriving at Salisbury and on the inside was an editorial about the Foreign Secretary's visit. It transpired that an official car for use during his stay had been driven up to Salisbury from South Africa, so that he could not be seen in any way to be beholden to what the British Government still regarded as an illegal regime in Southern Rhodesia. The article ended by expressing the hope that the Foreign Secretary would

---

[1] Since the granting of independence to Southern Rhodesia, Salisbury has been renamed Harare and the country is now called Zimbabwe.

not need to refuel his car while he was in the country. Only then did it dawn on me that for the past 16 years the British Government had been enforcing sanctions against Rhodesia, and that one of those sanctions was an oil embargo imposed by means of a standing naval patrol off Beira, a port on the coast of Mozambique from where ran a railway line to Salisbury. I telephoned my contact in the Foreign Secretary's party and said, regarding the article in the paper, that he ought to know that the previous day I had loaded something approaching 7,000 gallons of fuel into the VC10. He seemed unconcerned and, much to my relief, he told me not to worry about it. The incident did go to show, however, as many in the UK had long suspected, that the oil embargo, which had been maintained for some 12 years since UDI, had not been very effective.

From an aviator's perspective, the final two legs of our itinerary were fairly uneventful, and we landed safely and on time in Lagos late in the afternoon. A slip crew had been positioned at Lagos for the final overnight leg of the journey to Heathrow and, after a few hours on the ground, while more talks were conducted, my crew and I took our seats in the cabin of the aircraft and slept soundly all the way home. It had been a long and complicated journey, carried out in the full glare of international publicity. There were many potential pitfalls to be avoided, but my crew had performed their individual roles superbly, and they fully deserved the plaudits that were heaped upon us when we returned to Brize Norton. Furthermore, the talks which had been facilitated by our efforts were instrumental in bringing about a settlement of the Rhodesian Crisis, a settlement that gave birth to the independent state of Zimbabwe in 1980. Looking back on the task after many years, I was able to see that it was the highest peak of my lengthy flying career. Although I had many more challenges yet to come, none of them would place quite the same demands on my leadership and skill. This view was clearly shared by others in my chain of command because, at the end of the year, as I was completing my last operational flight on the squadron, I learned that in the New Year's Honours I had been awarded a Queen's Commendation for Valuable Services in the Air.

CHAPTER 8

A Brief Interlude

MY TOUR AS a Flight Commander on 10 Squadron now at an end, I was posted at the beginning of 1978 to a staff appointment at Headquarters 38 Group, the Group responsible for air transport operations. The Headquarters was located at RAF Upavon on the northern edge of the Salisbury Plain. From Faringdon, where I still had my home, the journey was rather tortuous, along narrow winding country lanes and through the small Wiltshire towns of Highworth, Marlborough and Pewsey. The journey, which took just over an hour, meant an early start and a late return home each day. Fortunately, there were other ex-10 Squadron colleagues also travelling the same route, so car-sharing not only eased the travelling but also provided company on the way.

The Headquarters building was fairly modern, with spacious and comfortable offices, one of which I shared with a colleague. When I first joined the air transport force at Thorney Island in 1963, it had been Headquarters Transport Command. In those now distant days, the RAF had been a vast organisation, with five operational Commands based in the UK, and several independent Air Forces in various locations overseas. It also comprised more than 350,000 personnel. Under successive defence cuts, however, and particularly with the withdrawal from the Far East, it had contracted considerably in size. The various home commands had been rolled into a single organisation known as Strike Command, to which the individual Groups were now subordinate.

My post was designated Task Plans 2, and I was responsible for planning the itineraries for various special tasks undertaken by 38 Group aircraft around the world. Most of these tasks were carried out by the C-130 Hercules, based at RAF Lyneham, but I also had responsibility for some of the non-scheduled tasks carried out by the VC10s at Brize Norton. Many of these tasks were quite complicated, particularly as some of the loads carried were politically sensitive. In planning the itinerary, I had to take account of the range and payload of the type of aircraft allocated to the task. I also had to consider the nature and capability of the various staging posts en route to the destination, together with the opening and closing times of the airfields involved in the operation. Some airfields suffered from limited capacity and there were restrictions on the number of aircraft that they could handle at any one time. This aspect of route operations was handled by a specialist cell in the Operations Centre at HQ 38 Group known as the 'Flow Cell'. For some obscure reason this small department was always known as 'Auntie Flow'. Whatever the name, all itineraries had to be cleared by the cell before a final itinerary for the task could be issued. The itineraries for VC10 flights were also affected by the jet bans imposed by many airports around the world. Flights also had to comply with the relatively complex regulations governing the crew duty day and the amount of rest required by the crews as they progressed around the world on their various tasks. Fortunately, my lengthy spell of world-wide operations on the VC10 had given me a sound practical grasp of these complexities, and I was soon able to issue the tasking orders known as 'TRANSOPS' without further supervision.

Each month the customers, who came from all three Services, would submit their bids to the Air Transport staff in the Ministry of Defence (MOD). These bids would subsequently be further refined at a tasking conference held at Headquarters Strike Command. The outcome of this conference would then be passed down to me and my three fellow task planners in the form of an aircraft type, a payload, a destination and the number of days allocated for the task. It was then up to us to produce an itinerary that met the requirements and which could subsequently be passed in the form of a TRANSOP to the RAF station detailed to carry out the task. Consequently, shortly after the beginning of the month, I knew what my workload would be for the next few weeks and I was able to complete the task at my own pace. With my liking for intellectual puzzles, I enjoyed the work, which I humorously likened to attempting to complete The Times crossword over breakfast. I also enjoyed the environment in which I worked. My colleagues were all air transporters of long standing and knew the business inside and out. Most of them were older than me, but they made me welcome, and soon a close camaraderie developed between us. We worked regular hours, with a break at mid-day for a snack lunch in the Officers Mess and even a few minutes afterwards to read the papers. I was surprise and amused to find that several of my older colleagues took this as an opportunity for a brief nap in one of the comfortable anteroom armchairs. Every Friday lunch time, by tradition, we took ourselves off to the Red Lion in a nearby village, where we enjoyed a pint and a pie before returning to our desks. RAF Upavon also had its own 9-hole golf course and I played for the station in matches against other clubs in the locality.

Because of my current operational experience, I was sometimes called in as a trouble-shooter when particular problems arose. Not long after my arrival in the Headquarters, concern arose over the handling arrangements in Calgary that were being undertaken by Air Canada. I suggested that, as I was familiar with the Canadian operation, I should fly out to Calgary to see if I could identify and resolve the problem. This was agreed, and I duly travelled as a supernumerary crew member on a VC10 flight from Brize Norton. The day after my arrival, I attended the daily briefing held by Air Canada for their workforce at the airport. Fortunately, I had taken the precaution of arming myself with a number of Captains Reports, in which some of the shortcomings of the operation were laid out in graphic detail. I passed these around, giving the Air Canada representatives time to digest them, before expressing the hope that we could work together over the next few days to identify and eliminate the cause of the problems. This approach brought a favourable response, and for the rest of my time at Calgary I received excellent co-operation and support from the company.

The main cause of the problem seemed to be that, because of the military nature of the operation, the VC10s were being parked right at the far end of the terminal during their turn-rounds, and it was very much a case of 'out of sight, out of mind'. Consequently, when small things did go wrong, the problems escalated, either because no-one was aware of them or because nobody from Air Canada was on hand to fix them. The company representatives were quick to grasp the nature of the problem, and solved it by not only improving communications between the aircraft and their operations but also by allocating a dedicated member of staff to the turn-rounds. During my stay I established a good rapport with the operations staff and the end of my visit was marked by a golf day at a beautiful course in the foothills of the Rocky Mountains with the Chief of Operations and two of his staff. After my return to Upavon, I never again heard of a single complaint about the service provided by Air Canada at Calgary.

On another occasion a problem arose with the scheduled closure of one of the runways at RAF Gatow in Berlin for resurfacing. The station was surrounded by woodland, the trees on the approach to the main runway having been cleared to leave an avenue along which an arriving aircraft could safely descend. A second, parallel alternative runway was also available, but the trees had not been cleared to anything like the same extent, and station was concerned that they might pose a safety hazard to aircraft on the approach. I suggested to the head of my department that what was needed was for an experienced VC10 pilot to travel out to Berlin and assess the situation, and he agreed that I should go. Before leaving Upavon, I made arrangements with the Army Air Corps Flight based at Gatow to fly in one of their helicopters on a reconnaissance mission, and then I flew out on a British Airways flight to the commercial airport at Tegel in Berlin. Before the flight, I made arrangements with British Airways to sit on the jump seat of the aircraft for the arrival so that I could see for myself the operation into Tegel. Arriving in due course at Gatow, I met with my Army Air Corps pilot and discussed the purpose of the mission with him. To guide aircraft down on a visual approach, the airfield was equipped with Visual Approach Slope Indicators (VASIs). The system, which is in common use at most major airports, consisted of two sets of lights on either side of the runway embracing the point of touchdown. If an approaching aircraft was on the optimum 3° glideslope, one set of lights would show white and the other red; too high, and both lights showed white; too low, and they showed red/red. What I wanted the pilot to do was to fly an approach and hover at any point where the trees posed a problem. We would then descend to a level where the VASIs showed red/red and assess the proximity of the trees. This plan worked well, and we assessed both ends of the runway, followed by an exhilarating sight-seeing trip over Berlin. After we landed, I asked him what he thought of flying a large aircraft on the approach to the alternative runway. 'F***ing dangerous,' was his response, and I agreed. On my return to Upavon I recommended that RAF flights to Berlin should use Tegel while the runway at Gatow was being resurfaced, and my recommendation was accepted.

One of my other responsibilities was the preparation of the annual Operation Order detailing the arrangements for the Suffield Airlift. The purpose of this exercise was to airlift Battle Groups of troops and their equipment from various airfields in Germany to Calgary for tank training at BATUS. For my first year in charge of the airlift, I followed the plan for previous years, which was to position a couple of slip crews at Gander airport in Newfoundland. The first crew would operate Brize Norton – Germany – Gander. A second crew would operate Gander – Calgary – Gander, while the third crew would complete the return flight to Germany and back to base. This pattern would be repeated over subsequent days until the entire Battle Group had reached its destination. By this method, six Battle Groups were transported to and from Calgary over the summer months. There were, however, a number of drawbacks to this pattern of operations, not least being the adverse weather at Gander airport, which was often covered by fog. If an aircraft full of troops had to divert to an alternative airfield in Canada, there was no easy way for the slip crew at Gander to reach it, and several days of chaos ensued until Gander re-opened. I recalled from my time on 10 Squadron that in the early days of the airlift we used to operate these flights through Keflavik in Iceland. Looked at on a globe or a map showing a polar projection rather than the normal Mercator projection, with its associated distortion of the northern latitudes, Keflavik lies on the great circle or shortest route between Germany and Calgary, while Gander lies well to the south and consequently involves a much longer route. We had stopped using Keflavik in 1976 during the so-called 'Cod Wars' with Iceland, when there had been a resurrection of a long-standing dispute over fishing rights, and Iceland had threatened to ban the use of the airport by NATO aircraft. The dispute had, however, long since been resolved, and there seemed no reason why we could not revert to using Keflavik once more. Enquires through the Foreign Office elicited the response that Iceland would indeed accept military flights. Accordingly, over the winter months, I flew out to Iceland with a fellow staff officer, and made a provisional agreement with Iceland Air that the company would handle our flights if we were to resume operations through Keflavik the following year. Returning to Upavon, I presented my plan, pointing out not only that the operation would remove most of the problems brought about by operating through Gander but also that the saving in flying hours over the summer would be enough to allow, if required, an additional Battle Group to be flown out to Canada free of charge. Needless to say, my proposals were accepted.

The long daily journeys between Faringdon and Upavon through the dark winter months were very fatiguing, and I discussed with my wife the possibility of selling our house in Faringdon and moving somewhere closer to Upavon. It seemed unlikely that I would return to Brize Norton, and more probable that, as a career officer, I would eventually find myself working in the MOD. Accordingly we looked for a place that afforded a good rail link to London. We were not concerned about schooling, as we had already arranged for our boys to undertake their secondary education as boarders, and they were both now pupils at the Duke of Kent's School in Surrey. At the time of our prospective sale, in the summer of 1978, house prices were going through one of their periodic spurts. Although we had resided in Faringdon for less than three years, the house sold for our asking price the same day that we put it on the market and we made a handsome gain on our original purchase price. After much searching, and being 'gazumped' a couple of times, we eventually bought a house in the village of Penton Mewsey, some two miles west of Andover in Hampshire, and about 20 minutes by car from Upavon. Hardly had we moved into our new home when I was informed that I was being short-toured at Upavon as I had been selected for the RAF's Advanced Staff Course at Bracknell in Buckinghamshire the following year.

In March 1978 I joined some 60 other students for a ten-month course at the RAF Staff College Bracknell. In addition to students from the various Commands within the RAF, there were officers from the Army and the Navy, from the Air Forces of some of the countries in the NATO alliance, from the Commonwealth, and from various other foreign countries. This eclectic mix of nationalities and operational experience gave rise to some lively discussions as the course progressed. It also led to a very hectic social life, much of which involved drinking in the bar. The course was designed to give the students a wider understanding of the theory and practice of air power. To this extent we attended numerous lectures, we took part in a range of desk-top exercises to give us practical experience in the employment of air power, and we visited various operational stations around the UK and in Germany. At one point our itinerary took us Berlin, at that time still a city divided between East and West by the infamous wall. In the course of our visit we had a presentation by the Military Commandant of the British Sector, an Army General. During the question period I asked why, if RAF Gatow was to serve as one of the main reception airfields in the event of a repeat of the Berlin Airlift, trees had been allowed to grow on the approach to one of the main runways to the extent that they now endangered arriving aircraft. The answer given was to the effect that the Berliners loved their trees and regarded them as sacrosanct. By no power on earth could the city be persuaded to cut them down. I did, however, have the satisfaction of learning sometime later that contingency plans had subsequently been drawn up to cut down the trees in the event of a major emergency.

Another function of the course was to develop the skills required to undertake high-grade staff duties. This inevitably involved a lot of writing, all of which had to be done in long-hand, since we were still in those far-off days before the advent of the lap-top or the personal computer. Over the years, I had maintained my habit of regular study, and I was currently working towards a degree with the Open University. I was, therefore, able to cope reasonably well with the more intellectually demanding phases of the course. We also had to develop our presentational skills, a requirement that involved giving talks on various subjects. We started in a small way in our syndicates, gradually worked our way through larger audiences until, finally, we each had to give a ten-minute talk on a topic of our choosing to the assembled staff and students of the entire Staff College. This latter task, with the most critical audience that we were ever likely to face, was very daunting, and not everyone was able to rise fully to the mark. I chose as my topic the Suffield Airlift, a subject in which I was well-versed, and one that I thought would be of interest to such a diverse audience. Addressing a sea of faces in the Staff College's huge lecture theatre, I started confidently, but after a few minutes I developed a 'frog' in my throat. My eyes watered to the point where I could hardly see my notes, and my voice became a croak. Panic seized me and in desperation I looked around for a source of relief. Noticing a glass of water that had been placed on the podium, I stopped for a moment and took a large gulp. There was a pregnant pause among the audience, as no previous student speaker had had the temerity to halt the proceedings in such a way. Observing the audience's reaction, I said, apropos of nothing, 'I know you have been dying for someone to do that.' There was a bust of laughter, in which I joined. My throat relaxed, and I was able to finish my talk on a strong note, emphasising that the accomplishment of the Suffield Airlift each year clearly demonstrated the RAF's capability to mount strategic transport operations on a global scale. The episode also gave me an insight into the use of humour when addressing an audience that came in handy later in my career.

During the course we also looked at various aspects of leadership. Each lecturer adopted a different approach to the subject, many of them being of a theoretical nature. While these topics were interesting from an organisational point of view, they did not relate very closely to the problems of leadership as I had experienced them in the air. Indeed, they reinforced the idea that was gradually forming in my mind that the RAF had no real intellectual basis for the various methods used to develop the kind of high performance teams that were essential in the cockpit if crews were to operate with optimum proficiency. Based on many years of practical experience, the organisation had developed a first-class system for teaching the 'stick and rudder' skills of flying, but had little or no method of developing leadership. It relied instead on the brief introduction to leadership acquired in basic training, supplemented by lessons learned from individual experiences in the early years of flying brought out in the time-honoured debrief that followed each training sortie. On the basis of these rudimentary but pragmatic methods, and through a process of observation and intuition, most aircrew acquired over time the skills necessary to perform a leadership role. There was, however, no system in place to help those who were unable to make the grade of their own volition. While these lectures and discussions gave me food for thought, it was to be some time before my ideas about leadership in the air crystallised sufficiently for me to formulate a practical approach to the problem.

Under pressures brought about by further cuts in the defence budget, the Staff College course had undergone various changes over the previous couple of years. Originally, it had been one year in length, but then, to make 'savings', it had been cut drastically to six months. In their post-course critique, the student's of the previous year had protested vigorously about the truncated nature of the course, and the intense workload that it entailed, so a decision had subsequently been taken to extend the term to ten months. When we arrived in March, the new syllabus was still a work in progress, so the course that we undertook was, as the cynics amongst us put it, 'a six-month course crammed into ten months.' From my point of view, one of the major attractions of attending the course at Bracknell was that the Staff College students enjoyed a concessionary arrangement at the nearby Wentworth Golf Club, where the cost of membership for the year was only £100. As quite bit of the spare capacity on the staff course was filled up by 'private study' periods, the golfers amongst us were able to take advantage of this arrangement and enjoy the facilities provided by one of the best and most famous courses in the country. Fortunately, the arrangements within the Staff College were such that its excellent library was open to students 24 hours a day, so any catching up that had to be done could take place in the evening.

As we approached the end of the course our postings were announced. I had fully expected to go to a staff appointment, but to my surprise and pleasure I was told that I was to be promoted to the rank of Wing Commander and that I would take over Command of No 241 OCU at Brize Norton the following year.

CHAPTER 9

UNIT COMMANDER

HAVING PREVIOUSLY BEEN a student on No 10 VC10 Course for some six months in 1970, and having also returned to the unit from time to time over the following six years for periodic refresher training, I was treading familiar ground in taking command of 241 OCU. Furthermore, as all the instructional staff had previously served on 10 Squadron, I not only knew them all by name but I had also flown with them many times on our world-wide operations in years gone by. The only element of the training with which I was not familiar was the Andover Training Flight, which also formed part of the OCU. Following my two years on the ground, I was earmarked for a flying refresher course on the Handley Page Jetstream aircraft at RAF Finningley in Yorkshire, followed by a full VC10 conversion course starting the following July. As there was plenty of time in hand, I suggested to my desk officer that, as I was to be responsible for training aircrew both on the Andover and on the VC10, I should undertake the Andover conversion course as well. To this proposal he agreed.

THE JETSTREAM WAS A twin-engined aircraft that was easy and pleasant to fly. After half-a-dozen dual sorties I was sent off on my own with a fellow student on the course acting as my copilot. A few more dual sorties followed, finishing with a short trip along the airways to Prestwick in Scotland and back, and that was the end of it, having mustered some 15 hours flying on type in all. Although I was to continue flying with the RAF for many more years, I never again flew the Jetstream.

The Hawker Siddeley Andover C1 had been acquired by the RAF in 1966 as a medium-range tactical transport aircraft. The military aircraft was a derivative of a commercial airliner, the HS 748, but it had up-rated Dart turboprop engines and longer propellers. It also had a unique kneeling undercarriage, allowing the rear of the aircraft to be lowered almost to the ground, thereby greatly facilitating the on-loading and off-loading of passengers and freight. In the RAF the aircraft was operated by a basic crew comprising two pilots, a navigator and an air loadmaster. In earlier times, the aircraft had been used successfully by the RAF in both the Middle East and the Far East. Following the withdrawal of British forces from east of Suez, all the remaining Andovers were now based in the UK. No 115 Squadron, based at RAF Brize Norton, operated the Mk 3 version of the aircraft in the airfield calibration role, while two VIP aircraft were operated by No 32 Squadron at RAF Northolt in the communications role. A few C Mk.1 aircraft, maintained by 115 Squadron, were used by 241 OCU for converting aircrew to type. Unlike the set-up for VC10 training, there was no Andover simulator, so the training was carried out from scratch on the aircraft itself. The Flight Commander, Squadron Leader Jim Campbell, a highly experienced Andover pilot and instructor, took me through the early stages of the course. Pointing out various bits of equipment on the aircraft, we came to the Decca navigational system, located at the navigator's station. We looked at the complicated method of loading the system and the strange parabolic charts use for plotting the aircraft's position. 'Decca is for ships,' he said; and we moved on, never to mention it again.

Flying the aircraft on two engines was a relatively straightforward business, although asymmetric handling presented more of a problem. Shutting down one of the engines early in the conversion programme resulted in a lot of yawing as power was reduced and the large propeller turned itself to the feathered position. It was also unnerving to look out of the window and see the stationary propeller almost alongside the cockpit. After a few sorties, however, I gradually got the hang of it, and I by the end of the course I felt very comfortable in the aircraft. The military version of the Andover had been designed with a tactical landing capability that was truly impressive. The technique was to approach the runway at minimum speed for the all-up weight and then, at about 15 feet above the ground, throw the propellers into reverse pitch. The result was something like an aircraft carrier landing, but the roll out was the shortest I have ever experienced in a multi-engined aircraft.

The runway at Brize Norton was equipped with turning loops at either end, a legacy of the days when the airfield had been a bomber base for American aircraft. Using the short landing technique, it was quite possible to land, turn off into the loop, and ask for another take-off, almost before air traffic control had realised that the landing aircraft was not still rolling down the runway. The ability to land and take-off in relatively short distances also meant that the aircraft could operate into quite small airfields, a facility that allowed for visits to some interesting locations. Guernsey was a popular destination for a training flight, as it included some navigation along the airways, followed by an approach and landing onto a relatively short runway. It also facilitated a brief but welcome visit to one of the duty-free shops in the town of St Peter Port before making the return flight back to base. My course ended with a training flight that took us to RAF St Mawgan in Cornwall, followed by a flag-stop at Lisbon and then on for a night-stop in Gibraltar. The next day we routed through Decimomanu in Sardinia, Lyon in France and back to Brize Norton. The trip provided a satisfactory conclusion to what had been a very interesting and enjoyable course.

After I had completed the Andover conversion I started the VC10 course. With my previous extensive experience on type, I did not really need the whole course, and two weeks of periodic refresher training would probably have brought me fully up to speed. However, I was not due to take command of the unit until the end of October, so I gratefully took full advantage of all the retraining that was available to me. Consequently, I was able to take over my new command having regained my former category as an above-the-average operator. Shortly after completing the conversion course I qualified additionally as a flight instructor and an examiner. On taking command, however, it was not the flying side of the job that presented a problem but the difficulties brought about by yet another attempt to make 'savings'.

Within a few weeks of taking over the job I was asked to carry out a review of training. Accordingly, I set up a small working group drawn from the most experienced members of my staff, and together we went over the various elements of training with a fine-toothed comb. In any organisation, it is always difficult to quantify the amount of training required for a given post, and this is particularly so in aviation. No-one would argue that the pilot of a passenger-carrying aircraft needs to be adequately trained, but who is to define what is adequate? As there are no objective standards by which adequacy can be measured, organisations concerned with training aircrew have to rely on a subjective assessment by highly qualified staff who have acquired through long experience a thorough grasp of the degree of competence required.

Under pressure to make cuts, the working group struggled with the problem. The training courses had evolved over a number of years and were designed to provide just enough instruction to cover the essentials. Consequently, there was very little fat on them that could be trimmed away without a reduction in the knowledge and proficiency of the students completing the course. This was a compromise that my staff resisted, and I sympathised with their desire to maintain traditional standards. We did manage to make some reductions, particularly in the area where people such as me, returning to flying after a period of absence, were concerned, but I was conscious of the fact that my limited proposals would not be met with enthusiasm by the 38 Group staff.

One area of particular concern was the requirement for training flights to the USA. Following the withdrawal of forces from east of Suez, there was no longer much call for flights across the Pacific, so changes had been made to what had previously been the end-of-course global training flight. At the end of the course the students now undertook a flight eastwards to Hong Kong, returning to base by the reverse route. After a few days of rest and recovery, the Hong Kong trip was followed by a flight across the Atlantic to North America and back. This route training arrangement not only better reflected the kind of tasks currently being undertaken by 10 Squadron but also allowed the students to recapitulate on the inbound sectors some of the lessons they had learned on the outbound flight. From a training perspective, a flight to the USA was necessary to familiarise the pilots with the procedures for crossing the Atlantic, to acquaint them with the pilot navigation procedures in use in North America, and to expose them to the methods used by the air traffic control system to cope with the high density of flights.

Chicago O'Hare airport, one of the busiest airports in the world, was often included in the itinerary of these North American flights. On one such flight, approaching from the south-east, we were cleared to descend to 10,000 feet for an approach to runway 32 Left. It was a gin-clear day with a visibility in excess of 50 miles. As we descended, we could see nine aircraft ahead of us, stepped down at 1,000 foot intervals and all lined up for successive landings on the same runway. Not only that, but off to our right and parallel to our course, we saw another nine aircraft stepped down and heading for successive landings on runway 32 Right. Some time later I spoke to the captain of a Boeing 707 of the Canadian Air Force who told me that high-density training for their crews involved a flight across the Atlantic and a landing at Heathrow Airport.

Atlantic training flights also provided the navigators with an opportunity to practise the techniques of navigation in the higher latitudes, where the magnetic compass was unreliable and gyroscopic steering had to be used instead. During my time as a Flight Commander on 10 Squadron, I had supervised a number of such training flights and was well aware of value to be gained from them in terms of crew proficiency. It was not so easy, however, to convince the higher echelons of the Air Force, desperately searching for more 'savings', that these flights were an essential part of the training for crews who, after joining 10 Squadron, would be expected to undertake world-wide tasks with little or no notice. I had presented this case in writing on a number of occasions, but the pressure to cut out the flights had not gone away.

Support for my cause was to come from an unexpected quarter. The itinerary of North American training flights was often adapted by the task planners at HQ 38 Group to deliver payloads to various destinations in Canada and the USA that were not served by the regular VC10 scheduled services to Ottawa and Washington DC. On this particular occasion the flight had been extended to take the Deputy Commander-in-Chief of Strike Command to Offutt AFB in Nebraska. Offutt AFB was the location of the Headquarters of the United States Air Force's Strategic Air Command, and it was here that the RAF was presenting a Vulcan bomber to the air museum on the base.

We had taken our stations on the flight deck of the VC10 at Brize Norton and were almost ready for departure when the DC-in-C came on board. I had already asked the loadmaster to invite him to sit on the jump seat for the departure, and when he arrived on the flight deck it turned out to be none other than my former Wing Commander Flying at RAF Nicosia, the then Wing Commander Peter Bairsto, now Air Marshal Sir Peter Bairsto, KBE, CB, AFC, CBIM. Although it was some 17 years since we had last met, when I acted as copilot on his ill-starred final trip on the Hastings, he remembered me immediately and greeted me warmly. Before starting engines, I briefed him on the purpose of the flight and informed him that the copilot was new on type and had not previously flown in North America.

The departure proceeded smoothly and before long we had established our clearance for the Atlantic crossing and settled down in the cruise. At my suggestion, the Air Marshal returned to his seat in the cabin for the long flight to North America, having accepted my invitation to return to the flight deck for the approach into Dulles International Airport. Some eight hours later, as we were passing over New York, he reappeared on the flight deck and took his place on the jump-seat.

The descent clearance issued by New York Centre involved being at a particular height by a given navigation beacon along the route. For the copilot, who was flying the aircraft, this requirement meant that he had to navigate along the planned route from beacon to beacon while, at the same time, monitoring the rate of descent to ensure that we complied with the instructions issued by air traffic control. As usual, the airspace was extremely busy, and the controllers were rapping out instructions to a multitude of aircraft as they climbed, criss-crossed and descended through the airspace. Not uncommonly, it all began to get a bit hectic, and I could sense that the copilot was gradually losing the plot. At one point I had to nudge him quite forcefully to ensure not only that he stayed on track but also that he extended the airbrakes so that we completed our initial descent in compliance with our clearance. To give him his due, he did eventually catch up mentally with the aircraft, but it was apparent to everyone on the flight deck, including the DC-in-C, that he was working like the proverbial one-armed paper-hanger in order to do so.

In a quiet moment during the turn-round, the DC-in-C spoke to me about the flight. He had been surprised and disturbed by the copilot's difficulties during the descent, and complimented me on my handling of the situation. For my part, I took the opportunity to stress that such difficulties were not uncommon, and it was essential to ensure that crew members had the appropriate training before operating in the kind of high density environment often found in the air space of North America.

We delivered the Air Marshal on time to Offutt and left him there. The next day we resumed our training itinerary, eventually returning via Calgary and a polar flight to Brize Norton. I never met the Air Marshal again, although he did crop up in my life at a later date when I was being interviewed by my desk officer. He referred to one of my annual confidential reports on which the Air Marshal had endorsed the remarks made by two earlier reporting officers. Somewhat to my surprise, he had written, "I have known Adcock since he was a young Flying Officer, and I have always admired him." He then went on to complement me on my handling of the recent training flight to the USA, and added that he thought I would make a very good Group Captain. Reflecting on the interview later, I thought how strangely the wheel of fortune sometimes turns. Not only were my promotion prospects enhanced by that chance meeting but no-more was heard about cancelling USA training flights during my time in command of the OCU.

Meanwhile, my busy life continued. There were always a number of complicated technical issues to be resolved regarding the operation of the aircraft. Sometimes these arose from a directive issued by the aircraft or engine manufacturer. On other occasions they were caused by a change in the operating environment, or the introduction of new technology. More often than not they were brought about by the never ending search for more economies and 'savings'. Traditionally, the RAF controlled its activities in peace-time on the basis of the number of hours flown but, for a while, it seemed that the organisation was trying to run its operations on the basis of the amount of fuel that each sortie consumed. Following a steep rise in the cost of aviation fuel brought about by events in the Middle East, and in parallel with measures being undertaken by the commercial airlines, we had already introduced some extensive fuel-saving measures across the VC10 fleet. The introduction of these measures had to be carefully weighed against the flight safety implications of carrying less fuel that had hitherto been the practice, and the brunt of this exercise fell largely upon my staff and me. With the troubles in Northern Ireland now at their worst, there was also a constant security threat from dissident republicans, and extra measures were constantly being introduced to counter the perceived risk.

Along with every other unit in the RAF, the perimeter of Brize Norton was now protected by a security fence, while entry to the station was controlled by armed guards. As a senior executive on the station, I was involved in many of the changes that now impinged on our operations. One day, as Duty Commander, I was called upon to deal with an unattended package that had been left against the wall of the operations building. Loath to approach the package myself, I called for assistance from our remotely operated security device. While I watched from a safe distance, the small robot was directed toward the package by its handler. There was a sharp hissing sound as a projectile was fired at the package, and then the contents were flung harmlessly into the air. Walking towards the scene on being given the all clear, I came upon a passport and a pair of bikini bottoms. Later, through information gleaned from the passport, I got in touch with a young woman, the owner of the package, and informed her politely of the security risk associated with unattended packages. She was very contrite. It appeared that she had just arrived back from a holiday in Cyprus and had been waiting outside the passenger terminal located at the base of the operations building for a lift from a friend. When the friend arrived, she had jumped into the car leaving the package with her few small possessions leaning against the wall of the building. She was very relieved when I returned her passport to her and informed her that we would be taking no further action.

Another responsibility that I undertook at this time was that of being President of the Mess Committee (PMC). In this role I was directly responsible to the Station Commander for the effective functioning of the Officers Mess, both as a home for the living-in officers and also as the focus of social life on the station. To carry out this task I chaired a small committee of officers and I was also assisted by a Warrant Officer who served as the Mess Manager. As so often seemed to be the case, the main problem facing us was how to maintain standards in the face of a rising tide of costs. A particularly contentious issue during my time as PMC was the question of bar books. For many years, officers had been allowed to buy drinks in the Mess bar on credit. Drinks ordered from the bar were entered into the individual's bar book and signed for by the purchaser. At the end of the month the entries were added up and the total appeared on the officer's mess bill. This system, however, was very labour intensive; to the extent that, in a large Mess, such as the one at Brize Norton, it required an additional full-time member of staff to service it. Consequently, by the simple expedient of paying cash over the bar for any drinks that were purchased, a reduction in costs could be achieved. This change, however, was hotly contested by some of the die-hard members of the Mess, who saw it not as a savings measure but as an infringement of their status as officers and gentlemen. I sympathised with their point of view, but I also knew that costs had to be reduced. Accordingly, with the help of the committee, I carried out a thorough analysis of the savings that could be accomplished by the abolition of the bar books, and converted this into the significant rise in price that would have to be added to a pint of beer if the system were to be retained. I then spelt out the options in a letter to all Mess members. At an Extraordinary Mess Meeting called to resolve the issue passions ran high and, as Chairman of the meeting, I was hard-pressed to reach a consensus of opinion as to the way ahead. After all the arguments had been exhausted, I put the matter to the vote, and the motion to retain bar books was defeated by a small but significant majority. Inevitably, there was some grumbling by those who had lost the vote, but the issue had been given a good airing, and the outcome determined in a democratic and traditionally British way. Nevertheless, the matter was a small reflection of a gradual reduction in the status formerly enjoyed by officers that took place during this period, as society as whole began to level out.

Another function of the PMC was to take the chair at formal functions such as Mess Dining-In Nights, part of the duty being to act as host to any guests or VIPs who were attending the dinner. By now my wife and I had let our house in Hampshire and we were living in a married quarter on the base. One evening, as I was dressing in what I fondly assumed was good time for the dinner, I had a telephone call from the Mess Manager, who said that the AOC, our guest of honour, had just arrived and was standing in the entrance hall to the Mess. Hastily throwing on the rest of my mess kit, and scrambling to correctly assemble my bow tie, I rushed down to the Mess to find the AOC enjoying a quiet drink alone in the bar. No-one else had yet arrived for the dinner. I apologised for not being present to greet him, but he seemed unperturbed and we chatted pleasantly until gradually other mess members began to arrive. After what was for me a traumatic start, the evening progressed smoothly. I had canvassed my colleagues for some good stories about the AOC and when I stood to introduce him towards the end of the dinner my remarks gave rise to laughter and were well-received. A couple of days after the event I received a very charming letter from the AOC thanking the mess members for their hospitality and apologising for mistaking the time of arrival. He ended by saying that his ADC was suffering from indigestion having eaten so much humble pie.

Another task that came my way in my new rank and status was to preside over a Court Martial. Earlier in my career I had attended three Courts Martial as an Officer Under Instruction. Along with several other junior officers, I had sat in on the proceedings, including the deliberations on whether the accused was innocent or guilty and, if guilty, what sentence was to be imposed. I had also taken a paper in Air Force Law as part of my promotion examinations. It is one thing, however, to look on as a bystander, or to read up on the theoretical aspects of the administration of justice, and quite something else to find yourself actually in charge of a trial. Consequently, when the court assembled at an RAF station in the Midlands, it was questionable as to who was the more nervous – the accused, or the President of the Board!

Fortunately the case was fairly simple and straightforward. A young airman had applied for leave, giving a location in Newcastle-upon-Tyne as his leave address. Later, he had put in a claim for leave travel but it had subsequently come to light that he had not actually made the journey for which he had claimed. He was, therefore, charged with obtaining money through false pretences. He pleaded guilty to the charge. The prosecution set out the circumstances of the offence. Word of the accused's intentions had leaked out and, as soon as he submitted his claim, he was arrested and charged. His admission of guilt in court was followed by plea of mitigation from the defending solicitor, who referred to the extreme youth of the offender and his clean record to date. He also mentioned that the airman was about to go on a tour of duty in the troubled province of Northern Ireland; therefore, if he were sent to prison, someone else would have to go at short notice in his place.

The airman was marched out and the courtroom was cleared while the other two members of the Board and I deliberated on his sentence. In general, the Armed Forces take a dim view of financial irregularity and such cases would normally involve a stiff sentence. There was, however, one factor about the case that concerned me, and that was why, when the potential offence first came to light, no-one in the airman's chain of command had thought to warn him of the consequences of being found out, particularly in light of his extreme youth and his general lack of service knowledge and experience. I felt that there had been a distinct failure of leadership by those involved in handling the case and, if prudent action had been taken when the possibility of an offence being committed first came to light, the airman could have been made aware that his scheme was illegal and the consequences of carrying it out were likely to be severe. In the event, no-one warned him. He was allowed to commit the offence and then charged with the consequences.

With this in mind, we accepted his plea of guilty and issued him with a moderate fine. We all felt that in the circumstances it would be a long time, if ever, before he was likely to carry out a similar escapade. The Court Martial did, however, help to focus my mind on issues relating to justice and the law, particularly in a military context. It also forced me think more deeply about the need for order and discipline, and how they could best be maintained through the exercise of leadership.

In April 1982, following the invasion of the Falkland Islands by the forces of Argentina, there was an unprecedented demand for the services of the air transport force. Following the invasion, a naval task force had been assembled at extremely short notice to mount a military operation for the recovery of the islands. While this armada sailed southwards, Ascension Island, in the South Atlantic, became the focus of intense activity, as further troops and equipment were air transported ahead to link up with the task force. The VC10s were heavily involved in this operation and a slip pattern was set up through Dakar in Senegal to cope with the demand. Under this arrangement, a crew would operate the first 5-hour sector from Brize Norton to Dakar and then hand over to a second crew, who operated the 6-hour trip to Ascension and return. A third crew then flew the return sector back to Brize Norton. Meanwhile, the first crew would be accommodated in rather pleasant hotels that normally catered for the French tourist industry in Senegal and whiled away the time until the arrival of the next aircraft sitting by the pool with a host of topless bathing beauties. Later, after temporary rest facilities had been established at Ascension, crews night-stopped on the island. Together with my crew, I spent a night there myself. We slept in a sort of blow-up tent, the whole crew together in a long line of beds: captain, copilot, navigator, flight engineer, loadmaster and three air stewards. The fourth air steward, a girl, slept in the island's jail. It was a far cry from the relatively luxurious living in Senegal, but quite amusing, nevertheless.

In due course, a new challenge for the OCU began to appear on the horizon. As the Victor tanker force approached the end of its operational life, the RAF had purchased a number of civilian VC10 airliners that had been phased out by their operators, and these aircraft were being refurbished and converted into tankers by British Aerospace at Filton airfield near Bristol. The time was fast approaching when 241 OCU would not only be required to convert aircrew to the VC10 in its air transport role but would also need to teach the techniques of air-to-air refuelling as well. As my unit had very little experience of air-to-air refuelling within its ranks, I arranged to visit the Victor air refuelling school at RAF Marham in Norfolk to gain an insight into what might be required in the way of additional training. My visit started with a trip in the Victor flight simulator in which we off-loaded fuel to a couple of fighter aircraft and then to various other customers who appeared on the scene from time to time. We were able to take advantage of one the simulator's most useful features, which is to 'freeze' the action at any particular moment of the sortie, thereby allowing the crew to discuss any specific issues arising in the course of the sortie without having to monitor the flight path at the same time.

Later that day I flew as an observer on a Victor training sortie. As I had not previously flown in a Victor, I was given a comprehensive briefing by a member of the crew on the safety features of the aircraft, including how to escape in the event of an emergency. We took off at dusk with me sitting on the jump-seat and watching with interest as we progressed through a series of training routines not dissimilar from those that we employed on the VC10. Towards the end of the sortie the young copilot sitting in the right-hand seat was carrying out some night visual circuits at Marham. The was a strong cross-wind blowing, creating quite a lot of drift that had to be allowed for on the final approach and kicked off by the judicious use of rudder just prior to touchdown.

The copilot had carried out a couple of touch-and-go landings during which he had coped well with the tricky conditions but, as we touched down for the third time, the aircraft took a sickening lurch to the right and there was a loud cracking sound from the undercarriage. The captain immediately took control and brought the aircraft to halt on the runway. Meanwhile, the navigator reported that he could see flames coming from the starboard undercarriage, and the Captain ordered the crew to abandon the aircraft. Sensing an impending disaster, I had already freed myself from the complicated series of straps that held me in the jump seat, and when the navigator opened the door and lowered the escape rope I was one of the first to egress from the aircraft. Knowing that the aircraft was full of fuel, and seeing the flames licking around the underside of the wing, I took off across the darkened airfield like a startled hare until I reached what I thought was a safe distance away. I was hotly pursued by the rest of the crew. Luckily, the fire crew were quickly on the scene and within a few minutes they had the blaze under control, so no great harm was done. It was, though, one of the most exciting few minutes that I have ever spent in an aircraft, and one that I would not like to repeat. Needless to say, I never flew in a Victor again.

A subsequent technical investigation into the incident revealed a fatigue fracture in one of the undercarriage supporting struts that had given way under the strain of repeated cross-wind landings, and in the end the entire fleet of aircraft had to be modified. The exciting flight in the Victor notwithstanding, I had gained a useful insight into the likely future demands that were to be placed on 241 OCU, and I put in hand some preliminary measures to prepare for the additional task. Unfortunately from my point of view, the new aircraft did not start to arrive until long after I had handed over to my successor and moved on to a new assignment, so I never had a chance to try my hand at air-to-air refuelling in the VC10.

THROUGHOUT THAT SUMMER, THE VC10s continued to support operations in the South Atlantic, creating additional tasks that stretched the resources of 10 Squadron to the limit. Consequently, the crew members of 241 OCU were often called upon to give a helping hand when they could be spared from their regular training duties. On one such occasion the squadron asked if the OCU could provide a pilot to make up a crew for one of the regular scheduled flights to Dulles airport in Washington DC. There was only one pilot available at the time and that was me, so I agreed to do the trip. The other pilot scheduled for the mission turned out to be an American pilot who was serving on exchange with 10 Squadron. I had first met him when he came through 241 OCU on his VC10 conversion course earlier in the year and we had met professionally and socially on a number of occasions since. I knew that before coming to the UK he had been a flight instructor on the huge C-5 Galaxy aircraft operated by the Military Airlift Command of the United States Air Force (USAF).

During my long association with the VC10, we had always had exchange officers from the USAF and also the Canadian Air Force serving with 10 Squadron, both pilots and navigators. To a man, they were all first class aviators, who not only brought a usefully different perspective to our operations but also added a dash of colour to our lives. In view of the excellent track record of these exchange officers, the pilots, having completed the conversion course, were given a few screened rides to familiarise them with RAF operations and then authorised as aircraft captains. In this respect they differed from RAF pilots posted onto the VC10, who served initially as copilots, and were only converted to captain in strict order of seniority on the squadron, usually after about three years in the right-hand seat. Notwithstanding the fact that I was senior in rank to the exchange officer with whom I was to fly, and considerably more experienced on the VC10, I said that I would merely fill the duties of copilot and leave him in his normal role as captain of the aircraft. I was, therefore, both surprised and concerned when he made something of a meal of the departure from Brize Norton. It was not that he did anything wrong, but he did not seem to have much of a grip on the pre-departure procedures, and I had to prompt him several times as tactfully as I could so that we were not actually late off the chocks. After this rather inauspicious start, things went reasonably well as we obtained our clearance for crossing the Atlantic and settled down for the eight-hour flight to Washington.

Approaching our destination, however, things began to go awry again. Once more we were in the busy airspace between New York and Washington when we were given a clearance to descend to a particular height by a set navigation point along the route. The captain was slow to react to the clearance, and it was obvious to me and to the navigator that we would not make our cleared height in time unless we increased our rate of descent by extending the airbrakes. He appeared oblivious to the requirement. Once again I prompted him as tactfully as I could and only then did he take action. We just made our cleared height in time and it was evident to me that without my intervention we would not have made it. Failure to do so would have had serious consequences, since the instructions issued by Air Traffic Control to other aircraft in our vicinity were predicated on the fact that we would abide by the clearance we had been given, so that a failure to do so could conceivably have jeopardised the safety of other aircraft. The approach and landing were handled competently enough and we landed safely at Dulles International Airport.

The next day, after a night's rest, I took the captain aside and, wearing my flight examiner's hat, I expressed my concerns about his handling of the flight. I drew attention to his somewhat lackadaisical approach to the departure from Brize Norton, his failure to initiate a prompt descent when instructed to do so by New York Air Traffic Control Centre, and his general lack of awareness throughout the flight. I also told him that, in view of these shortcomings, I would give him a formal route check on the overnight return flight to Brize Norton. Despite these strictures, his handling of the return flight was no better. I told him that I thought he would benefit from a further period of supervised route flying with an experienced captain, and that I would advise his Squadron Commander accordingly. This I did, and my recommendation was accepted.

In view of the pilot's status as an American exchange officer, the circumstances had to be reported up the chain of command, and they caused a minor diplomatic hiatus. The American Air Attaché in London became involved in the subsequent discussions about the pilot's future, and was naturally concerned as to why a pilot of the United States Air Force with a hitherto good track record could not make the grade as the captain of an aircraft in the RAF. Once again it came down to a matter of poor 'airmanship', a term difficult if not impossible to define, but a trait that was easily recognisable by those charged with the supervision and maintenance of flying standards. To our dismay, and in spite of our best efforts, the pilot never fully acquired the degree of competence required to fly in command of a VC10. In the end, his tour of duty with the RAF was brought to a premature end, and he and his family returned to the United States.

For my part, I was disappointed and frustrated. Notwithstanding our excellent record in teaching pilots how to handle these large aircraft, I could see that there was a problem with our methodology when it came to the art of captaincy. Indeed we had no method. We simply relied on a pilot acquiring through observation and intuition the necessary skills during his period as a copilot, and we had no means of helping those who failed to do so. Not only that, apart from a nagging feeling in the back of my mind, we had barely identified the problem, let alone found a solution.

I was to meet these problems again during my next tour, because I had by now learned that I was myself to be posted as an exchange officer, and my future duties would lie with the Military Airlift Command of the United States Air Force, located at Scott Air Force Base in Illinois.

CHAPTER 10

Flying with USAF Military Airlift Command

For several months before taking up my new appointment in the United States I attended No 44 Air Warfare Course at the RAF College Cranwell. My wife and I moved back into our house in Penton Mewsey and I commuted on a weekly basis. Fortunately, there were several other officers attending the course who lived in my vicinity, so we were able to share the transport arrangements as we hurtled up and down the A1 on Sunday nights and Friday evenings. During the week were comfortably accommodated in the York House Officers Mess, an establishment that I had not visited since my days at Cranwell as a QFI. The Air Warfare Course, which was designed to prepare senior officers for operational appointments, comprised a series of lectures, seminars and visits to various operational stations and defence establishments. There was a vast amount of new information to absorb, but perhaps the hardest challenge of the course was to avoid putting on weight, as we were wined and dined most hospitably wherever we went, and particularly during visits to commercial aviation companies. The course also involved visits to various operational units in RAF Germany and other NATO units in Central Europe. I gave a talk to the course on the new VC10 tanker that was shortly to come into service and I wrote a paper about the optimum use of the Tristar aircraft that was also about to be acquired by the RAF in the tanker/transport role. Overall, the course was extremely broadening, and I was to be very grateful for the insight that it gave me into the British perspective on the role and function of air power in peace and war, as I was to field many questions on this subject during my time in America.

Arriving back in our home at the beginning of the year, my wife and I decided to create more space by building a second floor over an existing ground floor extension. We obtained the services of an architect who drew up plans that were subsequently approved by the local authority. Based on the recommendation of a friend, we then hired a local builder to carry out the work. The finished product was intended to provide an extra bedroom with its own en suite bathroom, and this involved knocking down some interior walls and a certain amount of re-ordering of the upstairs rooms. Inevitably, the work caused considerable disruption, and my wife and I worked long hours after the builder had gone home for night to prepare the house for the next day's onslaught. At the same time, we were busy packing up our belongings and ordering our affairs ready for our posting to America.

Fortunately, I had by this time completed the Air Warfare Course, and I was enjoying a few weeks of 'gardening leave' which allowed me to concentrate full-time on the task in hand. During our absence overseas, we intended to let the house again, and while the construction work was in progress we were visited by some prospective tenants. One such viewer was an officer of the United States Air Force who was taking up an assignment at nearby Greenham Common. He and his wife liked the house and were absolutely enchanted by the village, which was, to say the least, rather quaint. We stood in the living room surrounded by packing cases, with the sound of hammering and construction work coming from above. They asked me when I thought the work might be finished. I said, with more confidence than I actually felt, that it would all be completed and ready for occupation in three weeks time. A look of incredulity crossed their faces. Nevertheless, they agreed to rent the house, and we were as good as our word. The evening before we left for America the builder appeared and I gave him a cheque for the work that he had completed in record time. I just hoped that the funds from the building society, with whom I had arranged to extend my mortgage, would arrive in my account in time to cover the considerable expenditure that I had incurred.

My two teenage boys were now boarding at Lord Wandsworth College in Hampshire and under the rules prevailing at the time they were to be allowed three passages a year to visit us in the United States. As we were now in the middle of the summer holidays, they were entitled to accompany us on the journey to America. Accordingly, in August 1983 we flew together as a family in a VC10 from Brize Norton to Dulles Airport in Washington DC. Arriving on a Friday evening, we spent the weekend in Washington, as I had to attend a briefing with the British Defence Liaison Staff (BDLS) on the Monday morning. On Saturday we enjoyed some of the sights of the city, and on Sunday we took a trip on the Potomac River to visit George Washington's house a short distance downstream from the capital. Thus culturally imbued with the sights and sounds of America, we flew on Monday afternoon from Washington National Airport to St Louis in Missouri. For several weeks the mid-west had been enduring a heat-wave of biblical proportions, and when we disembarked in St Louis it was like stepping into a blast furnace. Fortunately, it was only a few short steps to the air-conditioned terminal, but it came as shock to realise that we would be living and working in such heat.

As this was an internal flight there were no customs to clear and we were met at the gate by my predecessor in the post, Wing Commander Dave Edwards, who had travelled out to the airport to collect us. We drove on a four-lane highway through the centre of St Louis and crossed into Illinois via a bridge over the vast Mississippi. The boy's gaped in astonishment at the strange surroundings and we were all keyed-up with excitement at the prospect of the tour ahead. Dave Edwards and I had been in touch since I had learned of my posting and he had arranged for me to take over his married quarter on Scott Air Force Base at No 235 E Street. I had also arranged to buy his furniture and his automobile, a green 10-seater Plymouth Fury estate car that had been handed down from one exchange officer to another over the years. When I acquired it, for a mere $300, it had more than 100,000 miles on the clock but it was still mechanically sound and ran as sweet as a nut. I drove it for the duration of my tour and eventually passed it on to my successor for $250.

Our new house was a compact two-storey building surrounded by an open garden. It was well-equipped and air conditioned, which was a mercy given the searing daytime heat. After a few days our packing cases arrived and we soon settled in to our new location. One of our first tasks was to register on the base and obtain our military ID cards, which allowed us to shop in the Commissary, a sort of giant supermarket on the base, and also to visit the Base Exchange (BX), which sold almost everything needed for day to day-to-day living. We registered my wife with a dentist in the local town of Belleville, where we also joined the AAA (Automobile Association of America). Also nearby was the residential area of Fairview Heights, in which was located a huge air-conditioned shopping mall. The mall contained a vast range of stores where it was possible to buy anything from a potato peeler to a grand piano. As this was long before shopping malls began to appear in the UK, it was something of a novelty. What was even more amazing to British eyes was that the enormous shopping complex was surrounded by enough parking spaces for about 10,000 cars.

Beyond Fairview Heights, on the western bank of the Mississippi River, was St Louis, a city of some 300,000 people. Located at the confluence of the Mississippi and Missouri Rivers, St Louis had been the jumping-off point for settlers opening up the west in the 19th Century. That period of mass migration is today commemorated by a 630ft high steel arch on the riverbank. At the top of the arch an internal viewing platform, reached by a lift, affords a tremendous view of the city and the surrounding countryside. The city also has several theatres, a well-stocked art gallery and its own symphony orchestra, as well as a major league baseball team and an American football team. During our stay of nearly three years at Scott AFB, we were to take full advantage of the many cultural, sporting and social activities that the area had to offer.

Meanwhile, I was introduced by Dave Edwards to my new working environment in the headquarters of Military Airlift Command (HQMAC), a large, brick-built, open-plan modern office block located about a 10-minute walk from my house on the base. MAC was a Major Command of the USAF, responsible for airlift around the globe and comprising about 120,000 personnel. Subordinate to HQMAC were two numbered Air Forces, whose areas of responsibility extended across the globe east and west of the Mississippi River. 21st Air Force, with its HQ at McGuire AFB in New Jersey, tasked flights operating across the Atlantic to Europe and beyond. 22nd Air Force, located at Travis AFB in California, controlled flights across the Pacific. The air transport bases associated with 21st Air Force were located from north to south down the eastern seaboard of the United States, while those of 22nd Air Force were located down the western seaboard. Within HQMAC, I was assigned to the Department of Standardisation and Evaluation (STANEVAL), which came under the Deputy Chief of Staff for Operations – the DO. Thus, under the nomenclature adopted by the USAF, our department was known as DOV. Within the department, I was part of a sub-section – DOVA – that dealt with MAC's largest aircraft: the C-5 Galaxy, the C-141 Starlifter and the C-130 Hercules, all aircraft built by the Lockheed Aircraft Corporation.

The Chief of DOVA was an amiable USAF Lieutenant Colonel, Roy Dent, and I was known as the Assistant Chief. The function of the department was to ensure that all flying units complied with MAC regulations and operating procedures. This task was accomplished through a series of visits to MAC bases known as ASETs – Aircrew Standardisation and Evaluations Tests – and for almost three years I was to be actively involved in this area of MAC operations, both within the Continental USA and around the world. Although my post was nominally a staff appointment, I found that I was to be employed as a flight examiner, and in order to fulfil that role I needed to become a qualified pilot on one of the MAC aircraft. In view of my VC10 experience, arrangements had been made prior to my arrival for me to attend a C-141 conversion course at Altus AFB in Oklahoma.

Until I was suitably qualified, there was not much that I could usefully do within the department, apart from familiarising myself as far as possible with the working arrangements. Consequently, I arranged with my new boss, Colonel Al Johnson, to take a few days leave before our sons had to return to the UK for the autumn term. As a result, we were able to spend an enjoyable family holiday in the Ozark region of Missouri, a vast area of woodland and lakes, where we discovered some of the delights of the great American outdoors. Not long after our return to Scott AFB, we drove the boys to the airport in St Louis from where they were able to take a direct flight on a British Caledonian aircraft direct to Gatwick, and from there travel by train to the school. For the duration of our tour, much of our time was to be taken up with arranging their flights to and from America for the holidays, and also finding somewhere for them stay with their many relatives during the half-terms. In spite of these complications, the periods they spent in America were very educational, and helped them to develop a more international outlook on life. The boys were also very popular with the girls, who thought that, with their British accents, they were very 'cool dudes'. By the end of our tour, my wife and I had grown accustomed during the holidays to a succession of good looking young ladies arriving in their cars to take the boys out for a date.

TOWARDS THE END OF September I set off accompanied by my wife for the long drive of about six hundred miles to Oklahoma. In the meantime, I had purchased a second automobile from the 'lemon lot', an area set aside on the base for the sale of used cars. With some 12,000 people serving on the base, there was a considerable turnover of personnel, resulting in lively market for automobiles and a large range of vehicles from which to choose. I eventually settled on a fairly new Chevrolet Caprice Classic, a 2-door 5-seater vehicle of elegant design, which showed every sign of having been well-cared for and was in excellent condition. Not only was it very handsome in appearance but it was also a beautiful car to drive, with powered steering and soft suspension, making it a most comfortable form of transport for the many long journeys around the United States that we were to undertake during our tour.

Our route to Oklahoma took us south-westwards through Missouri, passing the cities of Springfield, Tulsa and Oklahoma City. For the entire journey, through undulating countryside, we travelled on a dual carriageway containing very little traffic. During an earlier fuel crisis, the Americans had imposed upon themselves a 55 mph speed limit on their highways, so we progressed in rather stately fashion, with the cruise control engaged, and the radio and the air conditioning on, enjoying the sights and scenery as we went along. From Oklahoma City onwards, the trees became more stunted, the vegetation sparser, and the terrain more desert-like, until we reached the town of Altus which seemed to be in the middle of nowhere.

Arrangements had been made for us to be accommodated on the base in a Visiting Officer's Quarter (VOQ), which took the form of a one-bedroom apartment with a small living area and a separate kitchen. Here we soon settled in, glad of a night's rest after our long journey.

The next day, I started the ground school phase of my conversion course on to the C-141. Having commanded an OCU myself, I knew more or less what to expect but, to my surprise, the course began with a comprehensive lecture on various aspects of living in Oklahoma. It covered the local geography, the climate, the facilities available in Altus (and those not available), local State regulations – particularly those relating to speeding and the consumption of alcohol – and local wildlife, including various varieties of deadly snakes. The lecture helped to impress upon me, if help was needed, the vast continental spread of the country in which I was now serving. Being a senior officer of a foreign Air Force, not to mention a scion of MAC DOV, I also found that I was something of a celebrity on the base, and my wife and I were to enjoy considerable hospitality during our stay.

In the course of my six weeks at Altus, I was befriended by a C-5 Instructor Pilot (IP) who one day asked me if my wife and I would like to join him and his wife for 'dessert'. Unused to this form of social invitation, we duly turned up at his house on the base having taken the precaution of eating a light main course before we went. After the initial introductions and a preliminary exchange of pleasantries, we were duly served with a pudding of sorts, followed by coffee, after which we spent a very convivial evening in their company. In the course of our conversation they asked us if would like to 'house sit' for them over an up-coming weekend while they were out of town. Staying in their house, we would keep an eye on things, and also feed and exercise their two beautiful Red Setters. This we agreed to do. We took up residence on a Friday evening and, after our hosts had left, we went to party on the base organised by the Catholic Church, where we over-indulged in the wine. Somewhat the worse for wear, we returned to the house, only to discover that we were sleeping in a water bed. My wife was first into the bed and then, when I followed, my weight propelled her gently into the air. When she came down it was my turn to be lifted up, and so it went on for several oscillations. The more we laughed the longer the oscillations continued, so that the experience was rather like spending the night on a boat making its way through a good swell. The next morning, feeling somewhat the worst for wear, we decided to take the dogs for a walk. The house was located near the edge of the base and soon we came to vast cornfield that stretched as far as the eye could see. Walking along the edge of the cornfield, we decided to let the dogs off the leash so that they could have a run. Within seconds, and to our absolute horror, they both shot into the cornfield and disappeared. In the words of the song from the musical *Oklahoma*, 'the corn was high as an elephant's eye', and we could see nothing of them. For half an hour we called and whistled, but no dogs appeared. We imagined a scenario where our hosts returned and we would be obliged to say, 'Well, the good news is that your house is OK, but the bad news is that we have lost your dogs!' Fortunately, just as we were beginning to despair, there was a rustling in the corn, and both dogs reappeared as quickly as they had vanished in the first place. We soon had them back on their leads, and although we walked them several times over the weekend, we never let them free again.

MEANWHILE, I COMPLETED THE ground school phase on the C-141 and, after a few sessions in the flight simulator, started the flying phase of the course. The C-141 had entered service with the USAF in 1965, about the same time that the RAF was acquiring its VC10s. The two aircraft were similar in size and performance, the main difference being that the VC10 was a military derivative of an aircraft designed primarily as an airliner, while the C-141 was designed specifically as military aircraft. To this end, the fuselage was slung under the wings, thereby allowing for a cargo hold the size of a small cathedral. The aircraft was also equipped with a rear freight door that not only facilitated the loading and unloading of the aircraft but could also be opened in flight for the air delivery of freight by parachute. In addition, there were also two side-doors at the rear of the aircraft that could be used for dropping paratroops. The version of the aircraft now in service – the C-141B – had a stretched fuselage and was also equipped for air-to-air refuelling.[1] I found the aircraft pleasant and easy to fly. Unlike the VC10, however, where the engines were situated close inboard at the rear of the aircraft, the engines on the C-141 were in pods slung underneath the wing. The failure, or simulated failure, of an engine on take-off was, therefore, a more dramatic event that it was on the VC10, and called for a prompt and generous application of rudder to prevent the aircraft from yawing off course. On my first sortie, flown with Captain Mahnken, a staff instructor at the school, we carried out some upper air work and then returned to Altus for some visual circuits and landings. My first attempt at landing the aircraft was a bumpy affair, but during the final stages of the approach, feeling some resistance to the controls, I noticed that the instructor had his hands on his yoke. After the touch and go landing, and as we were preparing for a second approach, he made a comment

[1] What the RAF refers to as 'air-to-air refuelling' (AAR) the USAF terms 'air refueling" (sic). I have compromised by using the term 'air refuelling' (AR).

about the first landing. 'I might do better,' I said, 'if you would let go of the controls'. He withdrew his hands as if the yoke had suddenly become red hot, and after that my landings improved considerably. My four conversion sorties completed, I was signed up as an aircraft captain on the C-141.

During our stay at Altus we took the opportunity to visit places of interest in the area. Altus itself was a typical American small town and we found the local people very pleasant. They were always charmed by our accents - mine English and my wife's Irish - and neither of them heard very often in that part of the world. We also met several men who had served as aircrew in England during the war and who all seemed to have fond memories of their stay. We visited the small town of Lawton, some 50 miles away, and shopped for Christmas presents in the Post Exchange (PX) at Fort Sill, a large military base in the locality. Fort Sill had played an important role in the pacification of the territory, which had been largely occupied by native Indians until the westward expansion of the white settlers. Later that day we visited the grave of Geronimo, a famous Indian Chief who fought for many years against the encroachment of Mexico and Texas into what were Apache tribal lands. As I remarked to my wife at the time, 'You haven't really been to America until you have stood by the side of Geronimo's grave!'

Not far from Lawton in the Wichita Mountains was a National Park where herds of buffalo roamed freely as a protected species. Looking around at the landscape, it was easy to imagine that you were a settler in the old Wild West. On another occasion we spent a weekend at Fort Worth in Texas, after a drive of 200 miles, most of it in a dead straight line across the flat northern part of Texas. During our stay, we visited a local museum that told the story of the cowboys who drove the cattle along the famous Chisholm Trail to the stockyards of the Kansas Pacific Railway at Abilene near Kansas City. At its peak, in 1867, some 35,000 head of cattle were shipped out by this means. In this same museum, we also saw a representation in which all the countries of Europe, drawn to scale and turned on their side, fitted neatly into a map of Texas.

With our introduction into the American way of life now complete, we returned to Scott AFB in mid-November. When we had departed from Scott for Oklahoma, the daytime temperature had been over 100°F but, as we crossed once more the Mississippi River in the early evening, we discovered with a shock that the temperature had fallen to the low fifties and it was raining. It was one of the features of life in the Mid-West to which we had to become accustomed – the extreme weather – with blazing hot summers and freezing cold winters. I used to joke to our visitors from the UK that there were only two comfortable weeks in the year: one in May, as we passed from the cold of winter to the heat of summer, and one at the end of September, as the process was reversed. Luckily it was still warm enough to play golf, and I arrived back at my desk in HQ MAC just in time to organise a farewell tournament on Scott's championship golf course for my first boss, Colonel Al Johnson, who was retiring from the Air Force. Before he left, I took the opportunity to purchase from him a television, a set of golf clubs and a jet-ski. This last item was in effect a surf board with a petrol-driven impeller mounted at the back. Standing up on the board as you skimmed across the water, you controlled the speed by a hand-held throttle at the end of a long flex, while the device was steered by leaning left or right. A waist-belt was attached by a chord to a dead-man's switch; so if you fell off, the engine cut out, and you could re-board at your leisure. The jet-ski could be carried on the roof rack of the Plymouth Fury and, during the summer months, when our sons were home on holiday, we had enormous fun with it on the many lakes in the local area.

A new head of DOV, Colonel John Vilensons, arrived at Scott with his wife, Ginny (Virginia). His parents were immigrants from Latvia. Arriving in the USA as a small boy, he had rapidly assimilated the American way of life, although there was still a vestige of his origins in his accent. He had previously held a number of senior appointments at different MAC bases, many of them associated with STANEVAL. Not only did he know the business inside out, but he also proved to be a very good leader. During my time in DOV, I flew with him many times, and I would rate him as one of the best commanders of an aircraft that I have ever come across. Unlike the RAF, where relations between the ranks were formal, and senior officers were always addressed as 'Sir' by their subordinates, the staff I met at HQ MAC were much more relaxed, and the use of first names was common. At our first meeting, he asked me to call him John, and this set the seal on our relationship. We became not only colleagues but also firm friends as we travelled to various bases around the world in the course of our duties. John was very proud of the Air Force, and anxious for me to see as much of it as possible during my tour, so I gained unprecedented access to many aspects of air operations that I might not otherwise have seen. I suggested to him that now I was qualified on the C-141 it would be helpful to have some first hand experience of MAC operations, and he agreed. I therefore took part in a mission across the Pacific commanded by Captain Dennis Kirby, one of my subordinates in the office. Picking up an aircraft at Travis AFB just outside San Francisco, we repositioned at McChord AFB, a short flight up the coast to Washington State.

Taking off from Travis in the late afternoon we headed west on our initial departure before turning north. As the sun sank towards the horizon, the whole sky was filled with an enormous golden glow. Crossing San Francisco Bay, I could understand for the first time why the harbour is traversed by what is known as the 'Golden Gate Bridge'. The next morning we flew from McChord AFB to Yokota AFB in Japan. The sector was beyond the normal range of a C-141, so the flight included a in-flight refuelling rendezvous over the north Pacific with a tanker that came from Eielson AFB in Alaska. The next day we continued to Osan AFB in Korea before returning to Yokota. The final overnight sector of a return to California involved a refuelling stop at Anchorage airport in Alaska.

Our destination was Travis AFB, near San Francisco, but the weather in California deteriorated while we were on route with low cloud, torrential rain and a strong cross-wind to such an extent that we were forced to divert to Beale AFB some distance away. To gain proficiency on the aircraft, I had carried out the approach and landing at the various destinations, but even at Beale the weather was so bad that I suggested to Dennis, who had far more experience on type than I did, that he might like to make the final landing of our mission. This he did with considerable aplomb and great skill. A week later I flew another mission, this time from Charleston AFB in South Carolina. On this flight I was accompanied by Captain John Puffenbarger, a very pleasant young aircraft commander from the STANEVAL department on the base. Our route took us across the Atlantic to Ramstein AFB in Germany, and then on to Cairo, before returning to Charleston by the reverse route. After our arrival back at Charleston, he asked me if I would like to join him and his girlfriend in the Officers Club for dinner, which I was very pleased to do. There was Mexican food on the menu, which we all enjoyed. At the end of the evening, when he and I were saying goodbye, he said that his girlfriend had confided to him that she had never before seen anyone eat a Taco with a fork!

Now that I had qualified as an aircraft captain of the C-141 I had to maintain currency by flying the aircraft at least once a month, as did every other C-141 pilot in the department. There were no C-141s based at Scott AFB, but occasionally one would arrive bringing a senior officer from one of the Wings on the coast for a meeting or a conference at the Headquarters. When this happened, we would commandeer the aircraft for the day and carry out our training locally. On other occasions, I would travel out to one of the Wings and do my training there. Scott AFB was home to fleet of C-9 aircraft that were used in the aeromedical evacuation role, bringing patients from various MAC bases all over the USA to a large hospital on the base and delivering them home again when they had recovered from their treatment. I was able to travel as supernumerary crew on these aircraft and often made my way out to the coast on them as we zigzagged our way across the continent, stopping at various airfields en-route before we finally reached our destination at the end of the day. On one such occasion, I travelled out to Charleston AFB, carrying out my monthly continuation training the next day under the tutelage of the STANEVAL department on the base. I had planned to return the next day on a C-141 that was bringing the Wing Commander from Charleston to Scott for a meeting, but when I looked out of the window of my Visiting Officers Quarter in the morning I discovered that all the aircraft had disappeared. Apparently, a hurricane was moving up the coast from the Caribbean, and all the aircraft had been flown out during the night to a safe location. What was I to do? From my outbound journey I knew that a C-9 had night-stopped at Andrews AFB near Washington DC and was due to return to Scott via Charleston later that day, so I made my way to the passenger terminal and hoped that it would turn up. Although the winds were by now very strong and gusty, the conditions were still flyable, and at about 4.00 pm the aircraft duly arrived. With a sigh of relief I boarded the aircraft and arrived home safely later that evening.

The fact that the commander of a 'Wing' in the USAF was called the 'Wing Commander' – occupying a position that in the RAF would be called the 'Station Commander' – occasionally led to some confusion with my rank, which was that of a Wing Commander in the RAF. In the USAF system, I was classed as an O-5 – an Officer Grade 5 – while the commander of a Wing, a full Colonel, would be classed as an O-6. Not everyone knew that, however, and when I arrived on a base and announced myself as Wing Commander Adcock from HQ MAC, they automatically assumed that I was a visiting O-6 and assigned me to the VIP quarters. Rather than embarrassing my hosts by pointing out their error, I felt obliged to take advantage of their largesse. Consequently, I was always comfortably accommodated during my travels.[1]

In the early months of each year, MAC held a large airdrop competition known as VOLANT RODEO at Pope AFB, a C-130 base in North Carolina. John Vilensons was keen for me to see the event, which was not merely limited to MAC aircraft, but involved aircrew from different countries around the world, including some from the RAF. While we were at Pope, he decided to check me out as a Flight Examiner, so a C-141 was summoned from Charleston AFB to fly us the short distance across to the base. The next day I flew on a local mission with a pilot who needed a check. The aircraft had already been airborne for some time when the two of us arrived at Base Operations and it duly taxied into dispersal to pick us up. As I

[1] See Appendix 1 for a full list of equivalent military ranks.

climbed into the right-hand seat and looked across at the pilot who was to be given the check-ride, I was surprised to see that it was an attractive female with blonde hair.[1] I briefed her on the requirement and she flew the sortie competently enough apart from a few minor points, which I covered at the end of the sortie. So she passed her check-ride and I was duly signed up as a MAC Flight Examiner by John Vilensons, who had been observing the proceedings from the jump-seat.

By now, the department was well into its programme of ASETs. We would travel to a MAC base and stay there for a few days while our team of examiners, myself included, flew with the various aircrew trades and assessed them. Our main concern was to assure ourselves that the local examiners at the Wing level were doing their job properly. For my part, I would normally sit on the jump seat and observe the conduct of a flight check. If the check-ride went well, I had the authority to endorse the examiner's status; or, if things went awry, I could suspend it. Thus, if the pilot under test made an egregious error that the examiner failed to notice, and he or she wrongly assessed the pilot as proficient, I could fail both of them. In the examiners world, this was known as a 'double whammy'. Fortunately, this rarely happened, and I was invariably impressed by the proficiency and professionalism of the crews with whom I flew. At the end of the ASET, the Wing was given a grading, and the results were briefed to the Commander-in-Chief (CINCMAC) on a suitable occasion after we had returned to the Headquarters.

About half-way through my tour at HQ MAC, there was a change in the post of Deputy Chief of Staff for Operations – the DO, when General Donald D. Brown assumed command. Prior to becoming the DO, General Brown had held another appointment within the Headquarters, and I had occasionally had some dealings with him. He was an old MAC hand, who knew the air transport business inside out, and I had always found him pleasant and easy to do business with. He did, however, have one hang-up, as we quickly found out after he had taken up his appointment; he hated what he called 'homesteaders'. By his definition, 'homesteaders' were officers who had served in the same appointment within the Headquarters for more than five years, and an edict was issued that said they were to be moved on, pronto. Unfortunately for Roy Dent, my colleague who was the Chief of DOVA, he had held his appointment for more than six years, so he was quickly on his way to a new post at Altus AFB. But having moved

[1] The RAF did not, at that time, accept women for pilot training, a form of discrimination that has since been rectified.

him out, it was then discovered that there was no-one suitably qualified who was immediately available to fill the post. To my surprise, John Vilensons asked me if I would like the job and, having cleared it with the DO, I was duly appointed. Thus I became the de facto chief examiner for MAC's large aircraft, the C-5, the C-141 and the C-130.

To enable me fully to fulfil my duties, it was decided that I should qualify in the field of air refuelling, and in due course I travelled to the Boeing Aircraft Factory in Seattle, where there was a C-141 air refuelling simulator. Later, after completing the simulator phase of the AR course, I drove once again down to Altus for the flying. The refuelling orifice on the C-141 was located just above the cockpit. It was, therefore, a matter of flying in formation at the correct height and distance below the tanker, so that the 'boomer' could fly the probe down and engage with the refuelling aircraft. Contact was established by a satisfying thump just above the pilots head. A rendezvous with the tanker was accomplished by a head-on approach. At a given range, the tanker would diverge by about 30°and then, after a suitable period of time, turn onto the course being flown by the receiver. If all went according to plan, the tanker would then be just ahead and above the receiver, and all the pilot had to do was to advance slowly until the receiving aircraft was in the correct position for an engagement. In essence it was simple enough, but I had not flown in close formation since my days as a QFI, and those days were well behind me, so my early attempts were a bit of a struggle. However, I gradually got the hang of it until, by the end of the course, I could stay on the boom for the requisite 15 minutes. Challenging as this procedure was by day, it was even more taxing by night, as the receiver's position had to be maintained by reference to a series of lights on the underside of the tanker's fuselage.

A particularly demanding sortie was the 'night heavy', when the C-141 was loaded to a high all-up weight by concrete blocks in the form of ballast. The difficulty here was that the aircraft now had considerable inertia, so it took time for any change in the power setting to take effect. Furthermore, once the aircraft started to move fore or aft, it was reluctant to stop, and considerable anticipation was needed to hold station. My night heavy sortie took place over Texas with a clear sky. When I looked up from my seat in the cockpit at the dark shape of the tanker's tailplane above, the sweat pouring off my brow as I strove to hold station, and my heart thumping in my chest, I could see millions of stars illuminating the heavens above. Some time later, I flew a mission from Charleston to Mildenhall in the UK that involved refuelling at night off the coast of New England. After twenty minutes on the boom, I succeeded in 'getting the gas', and was therefore able to complete the journey, but I would easily rate that particular refuelling session as one of the most stressful events of my life.

Quite early on during my tour in America, I discovered that qualifying as a pilot in the USAF automatically brought with it considerable exemptions when it came to applying for a civil licence. After a short period of intense study, I duly took and passed the requisite exam in aviation law. There was a civilian flying club on the airfield at Scott that owned two Cessna-172 light aircraft. Some training with a club instructor led in due course to a Commercial Pilots Licence and Instrument Rating issued by the Federal Aviation Authority (FAA). The Scott Aeroclub had a full time manager but was short of suitably qualified supervisors to cover the weekends. Each day of duty qualified for one hour of flying, so by giving up a day over the odd weekend I was, over a period of time, able to build up a small bank of flying hour credits that I used to carry out several flights around the USA. On the first such trip I flew to Charleston accompanied by my wife and my sister, Elizabeth, who was staying with us at the time. On the way we stopped to refuel at Chattanooga, making use of the excellent flight planning and rest facilities on the airfield that are such a feature of light aviation in the United States.

After landing at Charleston, we hired a car, and stayed for a few nights in a condominium that belonged to John and Ginny Vilensons at the holiday resort of Kiawah Island. Over the weekend we attended a Battle of Britain dinner in the Officers Club at Charleston that was being hosted by an RAF exchange officer on the base, at which the British Air Attaché Washington was also present. The next day, a Sunday, we visited the old town of Charleston, before making the six-hour flight back to Scott on the Monday. Emboldened by this success, and some time later, I flew with my wife and two sons to Dallas/Fort Worth in Texas for a weekend. Ironically, we stayed with the USAF officer who had had such a torrid time during his exchange tour with the RAF, but with whom we had, nevertheless, retained cordial relations.

During our time in Dallas, we took the opportunity to visit the famous 'Southfork Ranch', location for the popular and long-running TV soap opera 'Dallas'. Taking off from Fort Worth on our return to Scott, we climbed slowly through a thin covering of low stratus until we came into clear air at about 2,500 feet. I noticed that the radar controller was vectoring us right over the centre of the adjacent Dallas International Airport while continuing to clear aircraft for take off immediately below us. Consequently, as we transited slowly overhead, and clearly visible under the bright blue sky, the occasional jumbo jet would burst through the cloud to the left or right of us en route to a distant destination.

Our final flight as a family took us to Toronto in Canada. I had intended to complete the flight in daylight but our departure from Scott was delayed for several hours by a technical problem with the aircraft. Heavy thunderstorms were forecast for Illinois later that day, so I decided to press on before the bad weather arrived, even though this would entail a night landing in Toronto. After some three hours flying we landed at a small airport south of Detroit to refuel. I had planned to go round the western edge of Lake Erie on the next leg, but no sooner were we airborne again than the controller routed us 'direct to Hamilton'. As I set the new course I realised that this would take us right across the centre of the lake, an over-water flight of about 150 miles. We climbed to 7,000 feet, and in the gathering darkness I could just make out the lights of the Canadian shoreline in the far distance. Fortunately, the engine purred along steadily, and in due course we landed safely in the dark at a small island airport just off downtown Toronto.

We spent the weekend in Toronto with a nursing friend of my wife's, now married to an Irish immigrant to Canada who had become a successful businessman in the city. On the Monday we arrived back at the aircraft only to discover that the battery was completely flat. Thinking back to my Tiger Moth days, I asked the ground handler, who had come out to the aircraft to see us off, if he knew how to swing a propeller. When he answered in the affirmative, we all climbed into the aircraft and, with the magneto switches off, he wound the propeller backwards a few turns to suck some air and fuel into the cylinders. Then, with the switches on and a call of 'contact', he swung the propeller forwards. The engine fired, hesitantly at first, but then with more certainty as I gingerly opened the throttle. I switched on the alternator, relieved to see the ammeter showing a steady rate of charge, and then we were on our way. The next leg of our trip took us along the shore of Lake Ontario to the Niagara Falls, where there was a race-track pattern that could be used by light aircraft making the scenic tour. Seen from right overhead at 2,000 feet, the falls were a fantastic sight, but the roaring torrent below us made my wife nervous, so we continued the flight and landed at Niagara Falls International Airport, on the American side of the falls, where we stopped for the night.

The next day we set off for Wright Patterson AFB in Ohio. The weather was poor, with low cloud, and I was forced to fly and navigate entirely by reference to the instruments in the aircraft. As we approached the single runway at Wright Patterson, the cross wind was close to our limits. I flew an ILS approach, and I asked the Control Tower to give me the surface wind as we neared the threshold. At about 400 feet we broke cloud with the runway dead ahead, and wind just within our limits. It eased slightly as we crossed the threshold and we landed smoothly. Almost immediately, before we had completed the roll out, the tower called me with an instruction to turn through 180° and back-track along the runway. I glanced down briefly to locate the hand-held microphone in the cockpit so that I could acknowledge the call and, as I did so, the wind gusted, lifting the starboard wing until we were at an angle of about 45°. Reacting instinctively, I slammed on full rudder and full right aileron. For a moment the aircraft hesitated, while the strength of the wind was opposed and balanced by the effects of the controls, then it settled down onto an even keel and came to rest facing the edge of the runway. Breathing a sigh of relief, I taxied to the dispersal and shut down. That incident was the closest I ever came in my entire flying career to having an accident in an aeroplane. After staying with friends overnight, we made an uneventful flight back to Scott in good weather the following day.

Throughout my tour I continued to lead ASET teams on visits to MAC bases within the continental USA, in Alaska and Honolulu, and around the globe. Because the bases were so large, the team was normally supplied with a fleet of cars to facilitate mobility during the visit. On the day of our arrival at a base there was traditionally a 'Grip and Grin' where members of the team could meet the senior staff of the base and the individual counterparts with whom they would be working over the next few days. On a visit to Norton AFB in southern California, I was making my way in my rental car from the Officers Quarters to the Sergeants Mess, where the meeting was to be held, a distance of some two miles. As I approached my destination, I missed the turn into the car park. Continuing along the road, I intended to go around the block for another try but, when I turned right at the next intersection, I found myself on a busy dual carriageway that led to the exit from the base. 'Never mind,' I thought to myself, 'I'll just go out of the base, turn around, and come back in again.' As I exited through the gates of the base, however, I now found myself on a four-lane highway with traffic moving at speed and carrying me further away from where I wanted to be with every passing minute. Eventually, after about five miles, I came to a set of traffic lights, where I was able to turn off the main road, reverse my course, and return to the base, eventually arriving about half-an-hour late for the gathering.

In the course of these ASET visits, I was careful to keep the senior staff briefed on how the evaluation was progressing. The results were important to the executives on the base, and I was always under pressure to speculate on what the final outcome might be. The grades progressed from 'Unsatisfactory' through 'Satisfactory', 'Good', and 'Excellent', with the highest award being 'Outstanding'. The results, however, depended on a number of factors, and there was a published table from which the final outcome could be determined. The table notwithstanding, a Team Chief had the authority to vary the grade in the event of extenuating circumstances. If the evaluation fell close to the boundary between one grade and the next, or if the pressure from the senior staff on the base became too intense, I had observed in the course of my travels that this authority was sometimes used, as a last resort, to advance the base from one grade to a higher one. On one of my later ASETs, which took place at Altus AFB, the table showed that the base qualified for an 'Outstanding' grade. I was concerned, however, that in a couple of significant areas, the staff had failed to take action on observations raised during the last visit that had taken place some eighteen months previously. There were, in addition, a number of minor shortcomings that were not covered specifically by the table. After considerable discussion with my team, I decided that, while the overall results of the testing were 'excellent', the failure to address the issues raised on the previous visit precluded the award of an 'Outstanding' grade. I therefore exercised my prerogative and withheld the 'Outstanding' grade, awarding an 'Excellent' grade instead. The executives on the base were aghast, and the Wing Commander was outraged. Within minutes telephone calls had been exchanged between Altus and HQ 22nd Air Force in California, and between 22nd Air Force and HQ MAC in Illinois. Nevertheless, I stuck to my guns and, when I briefed CINCMAC and his staff at a morning briefing on my return to base, I was relieved to find that I had their solid support. My decision not to award the topmost grade had repercussions that rippled out throughout the Command.

Some six years later, long after I had returned home from the United States, I had occasion to visit one of MAC's subordinate units, the 322nd Airlift Division, located at Ramstein AFB in Germany. In discussion with a senior Operations Officer, a Lieutenant Colonel of the United States Air Force, he suddenly paused in mid sentence and asked me again what my name was.

'Adcock,' I replied, 'Sid Adcock'.

'Oh,' he said, a light of recognition dawning in his eyes. 'You're the guy who bust Altus!'

In between ASET visits I was kept busy in the Headquarters resolving a variety of issues. The officers and Senior NCOs in my Section were very knowledgeable but generally more at home in an aircraft than sitting behind a desk. Although I knew considerably less about MAC and its operations than the members of my Section, I was nevertheless a staff college graduate and, by now, a very competent administrator. By combining our respective knowledge and skills, we were as a team able to produce some very creditable results. During the early part of my tour, MAC had suffered three major accidents, the causes of which could not easily be determined. In each case, however, the aircraft had been perfectly serviceable, and the accidents could, therefore, be attributed only to the actions (or inaction) of the crew. A conference was called at the Headquarters, involving senior operational, training and safety staff from the Numbered Air Forces and their various Wings, in an effort to determine what, if anything, could be done to prevent further such accidents in the future. At my own suggestion, I attended as an observer, with the intention of providing an outsider's perspective on the discussion.

During a break in the proceedings, I was approached by a Major from the Training Division of the Operations Branch at the Headquarters, who explained to me that he had been trying to arouse interest – so far without success - in some work being carried out by the NASA Ames Research Centre in California, which he thought might have some bearing on the proceedings of the conference. He passed onto me two bulky documents and I said I would take a look at them and report back to him. The following week I went to Travis AFB on the west coast for my monthly continuation training, travelling as supernumerary crew on a C-9 from Scott. As we zigzagged our way across the Mid-West, I took the opportunity to read the documents given to me by my colleague, which turned out to be the verbatim proceedings of a conference sponsored by the NASA Ames Research Centre and attended by most of the major civilian airlines in the USA. The aim of the conference was to address the problem of accidents that had occurred when there was nothing technically wrong with the aircraft involved, leading to the inescapable conclusion that they had been caused by human error. To my surprise, many of the speakers had raised as an issue the fact that their company had no real way of addressing the problem of aircraft captains who, while technically competent at flying the aircraft, had nevertheless made weak or inappropriate decisions at critical moments in flight. I was struck forcibly by the close parallel between the problem posed by the speakers and my experiences on the VC10 with captains who suffered from similar shortcomings, and the realisation dawned on me that here was a problem facing not merely aircrew on the VC10, or even in the RAF, but one that affected aviation world wide.

I was particularly taken by a paper presented by a NASA researcher, H. Clayton Foushee, entitled 'Dyads and Triads at 35.000 Feet'.[1] NASA had acquired one of the new dynamic flight simulators that were now in service and the paper drew on an experiment that had been carried out to try to

[1] 'Dyads' and 'Triads' are groups of two and three.

establish why some crews performed better than others. Eighteen airline crews took part and were given a relatively straightforward scenario. On a trans-Atlantic flight they suffered an engine failure that necessitated jettisoning fuel and diverting to Iceland. To increase the workload on the crews, various additional complications were added at critical times. Some crews handled the problem without turning a hair, while others made a complete hash of it, one crew even miscalculating its fuel jettisoning requirement by 100,000 lbs. By analysing the taped discussions on the flight deck, the researchers had tried to determine those actions and attributes that led to good captaincy, and those that detracted from it. Reading further through the proceedings of the conference, I noted that some airlines had already put in hand training programmes designed to improve crew performance on the flight deck, a process known as Cockpit Resource Management (CRM). In particular, United Airlines, a major carrier in the USA, had developed a programme to improve crew performance based on modern management and human resource training methods.

After returning to HQ MAC, and using notes that I had made at the recent conference, I wrote a paper entitled 'Aircrew Discipline and Situational Awareness'. In the paper I drew attention to the fact that the accidents under review occurred because of a breakdown of the crew process at a critical moment in the flight. Making the point that this problem was not confined to MAC but affected aviation world wide, I recommended that MAC should follow up on some of the work that had already been undertaken in this field with a view to incorporating the techniques into its own aircrew training programmes.

The paper was well received, and in due course it was arranged that selected senior aircrew, myself included, would attend a United Airlines CRM training course in Seattle run specifically for MAC personnel. One of my last commitments, before returning to the UK, was to attend a conference in San Francisco, jointly sponsored by MAC and NASA, and attended by a wide range of representatives from the military and civil aviation organisations, to discuss the way ahead for CRM training. I was invited by Clay Foushee, who had read my paper, to chair one of the four working groups and present its findings in a plenary session. This modest beginning sowed the seeds for a MAC CRM training programme that was eventually to embrace the entire Command.

As I approached the end of my tour at Scott AFB, I became more and more conscious of the fact that my age and seniority might preclude me from ever again holding a flying appointment while serving in the RAF. Looking at my logbook, I saw that I was close to accomplishing 7,000 flying hours. While this may seem a modest achievement in terms of civil aviation, in the field of military flying, where sorties tend to be shorter and much more intensive, it appeared to be a significant milestone. Consequently, I took every opportunity to fly, and with just a few months left to me I was within a few hours of my target. My final ASET visit in January 1986 took place at Norton AFB in southern California. I was absent from the base for few days while I evaluated some crew that were taking part in an exercise in Honolulu, and when I returned to Norton I had completed 6,997 hours and 15 minutes of flying time.

My last flight was as an examiner on an air refuelling sortie that took off from Norton and rendezvoused with a tanker off the Pacific coast. We travelled northwards up the coast while each pilot on board took his required ten minutes on the boom, passing as we did so the city of San Francisco, with the spires of its tall buildings just visible above the fog. Reaching the state border of Oregon, we turned southwards and retraced our flight path. I was the last pilot to take his turn on the boom and the training pilot in command of the sortie suggested that I stay in seat and complete the final approach back into Norton. When I landed the aircraft from what was to be my last sortie in the USA, we had logged just 3 hours, bringing me up to the grand total of 7,000 hours and 15 minutes.

In May 1986 we prepared to leave America and return to the UK. Several months previously, I had sold the Caprice Classic and reached the pinnacle of my motoring ambition with the purchase of a brand-new duty-free BMW saloon. Having been manufactured in Germany, the car was delivered to the UK, where it was registered, and then shipped to Baltimore, from where I had collected it. Now we were about to drive the car back to Baltimore so that it could be shipped back to the UK. From Baltimore, we would return to Washington Dulles airport and then by RAF VC10 back to RAF Brize Norton. Before that, however, we were treated to a farewell golf tournament and dinner by my department, at which I was presented with a memento of my tour in the form of a desk-top model of the St Louis Arch mounted on a wooden block. On the block was a Military Airlift Command shield. Beneath the shield the inscription read:

Wg Cdr C B Adcock RAF
HQ MAC STANEVAL
Scholar – Golfer – Socializer – Aviator
Aug 83 – May 86

CHAPTER 11

Flying a Desk in London

THE AMERICAN TENANTS of our home in Penton Mewsey had by now vacated the property and returned to the USA, allowing us once again to take up residence in the village. I had been posted to a staff appointment in the Ministry of Defence (MOD) in London, so the residential plan that we had adopted several years previously during my tour at RAF Upavon eventually bore fruit, and I was able to commute by train from Andover to London Waterloo without undue difficulty. Civilian clothes were the order of the day for military personnel working in the Capital, so I bought myself a smart new suit and several shirts and ties to go with it. On my first day at work I boarded the train and took a seat on the south side facing the direction of travel. After several intermediate stops along the way the train became very crowded, with people standing in the aisles. At Clapham Junction it came to halt, and there it remained for some two hours; a fire in the signal box - so we were eventually informed. As the sun rose, it gradually became hotter and hotter in the compartment, to such an extent that when we arrived belatedly at Waterloo my new shirt and suit were soaked in perspiration. When I eventually presented myself to my new Director, Air Commodore David Crwys-Williams, I looked like a survivor from a ship-wreck. Not only that but I spoke using idiomatic Americanisms that I had acquired through living and working for nearly three years on a base where there were 12,000 Americans and only half-a-dozen Brits. The Air Commodore must have had some justifiable qualms about this strange person who was coming to work in his department.

Not long after learning of my new appointment, while still at Scott AFB, I had telephoned Wing Commander Ian Headley, the current incumbent in the post, to find out what the job entailed. After our conversation, I asked him, by way of an afterthought, 'Is there any flying associated with the job?' 'The only time you get to fly here,' he replied, 'is when you go up and down in the lift!' And so it proved to be. In fact it was to be almost seven years before I was to fly as a pilot again in an RAF aircraft. Nevertheless, the intervening years would prove to be not only challenging but full of interest as well.

My new post was located in the MOD Main Building, a vast monolithic block of offices in Whitehall, situated right opposite Downing Street. Here on the fourth floor I shared an office with another Wing Commander. We were each equipped with a desk, a telephone and a large steel cabinet for the storage of our various papers, many of them of a highly classified nature. Our office looked over the inner well of the MOD and, as I was to find out in due course, it was difficult in winter to tell whether it was night or day outside. The Department within which I was to work for the next 3½ years was known as Air Force Staff Duties (AFSD), and my particular desk was responsible for matters pertaining to Transition to War (TTW). In essence, my job was to ensure that, in the event of a general war, the RAF would be able to transition smoothly from a peacetime footing to a full wartime posture. Consequently, in my new post, I found myself at the very epicentre of the political and military nexus that organised the composition and deployment of the Armed Forces in peace and war.

For many years, ever since the end of hostilities in 1945, the single biggest factor underpinning UK defence strategy had been the fear of a Soviet invasion of Western Europe, and it was this threat that still largely determined defence policy. Consequently, at the time when I took up my appointment, our thinking on defence matters was constrained to a considerable extent by attitudes developed during the long years of the Cold War. Another important factor – and one that was to exert ever-increasing pressure on our plans and resources - was that the UK could no longer afford the forces it had. The exponential rise in the cost of manpower and equipment that had occurred in the post-war period had led to an unsustainable financial squeeze. Successive defence reviews – reviews that were in effect little more than attempts to square the circle - had resulted only in bouts of 'salami slicing' as each individual service sought to save money yet still preserve its vital capabilities.

The immediate impact of these circumstances on my particular desk was a drive towards making greater use of reserve forces. Several trials to this effect had been put in place before I arrived in the department and I had barely had time to put my feet under my desk than I was called upon to provide a brief for the Assistant Chief of the Air Staff (ACAS) explaining our current plans for the deployment and use of reserve forces. I went to the Department's registry and pulled out the relevant files; then I took out a pad of foolscap paper and made copious notes in longhand about the various dispositions. Having condensed and compressed all the information into a logical and readable form, I took the draft to the typing pool, where there were perhaps a dozen typists all hammering away at their mechanical keyboards. The typists were supervised by 'Dottie', a civil servant who sat smoking at a desk at the head of the room. She appended a docket to my draft and placed it in a large pending tray.

'How long will it take?' I asked tentatively.

'About two days,' was the reply.

'Here, indeed,' I thought, as I made my way back to my office, 'is a stumbling block to progress.'

Nevertheless, the feedback I received after the finished product had been forwarded through the Deputy Director and the Director to the Assistant Chief was that the brief had been well received, and I felt that I had made a sound start in my new environment.

As I was soon to discover, a vast amount of paperwork flowed through the department. We drafted briefs and letters for our masters, wrote minutes and papers on a wide array of topics, commented on work originated by other departments that impinged on our area of responsibility and performed a host of other tasks. Our work schedule was determined almost entirely by deadlines and there was nearly always pressure to complete the various tasks on time. Merely to survive in this environment, I quickly established a routine. Catching the train from Andover shortly after seven o'clock in the morning I arrived in the office just before nine. Without further ado, I set to work on my most pressing tasks and applied myself solidly until about one o'clock, when I took a break for lunch. I left the building and went on a short stroll around central London to take in some fresh air and to buy a sandwich, which I ate at my desk on returning to the office. In the afternoon, I continued working until about a quarter to six, when I left the office and walked to Waterloo station to catch the train home. Arriving home just after seven in the evening, I enjoyed a meal and short period of relaxation before it was time to go to bed and then start the routine all over again.

By Friday I was exhausted and more than glad of a couple of days off at the weekend in which to recharge my batteries. After a few of months of daily commuting, the opportunity arose to take up lodgings in London. My new weekday home was just off Kensington High Street and a short ride on the Circle Line of the Underground from Westminster. The arrangement meant spending four nights a week away from home, which was not ideal, but it was far less stressful than the alternative of having to catch a train at a particular time twice each day.

A lot of my time was taken up with attending meetings. At that time the different MOD departments occupied numerous buildings in central London, so I was often required to travel the short distance from the Main

Building where I worked to one of the other nearby office blocks in the city. After a short period of experiment, I discovered that no matter whether you travelled by bus, by underground, or on foot, all the journeys took about the same time, so I chose to walk. Not only did this mode of travel allow me to take some exercise but I also had an opportunity to admire the many fine buildings along the way and to observe the great variety of goings-on as people went about their daily activities in the city.

One of my most important and time-consuming tasks in the MOD was to organise the regular six-monthly meeting of the so-called War Plans and Policy Group (WPPG). This committee comprised the 1-Star heads of about twenty departments, including some of the operational commands. My Director chaired the meetings, while I acted as Secretary. Some two months prior to a meeting, I would prepare and circulate an agenda. There would then be a burst of telephone activity as the relevant desk officer in each department prepared a brief for his 1-Star setting out the points for discussion. At the same time, I prepared a similar brief for my Director, summarising the progress made on each agenda item since the previous meeting and highlighting the decisions that had to be taken at the next meeting in order to move the issue forward. At the meeting itself, I would take the minutes, my notes often running to a dozen pages of foolscap, after which I would write up a draft of the proceedings and pass it to my Director for approval. Many of the issues discussed at the meeting were controversial, and it often took a great deal of tact and some judicious wording to reconcile widely divergent views. A final version of the minutes would then be circulated to the participants, allocating action as appropriate, and then the whole cycle would begin again.

Air Commodore Crwys-Williams and his successor, Air Commodore Tim Garden, were both first class Chairmen, and under their leadership the WPPG began to get to grips with some of the issues, both military and political, that had bedevilled for many years the RAF's preparedness for war. The minutes of the WPPG were read not only by the heads of the departments involved in the meetings but by a much wider audience as well, as I knew from telephone calls I had received from various branches of the RAF querying or seeking enlightenment on some of the topics under discussion. As the focal point for the desk officers working on these various problems, I played a central part in these discussions, drafting letters and papers for the Director that attempted to co-ordinate and resolve many of the issues that arose. After one particular minefield had successfully been crossed, the Director remarked to me, only half in jest, that I must be 'the most the powerful man in the Air Force!'

Writing all this material in long-hand was a slow and cumbersome way of going about our business, but help eventually came when I was about half-way through my tour. One day, out of the blue, a series of large cardboard boxes appeared in the corridor outside our offices, and when opened they were found to contain Personal Computers (PCs). This was the beginning of an electronic revolution that would transform the way in which society in general and the Armed Forces in particular conducted business. In these early days, however, hardly anyone in the department knew how to work a PC. We looked on them as rather clever toys and, as there were neither classes nor any formal instruction, we learned how to operate them from each other. Fortunately, one or two members of the Department already owned their own elementary home computers, and from these rudimentary beginnings knowledge of the operating systems soon began to spread. Wandering into someone else's office, you would notice that they has something different on their screen from what you had seen so far. 'Oh, that looks interesting,' you would say. 'How do you do that?' Then would follow a brief period of tuition, and back you went to your own office with a new string to your bow. Even though the new machines were of limited capacity and the material was stored on floppy discs, they brought two important advantages. First, they freed the desk officers from the tyranny of the typing pool and, secondly, they allowed material to be stored and reused without the necessity to write it in longhand all over again when it was needed once more but in a different context. Acquiring the necessary keyboard skills and learning the operating system involved considerable extra work in the short-term, but the vast improvement in efficiency made the effort well worth while in the long run.

In October 1987, when I was about half-way through my tour in the MOD, my daily routine was disturbed by an unusual event. In the evening I had gone to bed in my lodgings and slept soundly, although I was awakened briefly during the night by what sounded like a car alarm going off in the street outside. In central London, this was not an unusual sound, and thinking no more about it I went back to sleep. That morning I left my landlady's house at about eight o'clock and walked the short distance to Kensington Underground Station. When I arrived at the station I found the gates locked. A notice on a blackboard in front of the gates informed passengers that the train service was temporarily suspended because of storm damage, and it was only then that I began to realise that something was amiss. I decided to take the bus but, when I turned around, I saw that there were lengthy queues at all the bus stops. I joined the back of one of the queues, but every bus that came along was bursting at the seams with passengers, and it soon became obvious that there was not much prospect of travelling in to work by that particular mode of transport. Just at that moment, a colleague of mine from the MOD came by, and together we decided that our only option was to walk to work. Making our way past Kensington Gardens, we were astonished by the sight that we beheld as we saw huge trees, that had previously survived for hundreds of years, now felled by the ferocity of the overnight storm and lying on their sides with their roots sticking in the air. On the other side of the road were vehicles crushed by fallen trees, and everywhere there was debris and broken branches blocking the way. It looked like the aftermath of the blitz, a sight I had only previously seen on cinema newsreels. Continuing on our way, we crossed Green Park and St James's Park, where similar scenes of havoc and destruction met our eyes. Passing through Horse Guards Parade we crossed Whitehall and eventually arrived at our destination. When we entered the MOD building we found the place like a ghost town. Hardly any trains were running and only those officers living close enough to walk had been able to travel to work. It happened to be a Friday, and soon all thoughts of constructive activity were set aside as everyone concentrated their minds on the problem of how to travel home for the weekend. Fortunately for me, my Director, who lived not from my home, had arranged for his wife to come and collect him by car, and he very kindly offered me a lift which I gratefully accepted. By the time Monday morning arrived, following a huge effort by the transport authorities over the weekend, services were almost back to normal again.

Having worked under intense pressure all week, the weekends were naturally very precious. While we were in America, where there was a championship golf course on the base where we lived, my wife had taken up the game. Returning to the UK, we had subsequently joined Tidworth Garrison Golf Club on the edge of the Salisbury Plain, and most weekends, when the weather was fine, we relaxed by taking part in the various competitions organised by the club. Many members of the club came from a military background and we soon made a wide circle of friends. Initially, however, my wife got off to a rocky start. Having learned to play in America, where exuberance was considered to be a natural part of the game, she found the atmosphere of the Ladies Section rather starchy. Playing with three established members of the club, and delighted at having sunk a long put, she pumped her fist and shouted 'Way to go, baby!' This outburst of joy was greeted by a shocked silence, and it was pointed out to her later that such behaviour would be regarded as unseemly by other members of the club. This setback notwithstanding, she persevered with her game, not only achieving a respectable handicap but also serving on the Ladies Committee for several years as the Handicap Secretary.

I also found time to resume my studies with the Open University, a course of study that I had undertaken some years previously, but which I had had to set aside during my tour in America. Having specialised in the sciences at school, I had opted to broaden my education by studying in the Arts Faculty. Initially, I had completed a general course in the arts, including a week of Summer School at Keele University. This had been followed by courses in Greek and Roman culture, 'English Culture in the Seventeenth Century', and several other topics. My years at Cranwell, and my status as a graduate of the RAF Staff College, gave me some exemptions, and I had by now achieved enough credits for an ordinary degree. During my years in America I had taken a sabbatical, but now that I was back in the UK I decided to study for the two additional credits that would qualify me for an honours degree, and to this end I undertook two advanced courses. The first of these, entitled 'Conflict and Stability in Modern Europe' involved modern history. Having successfully completed that course, I decided to really expand my horizons, and for my final year I studied Modern Art. This latter course not only turned out to be the most interesting of all the different fields in which I had studied but also provided me with a lifelong interest in art that I was able to pursue during my subsequent travels around the world. It also gave me the satisfaction of attending a summer school in London involving visits to various central galleries while my colleagues were slaving at their desks just down the road in Whitehall. Following the successful completion of this final course, I was awarded my honours degree at Southampton University in December 1989.

Meanwhile, in the MOD, work continued at a frenetic pace. Efforts to reduce costs had resulted in the civilianisation and contractorisation of many tasks formerly carried out by service personnel, and there was growing concern that this process, if taken too far, would seriously impede the RAF's ability to function in the event of a general war. Consequently, a study was initiated by the WPPG called 'RAF Manpower in War'. The aim of the study was to determine the minimum manpower that the RAF would need to fulfil its expected wartime tasks. The study was also intended to determine which posts could be filled by civilians and reservists, thereby providing a definitive figure for exactly how many servicemen were needed. Intended primarily as a rearguard action against overwhelming pressure to further reduce manpower costs, the study was bedevilled from the outset by the complexity of the issues involved. At the heart of the problem was the rapidly changing nature of modern warfare brought about by the advent of air power. No longer were the protagonists divided by a clearly demarcated 'front line', the Forward Edge of the Battle Area or FEBA as it is known in Army terms. Instead, those employed in a supporting role on the home front were just as likely to come under attack as those facing enemy forces in the field. Not only could they be bombarded from the air but they were equally if not more so imperilled by acts of violence committed by terrorists. Given the amorphous nature of the threat, it was difficult if not impossible to draw up precise definitions of which category of manpower was best suited to which particular wartime tasks. For example, much of the maintenance required to keep a modern airfield fully operational was carried out by a highly qualified, experienced and dedicated corps of civilian staff. But what if the airfield were to come under attack from an enemy employing not only high explosive munitions but chemical and biological weapons as well? Service personnel were not only trained and equipped to deal with such an event but were also bound by the military ethos to go on fighting. But under such conditions, could the civilian staff reasonably be expected to continue their vital work as well? A similar problem attached itself to the use of reserve forces. In a protracted build up to war, there would be time to bring them up to the necessary degree of preparedness, but how much use would they be in the event of a sudden deterioration in the status quo or a surprise attack? Many of these issues were not only militarily significant but also had a political dimension as well, making them particularly difficult of resolution. So while the study was heading in the right direction, the unrelenting demand to cut costs meant that it was always in danger of being overtaken by events.

Having now been closely involved in these matters for more than three years my participation was about to come to an end. Towards the end of 1989 I learned from my desk officer that I was to be promoted to the rank of Group Captain and shortly posted to an appointment at the Supreme Headquarters Allied Powers Europe (SHAPE) based at Mons in Belgium. Just before Christmas I was given the traditional farewell lunch at a West End restaurant for an officer leaving the department, and with a full stomach and an unsteady gait I made my way for the last time to Waterloo station to catch the train home.

CHAPTER 12

Flying a Desk in Belgium

My new post at SHAPE was designated 'Chief of the Ace Mobile Force Movement Operations Section', thankfully almost always known by its abbreviated form 'Chief of AMF Mov Ops'. The Allied Command Europe Mobile Force – or AMF, as it was always termed – was a rapid reaction force whose task it was to reinforce the flanks of NATO in the event of an aggressive move by the forces of Russia and her Eastern European satellites, an alliance known as the Warsaw Pact. The AMF was made up of elements from the various providing nations, and it was the task of my department to co-ordinate the movement of those forces from their home stations to the theatre of operations.

To this end, I had a staff of five: a Lieutenant Colonel of the United States Air Force (USAF) and a Lieutenant Colonel of the German Air Force (GEAF), who together were responsible for movement by air; another GEAF Lieutenant Colonel who was responsible for movements by rail and by sea; and a Dutch Army Major who was responsible for communications in the field. The fifth and final member of the team was a Dutch Army Sergeant, who was responsible for the administration of the section. My immediate superior was Brigadier-General Thomas, a cavalry officer in the Dutch Army, who was Head of the Combat Management Branch. The Brigadier reported to the Assistant Chief of Staff for Operations (ACOS Ops), a 2-Star USAF General. With Armies, Air Forces, Navies, and Marines all represented from the 14 nations which at that time constituted the Atlantic Alliance, and with every rank present from the lowliest foot-soldier at the bottom to a Four-Star General at the top, SHAPE was a unique organisation that employed the full spectrum of military personnel in its integrated command structure.

Although French and English were the official languages of NATO, English was the main medium of communication within the Headquarters. English, however, came not only in a variety of different accents but was also spoken with various degrees of proficiency. For several months, until my ear became attuned to the different intonations, I found that the effort required to communicate effectively every day was absolutely exhausting. But the facility that NATO personnel had to switch from one language to another was remarkable. In my Section, for example, the two soldiers from the Netherlands might be speaking together in Dutch when they would be joined by one of the German officers. Immediately the conversation would revert from Dutch to German. If they were then joined either by me or by the American officer, everyone would instantly start talking in English. Although I spoke neither German nor Dutch, much of the discussion within the Section involved considerable use of technical terms, nearly all of which were English or anglicised words.

After a while, I reached a point where I could usually grasp the gist of the argument, even if the discussion was taking place in a language other my own. Because oral communication was a source of difficulty for everyone in the Headquarters, verbal slip-ups and misunderstandings were always the subject of great hilarity. Not long after I arrived at SHAPE I joined the officers club and went to collect my membership card. When I returned to the office, Volker Fritzemeier, one of my German officers, was sitting at his desk laminating a series of passes that were to be used in a forthcoming exercise. By way of conversation, I remarked that I had just been to join the Officers Club, and held out my new membership card for him to see.

'Would you like me to laminate it for you?' he asked in English. Because of his German accent, I misunderstood him, and I thought he had said 'Would you like me to eliminate it for you?'

'No, no,' I said, 'I've only just got it.' There was a puzzled silence while everyone tried to figure out the source of the obvious misunderstanding, but eventually the penny dropped and we all burst out laughing. Some time later, I mentioned this episode in a speech I had to make at a NATO gathering and the story gained a huge empathetic laugh from my audience.

Within two months of arriving in Belgium I was to experience at first hand the AMF in action. The exercise took place towards the end of February in northern Norway. The Norwegian Air Force Base at Bardufoss was the airhead for the exercise, and it was here that I set up operations with my team. Our task was to provide ground services for the aircraft that would be arriving from different departure airfields in Europe, Canada and the United States. To this end, my small team was augmented by ground handling teams from the various providing nations, so that I had some sixty or seventy allied personnel temporarily attached to my command.

The main purpose of the AMF was to send a political signal to the members of the Warsaw Pact reminding them of Article 5 of the NATO Treaty.

This Article stated that an attack on one nation would be regarded as an attack on all. To ram home this message, it was important that there was an even build up forces from the various providing nations, and this principle was enshrined in our operational plans. Consequently, at the airhead, there might be on the hour the arrival of a German aircraft. This would be followed at 10 minutes past the hour by an aircraft from Italy. A Belgian aircraft would take the slot at 20 minutes past the hour and a Canadian aircraft would arrive on the half-hour. And so on round the clock as the steady build up of forces continued throughout the deployment phase of the exercise or operation. Meanwhile, on the ground, the reception parties would also be multinational in composition, so that it would be clear to any outside observer that the alliance was working cohesively together to mitigate the threat. Controlling and co-ordinating all this movement was the task of my operations officers, and our set-up was known as the International Airlift Co-ordination Element (IALCE).

To test the plans, the deployment phase of the exercise was deliberately designed to be as intensive as possible, and we were stretched to the limit to keep the airlift running smoothly by overcoming the various logistical and operational difficulties that inevitably arose. Once the airlift was complete, however, and several thousand troops and airmen of the AMF had deployed into the field for the ground phase of the exercise, the pressure on the IALCE eased considerably. With only a few resupply aircraft now arriving each day, the members of the team were able to relax and enjoy the ambience of winter within the Arctic Circle, together with the hospitality of our Norwegian hosts.

We travelled through a vista of snow and ice to a nearby port to visit one of our supply ships. On another occasion we took a day trip to the distant town of Tromsø, looking spectacular in its winter garb. I also took the opportunity to carry out some cross-country skiing, a popular winter activity in Norway. With the ground phase of the exercise now at an end, we were once again fully engaged with the redeployment of the troops back to their respective nations. Returning from the field, they were accommodated in two large marquees that had been erected in the environs of the airfield.

With the daily temperatures well below freezing, and the nights even colder, it was clearly desirable to fly them out as expeditiously as possible. The weather had remained largely favourable throughout our stay. Although there was some impacted ice and snow on the surface of the runway, the braking action was good and aircraft movements were taking place at regular intervals. I was, therefore, astonished to discover that that the RAF had suspended its operations and the scheduled airlift by VC10 aircraft was not forthcoming. By this time there were several hundred British troops crammed into the marquees with more arriving by the minute. To head off the impending crisis, I telephoned the Station Commander at RAF Brize Norton and asked him what was causing the hold-up. He called me back to inform me that the weather reports from Bardufoss indicated that the runway conditions were unsuitable for the VC10 and that they were waiting for an improvement.

I told him that there was unlikely to be any improvement until the spring, and that every other nation was operating normally. I explained the situation with regard to the troops holding at the airfield, and said that, based on my own extensive knowledge of VC10 operations, there was no earthly reason why they could not operate from the airfield. If the RAF couldn't do it, they needed to charter the task as soon as possible to another operator who could. It seemed that my telephone call had its effect because within thirty minutes I learned that three VC10s were airborne from Brize Norton and on their way to Bardufoss.

Over the years, my team had developed an excellent rapport with the operational headquarters of the transport forces of the various providing nations. Well-established informal channels of communication often helped to resolve the many operational problems that inevitably arose in the course of an exercise. Quite often, they also helped to resolve some of the less pressing matters. At Bardufoss, for example, we acquired some splendid Norwegian smoked salmon that needed to be transported back to Belgium. It was agreed that an Italian C-130, en route from Bardufoss to its base at Pisa, would divert into Brussels International Airport and drop off the cargo at Melsbroek, the Belgian Air Force Base located on the north side of the airfield. Pieter Anbeek, the Dutch Sergeant who administered our Section at SHAPE, and who had remained at the Headquarters for the duration of the exercise, would meet the aircraft and transport its precious cargo back to base.

Unfortunately, on the day of the mission, strong cross-winds precluded a landing at Brussels, so the C-130 overflew the airport and continued on to its destination at Pisa. Nothing daunted, the next day, when the winds had abated, the Italians generously launched a 'resupply mission' to their embassy in Brussels, and the cargo of salmon safely reached its destination at SHAPE. Not long after our return from the exercise, we hosted a conference at SHAPE, involving the AMF Providing Nations, to carry out a periodic review of our contingency plans, and the salmon provided excellent fare at a dinner for our guests.

Following my return from Norway, I took over a SHAPE hiring in the small village of St Symphorien, some three kilometres to the east of Mons.

By now, my two sons had completed their secondary education and had both gained places at university. James, the eldest, was at Bristol on a cadetship, studying aeronautical engineering, with a view to becoming an Engineering Officer in the RAF. Meanwhile, Brian, the youngest, had started at Loughborough on a Royal Marine scholarship, studying Physical Education and Maths. With both boys now settled for the time being, we were able once again to let our house in Penton Mewsey and my wife was able to join me in Belgium. Crossing the Channel by ferry from Dover to Calais, she drove herself to Mons on a bitterly cold day at the beginning of March, and we began the process of settling into our new home. Within a few days our furniture and effects arrived from the UK in a removal van - a huge pantechnicon - which promptly broke down in front of our house. Fortunately, we had by this time managed to have the telephone reconnected in our name, and a rescue plan was put in hand.

Not long afterwards I took a telephone call in French from an agent in Namur. With some considerable difficulty, I managed to establish that a recovery vehicle was being dispatched to effect repairs. Could I give them directions as to how to find my house? At that stage, I could barely find the house myself, let alone give directions in my schoolboy French as to how to reach it, so a somewhat convoluted conversation ensued. I remembered, however, that St Symphorien was off the Rue de Binche, and that the turning was marked by 'une maison avec une lanterne rouge'. This information seemed to satisfy them as about an hour later the recovery vehicle arrived and the problem was lifted from my shoulders.

From then onwards, we adjusted gradually to life in Belgium, joining a local golf club, the Royal Golf Club du Hainaut, and taking part in the many other social and cultural events that were the inevitable concomitant of serving in a large multinational military headquarters. The town of Mons lies in Wallonia, the French-speaking part of Belgium, and although the language barrier posed a few problems, we found that English was widely spoken as a second language. Step by step, we gradually learned to make our way. Over a period time, we became very proficient at making ourselves understood on the golf course, particularly when playing in competitions with our Belgian hosts. This was not quite as difficult as it sounds, since most of the terms had been adapted from the English. So we had 'le tee', 'le green', 'le bunker', etc, etc. I once asked a Belgian lady with whom I was partnered, 'What do you call a hole that starts straight ahead and then veers to the left or the right?' Rather sheepishly she replied, 'We call it "le dogleg"!' We also played Bridge in the SHAPE Officers Club, where some of the Belgian couples spoke only a little English. So the bidding proceeded... '*un trefle*, one diamond, *un coeur*, two diamonds, *deux pics...'* etc. Notwithstanding the occasional difficulty and a few embarrassing linguistic gaffs, we nevertheless greatly enjoyed the opportunity to mix in such a vibrant international community.

Living in Belgium also greatly facilitated continental travel. Without the necessity to cross the channel, many parts of Western Europe could be reached in a day's drive, while even the more distant destinations required only a single night-stop en route. It is little wonder that some members of staff took the cynical view that the acronym SHAPE stood for 'Super Holidays at Public Expense'. Cynicism notwithstanding, my own department was required to undertake a lot of travel. There were two full-scale AMF exercises each year, each one in a different deployment area. Every exercise required two planning conferences: the first was usually held in the capital city of the host nation and determined the scope and scale of the exercise, while the second one was held at the planned airhead. Once again, good relations with the transport forces of the providing nations served to our advantage, as we were often able to hitch a ride on a military aircraft. The Belgian Air Force, in particular, had several communications aircraft based at Melsbroek, and they would normally offer us a ride if they were attending the various conferences. So rather than joining the scrum at Brussels International Airport, and perhaps having to change airlines en route, we merely arrived at Melsbroek shortly before our scheduled departure time and were carried in comfort directly to our destination.

In the late summer of my arrival at SHAPE I attended a Senior Officers Orientation Course at Oberammergau in southern Germany. During the course we had high-level briefings by various senior commanders in the NATO organisation. Apart from explaining in detail the scope and nature of their various commands, they also drew attention to the significant political changes that were taking place in Eastern Europe. Following the collapse of the communist government in Poland and the fall of the Berlin Wall, the way seemed open to some sort of rapprochement with the Soviet Union. As the NATO treaty had been signed specifically to mitigate the threat of a Soviet incursion into Western Europe, these developments clearly had important ramifications for the alliance. At that moment, no-one could foretell with any degree of certainty what changes the political developments would bring, and for the moment the alliance would continue to maintain its guard. From my particular point of view, this approach meant that the AMF exercises already being put in hand would go ahead, for the next few years at least.

Because SHAPE was the military headquarters of the NATO alliance, the organisation had a wider remit than mere contingency planning, and the development and fostering of good international relations played an important part in the life of the organisation. Consequently, wives were encouraged to accompany their husbands where circumstances allowed, albeit at their own expense. During my tour this arrangement gave my wife and I an opportunity to travel extensively around Western Europe. Following our week at Oberammergau, for example, I was able to take a week's leave, during which time we explored southern Germany and Austria as far east as Vienna, parts of Europe that we had never previously had the opportunity to visit. From time to time during my subsequent tour at SHAPE I was also required to attend meetings at the AMF Headquarters located in the ancient university town of Heidelberg. On these occasions we were comfortably accommodated in Visiting Officers Quarters provided by the US military in Heidelberg. One of these visits took place in December, so not only were we able to do some of our festive shopping in the local Christmas Market but we were also able to attend the AMF Christmas Ball held in Heidelberg Castle.

Meanwhile, the work of my Section continued apace, with a highly successful deployment to Værløse, a Danish Air Force base located on the outskirts of Copenhagen. Deployments to bases in Scandinavia were always relatively straightforward. Not only were the various airfields well equipped and organised but the majority of the staff spoke excellent English. I drove my car from SHAPE to Denmark, and thus was able to take advantage of any free time available during the redeployment phase of the exercise. Travelling overnight by bus, my wife joined me for a few days, and together we were able to visit the many places of interest that were located within and around Copenhagen. Another feature of the deployment was the excellent service provided by the RAF's Mobile Catering Support Unit (MCSU). This unit, which provided three meals a day for the 80 or so members of the IALCE, was staffed by Warrant Officers, SNCOs and airmen of the RAF'S Catering Branch. They were highly adept at sourcing themselves with local produce and consistently served meals of the highest quality under field conditions. We were often visited by high ranking officers who came to observe the AMF in action, and they were always astounded by the excellence of the fare that was provided. On one occasion we were joined by an RAF Mobile Air Movements Officer who was a vegan, and who could only eat meals prepared in a specific way. Faced with this problem, the MCSU found a vegan restaurant in Copenhagen and arranged for a daily supply of specially prepared meals for the duration of the officer's stay. Throughout my many detachments with the IALCE, the MCSU accompanied us to various different countries, and not once were we disappointed with the service they provided.

Much more difficult than deployments to the countries of Scandinavia were the exercises held in Turkey. Not many Turkish officers spoke English, and none of my staff spoke Turkish. We had, therefore, to rely heavily on a few interpreters in making arrangements with our hosts. Furthermore, the Turkish forces were commanded by means of a very rigid hierarchy, and junior officers were expected to obey orders rather than use their initiative. It was, therefore, often difficult to find the right man to get things done. Another factor that weighed heavily on us was the extreme heat of summer, with temperatures often as high as 46°C (115°F).

One of our most difficult deployments was to Çorlu, an airfield in Turkish Thrace. Çorlu had an excellent runway but almost nothing else in the way of infrastructure, so almost everything we need had to be either flown in or delivered by sea to the nearby port of Tekirdag. We even had to arrange for the Canadian Air Force to fly in and man a portable GCA unit so that we could maintain all-weather operations. As was customary during our deployments, we invited the Base Commander and some of his senior staff to a dinner in our tented accommodation. To our surprise, and unbeknown to us, he had arranged for music and a couple belly dancers to entertain us after dinner, making for a very jolly evening indeed.

While the AMF exercise was taking place in the field, a small group of NATO officers and I decided to take advantage of the relative lack of air transport activity to visit the site of the ruins at Troy. We drove in one of our minibuses to the Dardanelles and crossed by ferry to the south side of the straights. Another hour's drive brought us to the ancient citadel. After some time exploring the ruins, we returned to the port of Çanakkale and re-crossed the straights to the northern side. It was by now about four o'clock in the afternoon and we had intended to return directly to base, a drive of about an hour and a half. On disembarking from the ferry, however, we saw a sign for the beach-heads used in the First World War during the ill-fated Dardanelles Campaign, and we decided to pay them a visit before returning to Çorlu.

Having concluded our tour of the beach-heads at the magnificent Turkish war memorial, which stands on a high bluff overlooking the western end of the straights, we started our return journey in the gathering dusk. At that moment there was a loud bang from the engine compartment of the minibus and the generator warning light came on. A quick inspection confirmed our worst fears – the fan-belt had failed. So there we were, with night falling, a broken down vehicle, and about as far from civilisation as it was possible to be. Just at that moment, in the distance, at the foot of the hill on which the memorial stands, we saw a single light in a window. Without further ado, we pushed the minibus to get it moving and then free-wheeled down the hill to the source of the light. It turned out to be a small hotel manned by a single caretaker who was closing the place up at the end of the tourist season. By means of gestures and a few words of different languages, we explained to him that we had broken down and we needed help. Fortunately, he had a telephone that was working, and he telephoned a garage in a nearby small village, which sent out a mechanic to take a look. The mechanic spoke some German, and was able to communicate with a German officer in our party. After examining the vehicle he noted the requirement for a new fan-belt and said he would drive to Gallipoli in the morning and pick up a spare.

Meanwhile, we persuaded the caretaker to open up some of the rooms and accommodate us for the night. In the morning, while waiting for the mechanic to return, I took a look around and discovered that the hotel was situated between three enormous cemeteries containing the British, French and Turkish war dead respectively – perhaps about 100,000 graves in all. Although we all slept soundly, it was an eerie place to have spent a night, and we were thankful when the mechanic arrived later in the morning, fitted the new fan-belt, and enabled us to continue on our journey back to base.

On another occasion we were deployed to Erzurum, a military airfield in north-east Turkey, not far from the Russian border. Erzurum was one of the deployment options for the AMF and the purpose of our visit on this occasion was to check that all the support equipment written into the contingency plan by the host nation was in fact not only available but also in good working order. It was a difficult week, with the language barrier only exacerbating a certain amount of Turkish intransigence, and by the end of the stay our patience had been tested to the limit. On the final day of our visit we were guests at a lunch given by the Commander of the 9th Turkish Corps – an Army Lieutenant General.

As I was the senior SHAPE officer present it fell to me to sit next to the General at the lunch. Seated on a raised dais and flanked on either side with senior staff officers, we looked out over an assembly of some 40-50 officers. Although I had an interpreter next to me, I discovered at an early stage that the General spoke French. During my time in Belgium I had been attending a French class, and I was by now fairly proficient in the language. Consequently, the General and I were able to carry out a reasonable conversation, with only a little help from the interpreter, when something I said needed to be translated for the benefit of the other Turkish officers at the table. It also fell to me on behalf of the SHAPE team to thank the General and his staff on for their hospitality during our visit. Mindful of the difficulties that we had encountered during the week, I recalled an incident that had occurred in Turkey during a climbing expedition in the Taurus Mountains earlier in my career when I was a Cranwell Cadet. Passing through a small Turkish village high up in the mountains, two of our party aroused a great deal of local interest. Eventually, after some difficulty, they managed to explain that they were there to climb the mountains. Meanwhile, another word kept cropping up, and after a while they realised that they were being challenged to a wrestling match. Being good sports, they took part in a few bouts before proceeding on their way with smiles and handshakes all round. Prior to the lunch, I had rehearsed this story with my interpreter, who was well up to speed with the translation, so I achieved a great laugh from my audience when I concluded by saying that it never occurred to me at the time of the expedition that I might be back in their country, 30 years later, still wrestling with the Turks!

During this time our normal planning and exercise programme was affected directly by events taking place far outside the NATO area of operations. In August 1990, Iraqi forces had invaded and occupied Kuwait. This act of aggression led to a protracted spate of intense diplomatic activity which resulted eventually in the construction of a coalition, led by the United States, the aim of which was to liberate the occupied territory. As tensions rose in the Middle East, it was decided to deploy the air element of the AMF to eastern Turkey. Fortunately, we had a contingency plan already prepared for just such an eventuality, and we were able to mount the operation in short order and without undue difficulty. When the deploying fighter aircraft stopped to refuel at a military airfield in western Turkey, however, they were unable to proceed further because their destinations in eastern Turkey were covered by fog. Almost a week passed before the fog lifted and the aircraft were able to reach their planned area of operations.

Meanwhile, back at SHAPE, control of operations in support of the coalition forces had been relocated from the relatively soft office buildings to the hardened wartime bunker located well below ground. Furthermore, the staff were now working 12-hour shifts, and this arrangement, plus the speed and intensity of operations, imposed considerable stresses and strains on the personnel involved. In my own case, we had house guests over the Christmas period, so what with working all day and partying at night, I was exhausted by the time that the New Year arrived.

By the end of February 1991 Operation Desert Storm had succeeded in ejecting the Iraqi forces from Kuwait and the immediate crisis eased. Nevertheless, tensions in the Middle East remained, and the uncertain political situation led in due course to the relocation of an AMF exercise originally planned for southern Turkey in the summer of 1991. As an alternative venue for the exercise the UK offered the Otterburn Training Area in Northumberland, an offer that was readily accepted by NATO. It was suggested by the Army Command in North East England that Teesside Airport would be a suitable site for an airhead as it had been used a number of times in the past for troop movements. Accordingly, my staff and I arranged to visit the airfield to meet the airport management and carry out a survey of the available facilities. For this visit, we flew from the Belgian military base at Chièvres, near Mons, in a Russian-built Antonov aircraft. The aircraft was manned by a crew formerly of the East German Air Force that was now, following the recent reunification of Germany, part of the Luftwaffe. When my own multinational team disembarked at Teesside from this unusual mode of transport it must have brought home to the local population that the political map of Europe was beginning to change out of all recognition.

Teesside airport, which had been until recently an RAF base known as Middleton St George, was a well-established airfield with ample facilities for our needs. We were accommodated overnight in the St George's Hotel, which turned out to have been the Officers Mess of the former RAF Station. The airfield was owned by the Teesside Borough Council and some of its senior staff attended our discussions with the airfield management. It turned out that the airfield was in financial difficulty because of insufficient use of the facilities, there being at that time only some half-a-dozen flights per day. In the course of our discussions it came to light that we were planning some 350 movements for the deployment phase of the exercise, and a similar number for the redeployment, with possibly a considerable number of resupply flights in between. At the thought of all those landing fees, the meeting suddenly took wind, and from then on our hosts could not do enough for us. Given such warm and whole-hearted support from the airport staff, the actual exercise ran extremely smoothly, and my team and I enjoyed a most hospitable week.

During the resupply phase of the exercise, when things were relatively quiet, we decided to take a trip into the nearby town of Darlington. Arriving in the town on the local bus, we agreed to meet at a pub in the early evening prior to returning to the airport. The visit to the town having been a great success, we found the pub warm and friendly, and so we decided to have a meal there before our return. One thing led to another, and eventually we just made it onto the last bus of the evening. When we asked for tickets to the airport, the driver told that the last bus only went as far as a village some three miles short of our destination. 'Never mind,' we said, still full of bonhomie and good cheer, 'we'll walk the last bit.' And we thought no more about it, although it did seem to me, even in my euphoric state, that the bus was going rather fast in the dark along the narrow country lanes.

My team and I were the only passengers on the bus, and when we reached the last stop we prepared to disembark. To our surprise, however, the driver indicated that we should stay on board and promptly drove us the extra distance to the airport. All of us were astonished by this generous gesture, but my two German colleagues simply could not believe that a mere bus company employee would so far exceed the bounds of his authority; and forever afterwards, when we went away on detachment, that journey always came up as a topic of conversation.

Throughout my tour in Belgium my wife and I continued to play golf regularly at the Royal Golf Club du Hainaut, and during my second year I was elected Captain of the SHAPE Golf Society. The main purpose of this society was to play matches against other clubs in Southern Belgium and Northern France. For these events, which were eagerly anticipated by our opponents, we always fielded mixed teams of men and women, so that the matches were as much a social occasion as a sporting event. It also gave us an outstanding opportunity to play some of the excellent golf courses in the region. Our hosts on these occasions were invariably generous with their hospitality, and the multinational nature of the SHAPE team ensured that the post-match dinner was always a lively, multilingual and entertaining affair.

As Captain, it fell to me to thank our hosts on behalf of the SHAPE team. On one occasion, we were playing the Marache course at Royal Waterloo, a course that lies close to the route taken by the Prussian forces as they arrived on the battlefield during the early afternoon of the fateful encounter between Napoleon and the Duke of Wellington's forces in 1815. We normally travelled to these matches by coach but, because some members of the team wanted to go into Brussels after the match, we had on this occasion travelled in private cars. However, some of the team got lost on the way to the golf course and were late arriving. As the tee-off time for the first match approached, and with half my team missing, I had to hastily rearrange the pairings so that those members who had managed to arrive on time went off first. I was the last of these to tee-off, and as I made my way down the first fairway, I saw three cars come screeching into the car park. To my great relief, I saw the rest of my team disembark and rush off to the changing rooms to prepare themselves for the match. Speaking later after the dinner, I was able to liken my team to the Prussian forces, arriving late on the battlefield, but just in time to save the day. It was an analogy that went down well with our Belgian hosts.

Another feature of life in a major international military headquarters was that we had a very good Military History Society. Not only were we treated some excellent lectures on military events of the past but we also had visits to the sites of many famous historical encounters. Notable among these was the battlefield at Waterloo, located some 20 miles north of Mons on the southern outskirts of Brussels. Having visited the site a number of times in the company of several eminent historians, I became quite knowledgeable about the famous encounter, and took pleasure in showing our many visitors around the battlefield. Another visit of interest was to the Belgian fort of Eben-Emael. Supposedly impregnable, the fort was constructed in the 1930s, so that its powerful guns would guard against a potential German invasion across the bridges over the Albert Canal. On 10 May 1940, German forces landed on top of the fort by glider, blasted their way in using shaped charges, and occupied the building within a few hours. It was a classic example of the use of air power to overcome and outflank fixed defences. Another three-day visit to the area of the D-Day landings was also of considerable interest, and brought home with some force the huge risks involved in mounting the operation.

Also within easy reach of Mons were the infamous battlegrounds of the First World War. To visit the town of Ypres and see the 54,000 names of the dead and missing engraved on the Menin Gate was a truly humbling experience, as indeed was the Thiepval Memorial, erected in memory of the 72,000 allied troops killed or missing in the Battle of the Somme with no known grave. These losses, horrific as they were, paled in comparison with the French and German losses incurred at Verdun, where over half a million men from the two opposing forces were killed during 1916. I had by now served now in the RAF for some 30 years during the so-called 'Cold War' but, like most of my contemporaries, I had never been involved in combat. Visits to these battlefields served as a reminder, however, that warfare in a modern industrialised society had become a lethal and brutal affair. They also brought home the fact that the values of a free and democratic society could not be taken for granted, and that constant vigilance was necessary if they were not to be overwhelmed by the forces of tyranny.

Throughout my final year at SHAPE, the political situation in Eastern Europe continued to evolve. Evidence of the improvement in relations between Russia and the West came in the form of a visit to SHAPE by the head of the Soviet Military Forces, a visit that even included a tour of the Bunker. During the summer, in preparation for my eventual return to the UK, I took delivery of a brand-new duty-free BMW, and my wife and I decided to try it out with a visit to Berlin. We arranged to stay in a military leave centre in the city. As the day of our departure approached, however, I realised that I knew very little German, so I asked one of the members of my staff if he could give me a useful phrase for ordering a hotel room, as we would need to stop overnight en route. 'Haben ze eine dopple zimmer, bitte?' was the phrase he gave me – 'Do you have a double room, please?' Armed with this useful expression we set off on our journey. Somewhere, between Hanover and Berlin, we stopped in a small town and pulled up in front of a hotel.

'Haben ze eine dopple zimmer, bitte?' I asked the receptionist.

'Yes', she replied, in perfect English, 'How many nights would you like to stay for?'

The next morning we continued on our way, passing the now abandoned checkpoint in what was formerly the entrance to East Germany, and arriving in Berlin in the late afternoon. Having visited Berlin several times previously during my days flying the VC10, when the wall dividing East Berlin from the West was the main geographical and political feature of the city, I was amazed to find that it had disappeared almost completely. On our way to visit the excellent museums in the eastern part of the city, we walked through the Brandenburg Gate, with no sign of the wall and not a single check-point in sight. We did, however, find a stall-holder who selling 'authentic pieces of the Berlin Wall' so we bought a piece for 10 marks that we still have on display in our home. (I keep telling my wife that one day it will be worth a fortune!) In the absence of any physical evidence, I found it difficult to explain to my wife, who had never before visited Berlin, how the city had been divided. One day, however, we took a boat trip on the Wansee, a large lake on the outskirts of the city and, as we transited through a narrow passage, a section of the wall that was still standing came into sight.

'Oh,' said my wife, eying the fortifications and the coils of barbed wire, 'whatever is that?' She was amazed when I told her that what she was looking at was a section of the wall that had, for some 30 years, completely encircled the Western half of the city.

After three days in Berlin we headed south to spend a day in Dresden before stopping for the night in a small hotel just north of the Czechoslovakian border. The next day we continued our journey to Prague, making very slow progress along narrow roads clogged by tractors and horse-drawn vehicles. Approaching the outskirts of Prague, I was astonished to find myself on a long stretch of dual carriageway, with hardly any traffic in sight. Inevitably, I felt obliged to give my new BMW its head, and we roared along in fine stead. As we approached the end of the carriageway, however, and I began to slow down, I was flagged down by a policeman at the side of the road. A young man, who spoke excellent English, he pointed out that I was guilty of speeding, and proceeded to hand me an on-the-spot-fine of 50 crowns. It was a relatively small sum and, luckily, I had acquired some local currency at the border, so I was able to pay the fine and continue on my way. At that time, Prague had not long been open to western tourists, so the city retained much of its original charm, and we enjoyed a very pleasant 3-day stop over. On our return to Belgium, we had intended to break our journey with a night- stop in Germany and, having taken nearly six hours to travel from Prague to the German border, this still seemed to be a good idea. Once in Germany, however, we were soon on the autobahn and going like the wind. By supper time, we had already passed Frankfurt and, after a short stop for refreshment, we took the decision to continue to our home, which we eventually reached at about 11.00 o'clock at night.

Towards the end of the year, General Thomas, my Branch Chief, asked me to write a paper justifying the continued requirement for my Section in the light of the political changes that were beginning to impinge on the NATO structure. During my tenure of the post there had always been two separate movement planning organisations at SHAPE. My own section, responsible for the rapid deployment of the AMF, and another American-led section, that prepared contingency plans for the massive movement of troops and equipment from the USA that would be required in the event of a major conflict in Europe. Now that the direct threat from the countries of the Warsaw Pact was receding, NATO was considering a more mobile posture, so that its forces could intervene in trouble spots before they could develop into full-scale war. To this end, plans were afoot to develop an Allied Command Europe Rapid Reaction Force (ARRC), and it was evident to me, as I considered the options, that the two planning sections at SHAPE needed to pool their resources in support of this new force structure. I therefore recommended the setting up of new organisation within the Headquarters, the SHAPE Movement Co-ordination Centre, which would be responsible in a crisis for the deployment by land, sea and air of the ARRC.

As autumn approached, and the end of my tour loomed ahead, I began to give some thought as to what I might do in the four years remaining before I was due to retire at the age of 55. Given my age and seniority, another flying tour seemed out of the question, so I had opted at the time of my annual appraisal for another appointment in the Ministry of Defence. It was geographically convenient to my home in Hampshire and I had found the work interesting and congenial during my previous tour, so the MOD seemed like a good option. My tour in Belgium was due to end in January 1993, and a couple of months before Christmas my desk officer rank to say that a post as Chairman of the Joint Airmiss Working Group was about to become vacant and would I like the job? Given a few days to make up my mind, I telephoned the incumbent in the post and asked him what the job entailed. Explaining the details, he said that the job was interesting but not particularly time consuming. In fact, in addition to his primary duties, he was also Chairman of the RAF Fishing Society, and this gave him licence to spend a couple of days a week at his favourite sport. At that time the job was based at RAF Uxbridge on the western outskirts of London, which for me would have been a convenient location, but was I quite ready to be put out to pasture? After so many consecutive demanding tours of duty, the idea of spending the remaining years in a relatively benign environment had a certain attraction. On the other hand, I still had ambition, and the desire for one last challenge burned strongly within me. I discussed the dilemma with my various RAF colleagues, with my wife, and even by telephone with my father, but I could not make up my mind. Eventually, I decided to accept the post, the determining factor being that it might offer the prospect of further service after the age of 55. But when I rang my desk officer and he answered the telephone, I was surprised to find myself telling him that I didn't think the job would suit me, and was there anything else on offer? He didn't seem the least bit put out that I had declined the post (I suspect he may have had one or two other candidates in mind) but said he would call me back in a week or two with another option. When he did call me again not long afterwards I was surprised and delighted to be offered a post as a Station Commander.

In the normal course of career progression in the RAF, the post of Station Commander was regarded as a plum job and an essential stepping stone to higher rank. Such posts were normally the prerogative only of up and coming young men who were likely to fill eventually the top ranks of the Service. Given my age and background, this seemed unlikely in my case. Nevertheless, I was delighted to have been offered such a challenging assignment in the later stages of my career.

Just before my tour came to an end I learned that my proposals for a new SHAPE Movement Co-ordination Centre had been accepted, and discussions were under way as to how the merger was to be effected. With this final contribution to the new SHAPE strategy, I handed over to my successor and packed my bags for a return to the UK.

CHAPTER 13

Commanding an RAF Station

The Station that I was assigned to command was RAF Newton, located to the north of the A46 between Leicester and Newark. From my days as a Cranwell Cadet, I remembered it as a sort of light-blue blur in the hedgerow as I flashed by on my motorbike en route to enjoy the delights of Nottingham. Over the years, the Station had had a number of different roles, but a few enquiries revealed that it was now primarily a training station hosting a hotchpotch of different units. Amongst these were the Training Development and Support Unit, responsible for educational matters in the RAF; HQ Air Cadets; the RAF Police School; a Management Training Wing, preparing civil servants for a role in the Air Force Department; and the RAF Police Dog Training Wing. The good news from my point of view was that Newton also had an active airfield and two flying units: the East Midlands University Air Squadron (EMUAS), operating the Bulldog aircraft; and No 7 Air Experience Flight (7 AEF), operating the Chipmunk. The bad news was that the Station was earmarked for closure in two year's time, meaning that I would be its last ever Commander.

It was, and I believe still is, customary for the commander of a flying station in the RAF to be qualified on at least one of the aircraft based at his locality. Accordingly, before taking up my command, I was detached for few weeks to the Central Flying School (CFS), now located at RAF Scampton, near Lincoln, for a flying refresher course on the Bulldog. Although I was looking forward to being back in the cockpit, I was conscious of the fact that it was seven years since I last sat at the controls of an aircraft, and more than 30 years since I had flown a light propeller-driven aircraft. Furthermore, I was now nearly 52 years old. Although I was still quite fit and active, I realised that the task ahead of me might be a bit of a challenge. And so it proved to be.

As I taxied out to the runway, sitting cheek by jowl with my instructor in this tiny machine, and was cleared by Air Traffic Control for departure,

I remarked to him that this would be the first time in the past 20 years that I had flown an aircraft that weighed less than 300,000 lbs on take-off.

The Bulldog had entered service with the RAF in the early 1970s and was used primarily as an ab initio trainer by the University Air Squadrons (UASs). It was powered by a 200 hp Lycoming engine driving a two-bladed variable pitch propeller. The controls were light and well-harmonised and the aircraft was fully aerobatic. It was also equipped for instrument flying and could be flown in cloud, although icing conditions had to be avoided. Its tricycle undercarriage meant that even in the strongest cross-winds once on the ground it was a steady as a rock. I had no difficulty actually flying this well-designed training aircraft, and after a few dual sorties I could carry out stalling, spinning and aerobatics to the required standard. With my extensive large-aircraft experience, I was very comfortable when flying the aircraft on instruments, while my circuits and landings were also quite respectable.

Where I did have difficulty, however, was with the airmanship side of the sorties. I had not operated in free airspace for many years, and I struggled to keep up with its demands. To keep a check on my position in relation to Scampton and other active airfields in the locality, to maintain a constant look-out for other conflicting aircraft, to maintain a listening watch on the radio for transmissions from air traffic control and other aircraft while, at the same time, trying to absorb the lesson that was being imparted to me by my instructor – this I did find extremely demanding. From my days as an ab initio student and also as an instructor, I knew what it was that I was trying to achieve, but it was as if my brain had atrophied during those long years on the ground, and in my darkest days I began to wonder if my mental processes would ever regain the speed and flexibility required if I was successfully to pass the course. The prospect of a premature end to my flying career in the RAF loomed before me. Eventually I was given a couple of extra sorties to get up to speed and then, suddenly, it all clicked into place. I found that my former cognitive skills had returned and I was able to keep up mentally with the aircraft. When I came to take my final handling test with the Deputy Chief Flying Instructor, I felt alert and relaxed. The sortie was accomplished without a hitch, and I was signed up as a qualified pilot on the Bulldog.

I still had a few weeks remaining before I was due take command at Newton , so it was agreed that I would continue with my flying training in the hope of regaining my Qualified Flying Instructor (QFI) status. Throughout my flying career, I had been an instructor and flight examiner on various aircraft types, but most of my work had involved converting qualified and experienced pilots to a new type of aircraft. It was now more than 20 years since I attempted to teach a student to fly from scratch. There was, therefore, quite a lot to catch up on. Furthermore, like many things in education, the wheel had turned a full circle, and instructional techniques that were regarded as the accepted orthodoxy when I first undertook the CFS course in 1966 were now regarded as being completely beyond the pale. Consequently, instead of merely refreshing my instructional knowledge and skill, each exercise had to be more or less relearned from scratch. This was a tall order, and it soon became apparent both to my instructors and to me that I was unlikely to make the grade in the limited time available to me. Despite the fact that I was not, in the end, able to regain my former qualification as a QFI, the extra demands on my ability as a pilot were useful and I learned a great deal from the experience. I was therefore able to take up my new command confident that I could now fly the Bulldog to the high standards rightly demanded by the RAF.

AT THE BEGINNING OF April 1993 I arrived at Newton and, after a few days of handover from my predecessor, Group Captain Phil Langrill, who was retiring from the Service, I took command of the Station. Unlike my earlier concerns about regaining my flying skills, I had no qualms about my ability to undertake my new responsibilities as a Commander. My previous tours of duty had given me plenty of hands-on opportunity to acquire the leadership and management skills required for the job. Furthermore, compared with my previous tour of duty at SHAPE, I was now in a post where everyone wore the same uniform and spoke the same language. I was also older and more experienced than almost everyone under my command. Furthermore, on a unit where most people were serving in the ground branches of the RAF, I wore on my uniform a pilot's brevet, which gave me certain additional standing. I had an official car, with my own pennant flying from the bonnet, an imposing-looking office, and a Personal Assistant (PA), Sergeant Anita Bearcroft, who was not only very efficient but also very personable, and who told me every day where I had to be and exactly what I had to do. These were adequate trappings of office and of my new status, and I felt no need to put on any additional air or graces.

I was, however, slightly puzzled as to the scope of my command and the extent of my responsibilities. It was clear that some of the units on the Station were independent and reported not to me but directly to higher formations outside the scope of my command. Furthermore, I was not the only Group Captain at Newton , there being, in different departments, three other officers of the same rank, and also an Air Commodore who outranked us all. One of my first acts, therefore, was to draw up a draft diagram of the organisation, as I saw it, showing what units there were and who reported to whom. I then circulated this document round and asked for comment. It took about four goes before everyone was in agreement, but from then on my own responsibilities became clear. Most of the units were self-contained organisations reporting elsewhere; while my job and that of the station was to act as a support unit, providing messing, accommodation, transportation, and administrative support in all its many guises. My staff and I were also responsible for the maintenance of the airfields at Newton and nearby Syerston, including the provision of Air Traffic Control. Interestingly, the only major unit to fall directly under my chain of command was the RAF Police School, an area of training about which I knew absolutely nothing.

In running the station, I was ably supported by a team of mainly young, capable and enthusiastic officers and NCOs. From hard empirical experience, I had come to believe that the primary function of the leader was to define the 'vision' of the organisation. Once subordinates understood clearly what it was they were trying to do, and how they fitted in to the overall plan, they would, in my experience, push themselves to the limit to achieve the aims of the organisation. My 'vision' for RAF Newton was fairly easy to establish. Under what was known as the 'Ground Training Rationalisation Scheme' the RAF was reducing the number of ground training stations from eight to three, and perhaps eventually to two. This draconian measure was necessary to reduce costs in line with an ever-decreasing defence budget. Under this scheme, Newton was one of the stations earmarked for closure. Because there were no other suitable airfields in the locality that could accommodate the requirements of EMUAS and 7 AEF, the plan envisaged that after the run-down of the station the airfield at Newton would remain open, supported by a small administrative unit. My 'vision' was, therefore, to carry out the run-down in an orderly and efficient manner, so that resulting enclave of the airfield and its supporting administration could be handed over to whichever station was to assume responsibility for it on 1st April 1995.

Having established the 'vision', my next most important task was to create within the organisation a climate of openness in which even the most junior member of the team would feel free to put forward ideas as to how this complex task might best be accomplished. I was greatly aided in this process by my weekly inspections of some aspect of the work of the station. During these visits, I took pains to meet as many people as possible, to discuss with them the problems likely to be caused by the forthcoming closure of the station, and to listen sympathetically to their views on how these problems might best be overcome. Based on what I heard during my inspections, I decided at an early stage to set up a committee, under the capable chairmanship of Wing Commander John Pearce, the Wing Commander Admin, whose job it would be to assess the impact of the closure, to identify significant problems, and to draw up a plan for the run-down. Information and ideas that I gleaned from my inspections was passed to the committee for consideration and further action as required.

While these activities were taking place, I was greatly involved in one of the other main functions of a leader, which was acting as the figurehead of the organisation in relation to the surrounding community. I soon found that invitations to various Service, civic and social functions poured daily into the PA's office and I was heavily committed to attending these events. By this time, my wife and I had moved into the Station Commander's residence, a large comfortable house with an extensive garden, situated in a remote part of the grounds. One of the most fortunate things that I discovered shortly after taking up residence at Newton was that the Station Commander was entitled to have his grass mown by the company contracted for the overall maintenance of the unit, thereby ensuring that my lawns looked immaculate all the year round, and I was saved a great deal time and effort. Meanwhile, my wife, who had been looking forward to returning to our own house in Hampshire, and had indeed been living there while I was attending my flying refresher course at Scampton, loyally agreed to accompany me to Newton, but with the proviso that we kept our own house empty so that she had place out of the limelight to which she could retreat from time to time.

One of the first functions that we attended together was a service of commemoration for the local branch of the British Legion in the nearby small town of Bingham. I had mistakenly thought that this might be a relatively low-key affair, so I was surprise when we arrived to be met at the church gate not only by the vicar but also by a strong delegation of the leading lights of the local Branch. When we entered the church it was absolutely packed and we were led to the only two vacant seats which were in the foremost pew. During the service, when it came time for the collection, the plate appeared in front of me almost before the organist had finished playing the opening bars of the hymn, and in my haste to respond I dropped my offering on the floor and had to scrabble around for it. After the service when I took the salute as the Legion marched past, I thought how pleased Sergeant Ross and Flight Sergeant Holt, my one-time drill instructors at Cranwell, would be to see one of their former protégés occupying such an eminent position. After the parade I joined members of the legion for a drink in the local pub, and soon we were all agreed that it had been a jolly fine affair.

One of the invitations I received almost as soon as I had taken up my command was from an organisation calling itself 'The Nottingham Flotilla'. As Nottingham is about as far from the sea as it is possible to be in the UK, and it was also perilously close to April 1st, I was concerned that this might be some sort of inter-service April Fool's joke, and I asked my PA to make quite sure that this invitation wasn't a send-up. A few days later, the secretary of the organisation called personally to ask if I would propose a vote of thanks to the Naval Secretary, who would be the main speaker at the event. On the appointed evening, I arrived at a large hotel in the centre of Nottingham, dressed in my mess kit, where I was both relieved and astonished to find about 400 people gathered for the dinner. Among the many distinguished guests, in addition to the Naval Secretary, was the Captain and some of his senior officers from the warship HMS Nottingham. Up to that moment, I had no idea that there was such strong support for the Royal Navy in a land-locked city such as Nottingham. My earlier reservations about the viability of the event notwithstanding, the evening passed very pleasantly, and my short vote of thanks, which included at least one joke at the expense of the Royal Navy, was well received. In the event, this commitment, and the earlier one at Bingham, were indicative of the huge range and variety of functions in the Nottingham area that I attended during my two years in the post, either on my own or accompanied by my wife. Throughout my tour, I was continually impressed by the tremendous support and admiration there was for the armed services. It was comforting to know that, despite the many cuts they had endured, the forces were still held in the highest regard by the vast majority of the civilian population.

On another occasion my wife and I were invited to a Summer Ball at the Polish Club in Nottingham. During the Second World War, many Polish airmen had been trained to fly at Newton , and as a mark of respect for their contribution to the war the White Eagle of Poland had been incorporated into the Station's Badge. Quite a few of the airmen had married local girls and settled in the area, and there was still a considerable Polish contingent living in Nottingham. On a wet summer evening, we were driven into Nottingham and dropped off at what we thought was the Polish Club. I was wearing my dinner jacket and my wife was dressed in a ball gown. When we entered the building, however, I saw immediately that those present were dressed informally and appeared to be taking part in some sort of square dance. A quick word with the barman revealed that we were in the wrong place and that the Polish Club where we were expected was about two blocks away. Emerging from the building with a borrowed umbrella, we discovered that our transport had departed, and we were left to make our way through the pouring rain to our proper destination. Eventually, to the relief of our hosts, who were waiting for us to arrive, we appeared on foot, wet and rather bedraggled from the walk. Once inside, however, we were made extremely welcome, and after a rocky start we enjoyed a very pleasant evening.

Many Polish airmen were buried in the cemetery at Newark where, on another occasion, on a stiflingly hot day in the summer, my wife and I attended a memorial service to commemorate the 50th Anniversary of the death of General Sikorski, Commander-in-Chief of the Polish Forces during the Second World War. Something went wrong with the arrangements and the band failed to turn up. Nevertheless, there were some good singers at the service and we enjoyed some fine Polish hymns. The service was due to terminate with a flypast by an RAF aircraft, but the absence of a band meant that the service finished ahead of schedule and there was a lengthy wait for the climax. We had more Polish hymns. I was in my best blue uniform and, as the sun beat down, the perspiration poured down my back. More Polish hymns followed. Eventually, to everyone's relief, a lone aircraft flew low over the cemetery and the proceedings came to an end.

In spite of the many administrative and social demands that were made on me, I managed to make time to continue flying the Bulldog. This was made possible by the compact nature of the station and the fact that Newton was a grass airfield. It took but a few minutes to reach the flight line, and not much more than that to brief for the flight and taxi out to the take-off point. An hour's flying, a short taxi back to the dispersal after landing, a post-flight cup of tea and a chat with the staff and students of EMUAS, and then back to the office to catch up on the day's paperwork. What could be simpler or more delightful? Another advantage of flying from Newton, enjoyed by both the EMUAS students and me, was that it was almost impossible to get lost. Our local flying area, which lay to the north of the airfield, was bounded by the town of Newark to the east and the city of Nottingham to the west. At its most northerly point the area encompassed what remained of Sherwood Forest, wherein lay the unmistakable holiday resort of Centre Parks. Returning south, and just before reaching the airfield boundary, lay the River Trent, running from west to east, so that no matter how low the cloud-base, or how restricted the visibility, you could, as soon as you saw the river, always find your way home.

Although I was no longer a current QFI, which meant that I could not formally instruct UAS students, I could carry them as passengers, and in practice we often shared the flying between us. They were all as keen as mustard and most of them couldn't wait to graduate so that they could begin their flying training proper in the RAF. During the summer vacation, we also hosted visiting detachments from other UASs. In the main, they were very well behaved; but, being young and away from home, they were naturally high spirited, and sometimes things would get out of hand. I always briefed their Squadron Commander that any damage had to be paid for and, in the event of any significant lapses of discipline, the rule was, like that of baseball, three strikes and you're out! As well as flying with UAS students I also took the opportunity to fly airmen and NCOs from the station who showed a particular interest. Almost all of them were serving in one the ground branches of the RAF, and it provided a useful opportunity to press home the message that, no matter how far they were from the front line, the ultimate aim of their contribution to the organisation was to keep men and machines in the air.

It was not long before I discovered in Queen's Regulations that I could also fly civilians 'in the interest of public relations' and I often used this permission to good effect. From time to time, EMUAS held a briefing session for people of influence in the locality to make them aware of the flying commitment and what it was attempting to achieve. Attending one such briefing, I was severely taken to task by one of the visitors who insisted that we were deliberately doing aerobatics over his house, which lay in a small village about 10 miles to the north of Newton and well within our local flying area. Although I tried to explain to him how we were often constrained by time or weather from spreading the noise footprint as widely as possible, nothing would pacify him. In the end I invited him to come for a flight and see for himself.

On the appointed day I took him up and flew him round the local area, explaining things to him as if he were an ab initio student on his first sortie. After about 30 minutes, during which he had clearly enjoyed himself, I asked him if he would like to loop the loop. Although a little apprehensive, he said that his children would never forgive him if he didn't have a go. So after a clearing turn, during which I pointed out that we were well away from any significant built-up areas, I pulled up into a loop. And there, just as we reached the inverted position at the top of the manoeuvre, was his house, framed clearly in the windscreen. After we landed he admitted to me that he had no idea how much distance an aircraft could cover in such a short space of time, and it was now evident to him, given the locality of his house, that some aircraft noise was inevitable. Shortly afterwards, he wrote me a very nice letter, saying not only how much he had enjoyed the experience but also how envious his children were. We never had another complaint from him.

Another distinguished passenger that I managed to fly was Councillor Ted Bonham, the Mayor of Rushcliffe, the borough in which Newton was located. A former seaman in the merchant marine, Ted was quite a character, and we got on well as our paths crossed at numerous civic engagements. I had played golf with him and some of his colleagues on several occasions and he had expressed a desire to see his local course from the air. He was by then in his mid-seventies, but he seemed fit and healthy so I agreed to take him up. Having taken him on a tour of the local area, including his golf course, I asked him if he would like to do some aerobatics, a suggestion with which he enthusiastically concurred. So I carried out a few gentle loops, barrel rolls and stall turns before coming back to land at Newton. After the flight he said he felt absolutely fine and thanked me profusely for giving him the opportunity. A few weeks later I received an invitation to attend the Mayor's Annual Dinner, where I was taken aback to find that half of his speech to the assembled distinguished guests was devoted to reliving the few minutes that we had spent together doing aerobatics in a Bulldog.

Several months into my tour, I discussed with Squadron Leader Bill Purchase, the commander of 7 AEF, the possibility of qualifying on the Chipmunk, a proposal to which he readily agreed. I had not flown the Chipmunk since my days as a QFI at Cranwell some 30 years previously, when I had flown cadets from the North Airfield during their summer camps. However, the aircraft was simple and easy to fly, and after three dual sorties and a solo I took and passed a handling test with an examiner from CFS. From then on, when the opportunity presented itself, I was able to give air experience to those cadets of the Air Training Corps (ATC) and the Combined Cadet Force (CCF) who fell within the Newton catchment area.

FLYING CADETS WAS AN enormously rewarding experience. They were all tremendously enthusiastic, the girls as much if not more so than the boys. Furthermore, the Chipmunk was a benign and forgiving aircraft to fly, so with just a little instruction the cadets could handle the controls for most of the flight. The one drawback from which the aircraft suffered was its tandem seating, whereby the cadet sat behind the instructor and the only means of communication was by intercom. Giving instruction without being able to see what the student was doing presented a challenge, and it took a few sorties to develop a coherent instructional technique. Myself apart, all the other instructors on the AEF were officers who had retired from the flying branches of the regular services and now held a commission in the RAF Volunteer Reserve (Training) (RAFVR(T)) branch. Many of them I knew from my earlier days of service; while several of them, having held senior positions in the RAF, were now enjoying the opportunity to fly again in retirement. Except for the CO, they were all commissioned in the rank of Flying Officer. None of them stood on their former rank, and everyone was on first name terms. I enjoyed meeting them and they appreciated that I took the time to fly with them and spend time with them for a post-flight cup of tea and a chat. It struck me that this was a very pleasant thing to do in retirement and, as this was now not too far away, I decided to look into it when I had the time.

About five miles to the north east of Newton lay the airfield of Syerston, home to the Air Cadet Central Gliding School (ACCGS). This organisation reported directly to HQ Air Cadets and did not come under my command. Nevertheless, the maintenance of the airfield and its infrastructure was one of my responsibilities. Apart from ACCGS, which had offices in the control tower, and a few maintenance personnel in one of the hangers, there were no other units based at Syerston. Consequently, the domestic site, which had once housed a thriving RAF station, had been abandoned. A few of the buildings were used by the RAF Police Dog Unit for training the animals to sniff out drugs; that apart, the rest were in various states of decay. Thus one approached the airfield down a long avenue bordered by what appeared to be a ghost town. To foster good relations with the ACCGS, I arranged to qualify on the Robin, a chartered light aircraft used for towing the gliders. I also learned to fly the Vigilant, one of the school's powered gliders. Flying these different aircraft was not only tremendous fun but also kept me in close touch with the many different factors affecting safe flying from the airfield.

ANOTHER UNIT AT SYERSTON was the Four Counties Gliding Club of which I was, by virtue of my position as Station Commander, the nominal Chairman of the Committee. The club was run by an enthusiastic band of civilians who flew at the weekends, using as a crewroom an old double-decker bus that was towed out to the middle of the airfield. The club members owned a number of caravans that they used for accommodation at the weekend. They had also converted one of the rooms in the hanger into quite a serviceable club house. Unfortunately, their enthusiasm and initiative had also led them to convert one the abandoned barrack blocks into additional accommodation by tapping illegally into the station's electricity supply. This unauthorised activity greatly annoyed my staff, who wanted to close the club down. I was opposed to this, as the club provided an opportunity for the personnel at Newton to engage in an adventurous activity at a very low cost, and I did not want to throw away such a character-building endeavour for the sake of a few relatively small administrative problems. It so happened that during one of my visits to Syerston I discovered that the RAF Police had abandoned some spacious accommodation in the former Motor Transport Section, which was still in a good state of repair. Accordingly, I offered this to the Four Counties Gliding Club free of charge, having first asked my staff to provide whatever little help was needed in modifying the accommodation to meet the requirements of the club. For their part, the club agreed to forebear from making any unauthorised alterations to their new accommodation or to any other building on the site. From then on, relations between the club and the Station improved enormously. I learned to fly the ACRO glider, and I was able to entertain some of my personal guests at the weekend by taking them for a short flight in the club's aircraft. Syerston was located on higher ground south of a valley in which flowed the River Trent. In summer, when the wind blew from the west, which it mostly did, small thermals were created as the wind lifted over the escarpment. The gliders were launched by a winch, the cable being manually released at about 800 feet, and these columns of rising air, occurring as they did round about the release-point, provided a means of soaring for a few minutes and gaining height before turning down-wind and gliding in for a landing. Sometimes, by skilful manoeuvring, it was possible to remain airborne from a winch launch for as much as 30 minutes. Being aloft in a glider and sailing serenely along on the air currents with no visible means of support was an elemental and sublime experience.

To provide some relief from the arduous business of running the Station, my wife and I joined the golf club at the nearby course of Cotgrave. Playing in events organised by the station golf society was not only an enjoyable experience but also provided me with an opportunity to meet subordinates on an informal basis. On one occasion we took part in the Station Golf Championships, my wife being the only lady to participate. Not only did she win a prize for being nearest the pin on a designated short hole but she also won the prize for the longest drive, much to the chagrin of some of the big-hitters in the competition. To win the prize the ball had to finish on the fairway, which my wife's drive did, while some of the stronger players finished in the rough. Furthermore, no-one had appreciated before the start of the competition that the ladies tee was positioned well in advance of the men's tee, thereby negating the advantage that the men enjoyed by virtue of their greater strength.

On one occasion, my wife and I were relaxing by playing a few holes on a Sunday afternoon, when we were joined by a youth of some 15 or 16 years in age who was playing alone. He was a very pleasant young man and an excellent golfer for his age. We chatted on the way round and I asked what he hoped to do when he left school. When he said that he wanted to be a policeman, I asked him if he had ever thought about joining the RAF Police. If not, would he like to visit Newton and see for himself the opportunity that might be open to him as a military policeman? A few days later, accompanied by his father, he came to the Station and, after a cup of tea and a chat in my office, one of the officers from the Police School took them round and showed them the training set-up. So on that particular occasion I was not only able have a relaxing and enjoyable round of golf with my wife but also to carry out a bit of recruiting at the same time. That same summer we were also invited by the Chancellor of Nottingham University to play in an invitational event at Wollaton Park, an attractive golf course to the west of the city. Afterwards we joined other distinguished guests at a dinner in the impressive Chancellor's Dining Room. Such events provided an excellent opportunity for networking with influential figures in the local community.

With a busy schedule the months past at astonishing speed and soon Christmas was upon us. We were approached by the Rotary Club from Bingham. They had a musical sleigh that Father Christmas used to collect funds for the charity, but over the years it had gradually deteriorated until now it was almost beyond repair. Could we help? I knew that in our workshops we had a SNCO, Flight Sergeant Meakin, who was a very good craftsman. I asked the Officer Commanding the Engineering Flight if Flight Sergeant Meakin could undertake the job as a good-will gesture towards our local community, on the understanding that the work was not to use public money or materials, but only odd bits and pieces from other jobs that had previously been carried out in the workshops. The Flight Sergeant stripped the sleigh down to its bare bones, repaired it, repainted it, mended the sound system, and reassembled the machine so that it was then better than it had been when it was new. The refurbished sleigh was then returned to a grateful and delighted Rotary Club. A short while later I received an invitation from the Rotary Club for my wife and me to attend their annual Christmas Dinner. I telephoned the Chairman of the branch and told him that it was Flight Sergeant Meakin who had done all the work and would they be offended if he was to represent me at the dinner? 'Not at all,' came the reply, 'they would be delighted to see him.' So I asked the Flight Sergeant if he and his wife would like to attend the dinner, an invitation that they readily accepted. As it was an official event, I arranged for them to be driven to and from the venue in my staff car. Under these arrangements, the man who had done all the work had a memorable evening and gained some reward for his labours.

One of my sisters, Patricia Bradshaw, came to stay with us for Christmas with her two children. On Christmas Day, I asked my niece, Alison, who was then about ten years old, if she would like to come with me while I visited those sections of the Station that were having to work over the holiday. Having called in on the telephone exchange, the kitchen hands in the Messes, and one or two other sections that were working, I popped into the hanger and we had a look around one of the aircraft. Finally, we visited the kennels, where the police dogs were being fed. A couple days later, while we were out on a journey, I heard Alison musing in the back seat of the car about what she might do in the future. 'When I grow up,' she said, 'I would like to be pilot......or perhaps', she added, as an after-thought, 'a dog handler!' I related this story when I was speaking at a Guest Night some weeks later, much to the amusement of the audience.

WITH NOW BUT A year to go to the run-down and change in status of the Station, my main concern was to maintain the morale of the workforce in the light of the impending closures. The run-down of the station and the relocation of the various training organisations to other units necessarily meant huge disruption to the 600 service personnel under my command and their dependents. It also meant the loss of employment for some 200 civilian staff, many of whom had loyally served the station for many years. Rather than just fade away, I wanted us to go out in style; so, with the agreement of my executives, I arranged for a series of high-profile events to mark the closure of the station. The first of these was an Air Show that took place on a glorious summer's day. Thousands of people flocked to the Station to witness a magnificent flying display by a wide variety of aircraft, including an awe-inspiring performance by the RAF's premier formation aerobatic team, the Red Arrows. I mingled with the crowd, meeting with local people, and greeting the various veterans' organisations that had come from far and wide to see the show. Many stalls and side-shows were attracted to the show and, as an adjunct to these activities, my staff also managed to raise a large sum of money for charity.

The next major event was the granting of the Freedom of the Borough of Rushcliffe. I had suggested to Ted Bonham, when he was Mayor, that the Borough might wish to take the opportunity to show publicly its appreciation for the long-standing service to the community provided by RAF Newton since the founding of the Station more than 50 years ago. Having concurred with my suggestion, he had set the wheels in motion, and now the occasion for the parade was upon us. Meanwhile, a new Mayor, Mrs Joyce Dixon, had taken office, and it was she who was to join me in taking the salute during the march-past. Accordingly, I arranged for her to attend a parade rehearsal at Newton a few days before the event, where we went over in detail the procedure to be followed. On the appointed day the sun shone from a cloudless sky as the parade assembled in an open square near the centre of Rushcliffe. Flanked on one side by a posse of police dogs and their handlers, and on the other side by two massive police horses and their riders, the flight of Airmen and Airwomen were brought smartly to attention by the Parade Commander as the Mayor and I took our places. Escorted by the Parade Commander and myself, the Mayor then inspected the parade. As she did so, four Bulldogs overflew the parade-ground in close formation. With the inspection over, the band struck up and the parade marched through the streets of the town. As the Mayor and I made our way to the saluting dais, I saw that the streets were thronged with spectators, and huge cheers greeted the parade as it marched past. I felt immensely proud of the men and women under my command as we played our various parts in this ancient and dignified ceremony.

The following day my wife and I drove to Lincoln to attend the wedding of my son James to his bride, Sarah. As usual, it had been a busy and eventful week.

DURING THE AUTUMN, A new Air Officer Commanding-in-Chief, Air Chief Marshal Sir Andrew 'Sandy' Wilson, KCB AFC ADC FRAeS, had taken over at Headquarters Personnel and Training Command (HQ PTC), the formation to which I reported. Shortly after assuming command, he decided to visit all the Stations within his area of authority, including RAF Newton. The Air Chief Marshal and I had joined the RAF at the same time and as Flight Cadets at Cranwell we had both been members of 81 Entry all those years ago. We had got on well together then and relations between us remained cordial as we met up on a number of occasions in the intervening years at various Entry reunions, even though our subsequent careers took widely different paths. Consequently, I took the liberty of asking him through his Personal Staff Officer if he would be kind enough to present during his visit the Honours and Awards that were due to a number of personnel on the Station. This he kindly agreed to do. On the appointed day, he was due to arrive by helicopter, but bad weather in the form of dense fog intervened, and he travelled by staff car instead. I had arranged for an early warning system to be put in place to give me due notice of his impending arrival, and I was sitting in my office in my shirt sleeves attending to some paperwork when my PA rushed in and said, 'Sir, Sir, the C-in-C's car is outside.' Grabbing my hat and donning my jacket as I rushed down the corridor, I emerged from the front door of the Headquarters just as the C-in-C's driver was opening the car door. The great man had a thunderous expression on his face, and I thought for moment that the visit was going to get off to the worst possible start. But then he emerged from the car, straightened himself up, smiled, and said, 'Good morning, Sid. Very nice to see you again.' And from that moment onwards, everything went extremely well. I gave him a briefing on the current role of the station and our plans for the run-down, emphasising that even at this late stage his staff had still not decided who was to be responsible for the administration of the enclave. He was visibly impressed by the complexity of the task ahead of us and asked a number of pertinent questions about the arrangements. Then we went to the Sergeant's Mess for the presentation of Honours and Awards. After the ceremony had been completed, he was charm personified as he met and chatted with the recipients, their families and their friends. Among the recipients, I was particularly pleased to see the award of a Long Service and Good Conduct Medal to my PA, Sergeant Bearcroft, and a Station Commander's Certificate of Merit awarded to my housekeeper, Mrs Lily Brown, who had looked after my wife and I so assiduously during our tour of duty. After lunch, we drove to Syerston, travelling through the appallingly dilapidated domestic site before we reached the airfield. There, after meeting the staff of the gliding school, and the morning fog having by now cleared, he was whisked away by helicopter to his next port of call.

IT WAS NOT LONG after this visit that I was called to a planning conference at HQ PTC, where it was finally confirmed that the run-down would go ahead as planned and that RAF Cranwell would take over the administration of the remaining enclave with effect from 1st April 1995. From that day onwards, events leading to the closure of the station began to gather pace. The Police Dog Training Unit merged with what became the Defence Animal Centre at Melton Mowbray. We held our last major church service to commemorate the Battle of Britain with a congregation of several hundred people in a converted hangar on the Station. Shortly afterwards, the final Mass was said in the Station's Roman Catholic Church before that, too, was closed down. Further closures followed as more units left the station and moved to their new locations. My final act was to host a farewell Dining-In Night and Sunset Ceremony in the Officers Mess. The event was attended by a number of distinguished Service guests including the Air Officer Commanding the Training Group, the Provost Marshal, the Air Officer Commanding Air Cadets, the Deputy Commandant of the RAF College Cranwell, the Commandant of the Defence Animal Centre and two former Station Commanders. Amongst the civilian guests were the Lord Lieutenant of Nottinghamshire, the Mayors of Nottingham and of

Rushcliffe, and the Chairman of the Polish Club in Nottingham, representing all his countrymen who had been trained to fly at Newton during the Second World War. After the dinner and the speeches, we all assembled outside the Mess for the sunset ceremony. To enhance the ceremony, several floodlit Bulldog aircraft had been positioned facing the building. Against this evocative backdrop the RAF College Band played an evening hymn and the Last Post, while I took the salute as the ensign was lowered for the last time to signify the closure of the Station. It was a poignant and moving moment, and a fitting tribute to the ranks of men and women, both Service and civilian, who had served at the Station to the best of their ability over a period of more than 50 years.

CHAPTER 13

Crew Resource Management

For almost the past 10 years, ever since I returned from the United States, I had been pressing the RAF to adopt Crew Resource Management (CRM) as a formal part of its aircrew training programme, but my arguments had always met with stiff resistance. For several decades the Air Force had had in place a well-honed training system that produced aircrew of the highest calibre. It seemed to many in the organisation not far short of heresy to suggest that there was some aspect of the training that was lacking, particularly when criticism was being directed at a failure to train adequately those most prized attributes of leadership and captaincy. I had written articles on the subject for Air Clues, the RAF's flight safety magazine, but to no avail. Furthermore, even when I was filling staff appointments that bore no responsibility for aircrew training, I nevertheless wrote to the Inspector of Flight Safety on a number of occasions when accidents and incidents occurred that involved aircrew error, drawing attention to developments in CRM training that would help to mitigate or prevent such accidents in the future. I also drew attention to the fact that these programmes were now being implemented by commercial airlines and other Air Forces world wide, and that the RAF was, regrettably, now lagging well behind. After taking command at RAF Newton, where I was once again directly involved in flying, I wrote on several occasions in a similar vein to my immediate superior, the Air Officer Commanding the Training Group. I also took care to copy these letters to the Inspector of Flight Safety.

In the meantime, on my own initiative, I arranged to visit the British Airways Training Centre at Heathrow to see for myself how the company was addressing the issue. I was very impressed with the training programme that they had introduced, but what struck me most of all was a mention in an aside that I was now the eighteenth person from the RAF who had undertaken this particular visit. Clearly there was a lot of interest in CRM among RAF aircrew at the grass roots level. The problem was how to convert this interest into positive action by the senior staff. Eventually, my efforts, and those of others, gained sufficient traction, and the Training Policy Branch at HQ Personnel & Training Command (HQ PTC) was tasked to produce a paper charting the way ahead for the introduction of CRM training into the RAF. The officer drafting the paper was Wing Commander Pieter Hemsley, a former colleague and friend from my days at Brize Norton, who not only incorporated into his paper all the arguments that I had previously put forward but also added for good measure a few additional ideas of his own. In the paper he not only made a substantial case for the introduction of CRM training into the RAF but also recommended that this should be done by setting up a CRM Implementation Working Group at HQ PTC to be headed by a Group Captain supported by two Wing Commanders. His proposals were accepted, and not long afterwards, while still at Newton , I received a telephone call from my desk officer asking me if I would like to fill the new post. With just one year left in the RAF before I retired, I thought it was an appointment that would suit me very nicely, and I readily accepted his offer.

Once my new appointment became known, I was put in touch with Wing Commander Martin Henshaw. I was told that he had been involved in an earlier attempt to address leadership issues amongst Harrier pilots at RAF Wittering. Having arranged for him to visit me at Newton , I set out in the conference room, which was conveniently located next to my office, all the various articles, papers and documentation on CRM that I had acquired over the years, including the training materials with which I had been issued when I attended the United Airlines course in Seattle. Martin was not aircrew but a member of the Administrative Branch of the RAF. Nevertheless, he had at one time in his career been a Flight Commander at the Initial Officer Training School at Cranwell, where he had acquire some useful practical insights into leadership training. Having now read some of the literature that I had put at his disposal, he had quickly grasped the essence of what I was proposing, and it was evident to me from our subsequent discussion that he knew as much, if not more than anyone I previously met, about the issues involved. I therefore asked him if he would like to join my team, an offer that he readily accepted.

Not long afterwards, I was contacted by another officer, Wing Commander Jon Fynes, who also expressed an interest in joining the team. Jon had previously been a desk officer at HQ PTC, dealing with the careers of Junior Officers. Following promotion on graduation from the Staff College, he was keen to take up another appointment at HQ PTC to give his family some stability. A former Lightning pilot, he was a member of the fast-jet fraternity, and I thought that his experience in this field would complement nicely my own multi-engine and training background. He was also a very likeable individual, and on this basis I acceded to his request to join the team. The other two members of the initial CRM Implementation Working Group (CRM IWG) were Squadron Leader Andy Finch, an officer in the Education Branch, and Corporal Mark Waldron, who had latterly been my PA at Newton , following the departure of Sergeant Bearcroft, and who had asked if he could join me in my new enterprise. These two additional members of the team were to play an important part in the subsequent development and implementation of a CRM training programme. Meanwhile, Jon Fynes, who was already established at HQ PTC, had acquired for us a suite of offices in the new building, and had busied himself adapting them to our needs.

On 31 March 1995, I handed over command of what now remained of RAF Newton to a representative of the Station Commander at Cranwell, and returned to my home in Hampshire. My new offices were located at RAF Innsworth, near Gloucester. As this was too far to travel daily, I agreed with my wife that I would become a commuter, living in the Officers Mess during the week and travelling home at the week-ends. This arrangement worked well. I rose early on Monday mornings and drove the 50 miles or so to Innsworth. The Mess provided a comfortable and congenial place in which to live during the week, and I was able to return home at a reasonable time on Friday. To allow for some rest and relaxation at the weekend, my wife and I rejoined the nearby Tidworth Garrison Golf Club Our two boys were by now both well-established in their own military careers. After a tour in charge of the Propulsion Flight at RAF Leuchars in Scotland, James was serving as a Junior Officer on the staff at HQ Logistics Command, based at RAF Wyton. He and his new bride, Sarah, were living in rented accommodation near Cambridge. Meanwhile, Brian was now a Lieutenant in the Royal Marines. Having recently trained as a helicopter pilot with the Army School of Aviation at Middle Wallop in Hampshire, he was based with the Royal Navy at Yeovilton, and had bought a flat in Bristol.

The first task facing myself and my newly-established team was to determine the scope of the new form of training that we planning to introduce and then decide exactly how this training would be delivered. To this end we started by visiting a number of units whose task it was to undertake leadership training and development. These visits included the Central Flying School; the RAF's Adventurous Training Centre at Aviemore in the Scottish Highlands; and an RAF establishment at Fairbourne, on the west coast of Wales, that was responsible for training Junior NCOs. We also had some very productive discussions with the RAF Institute of Aviation Medicine at Farnborough. In addition, we visited several civilian flying organisations in the UK that already had in place embryo CRM training programmes. I had also discovered that the Civil Aviation Authority (CAA) were from time to time holding CRM workshops in their Headquarters at Gatwick Airport and we began to attend these on a regular basis.

By a stroke of good fortune, at the end of the financial year, a request had been circulated to the staff at HQ PTC asking for projects to use up what was known as 'underspend' money. This was money accruing in the current financial year that could not, because of the annualisation of the defence budget, be carried forward to the next. Showing commendable enterprise, and acting largely on his own initiative, Jon Fynes put in a successful bid for some airline tickets to the USA. Once there, we visited the US Navy's Air Training Establishment at Pensacola, Florida; the USAF's flying instructor training facility at Randolph AFB, near San Antonio, Texas; and the Headquarters of the USAF's Air Combat Command at Langley Field, Virginia. Our final port of call was the Canadian Air Force Base at Winnipeg, a major centre for aircrew training. All of these units had either set up or were in the process of setting up various CRM programmes, and we returned home with a rich store of ideas on which to base our plans.

During our travels, prompted by our talks with the various agencies that we visited, we had engaged in some intense discussions about the training programme that we were about to develop. These discussions tested my powers of leadership to the limit. My own style was collegiate, preferring as I did when time permitted to discuss the issues with my colleagues and subordinates until we had reached a consensus on the best way ahead. I would then sum up the arguments and state clearly the decision that had been reached. The advantage of this approach was that everyone had then participated in establishing the 'vision'. Having bought into it, they would then have a vested interest in seeing the 'vision' brought to fruition. By temperament and background, John Fynes preferred a more autocratic approach. He could not bear to wait while everyone chewed over the pros and cons, but wanted the issue closed out as soon as possible. He told us, for example, that in the past when he had been on detachment with the Flight that he commanded, he could not cope with the endless procrastination while everyone decided where and when they were going to eat. To overcome this problem, he appointed one of his subordinates as 'leader' for the day. It was the job of the 'leader' to decide where they would eat that night, to make the necessary reservation, and arrange transport if necessary. While not totally incompatible, our two styles of management were clearly at the opposite ends of the spectrum. I felt that he was constantly challenging my authority and in the early days this led often to clashes between us. Fortunately, Martin Henshaw's style was more middle-of-the-road, and he was able to smooth things over by acting as a mediator. So in our little group, as we approached the task of designing a training package, we were already experiencing at first hand some of the issues involved in small group dynamics that our training programme would be addressing.

The main point of contention between the three of us was not so much what subjects we should cover – we already had a good idea of those from the discussions we had had with others – but how long the training should last. I favoured a three-day course like some that we had seen on our travels. This would allow sufficient time not only to teach most of the skills we wanted to impart but also to give those attending the course the time and opportunity to practise them. Jon Fynes was adamant that a three day course would be completely unacceptable to hard-pressed fast-jet aircrew on the front line, and insisted that a one-day course was the maximum that would be tolerated. As was so often the case, it was Martin who provided the solution by suggesting that we run a one-day CRM Foundation Course for all aircrew and then develop a follow on package that could be delivered by specially trained instructors on the squadrons over a longer period time. The Foundation Course would be generic in nature, applicable to all aircraft types and roles, and to all aircrew trades. The follow-on packages could be tailor-made and adapted to specific operational environments. Ultimately, our aim was to see CRM fully integrated into aircrew training as a way of life. We ascertained that there were at that time some 6,000 aircrew in the RAF. If we had teams of two instructors working together, and four teams, we could accomplish the task of delivering a one-day foundation course to all aircrew in about a year. On this basis, we agreed that Martin would develop the Foundation Course, Jon would supervise the development of the follow-on packages and any other forms of equipment or training that would be required to integrate CRM fully into mainstream aircrew training, and I would draft a paper seeking endorsement from the Air Force at large for our proposals.

With some minor modifications, the plans were in due course approved, and eight junior officer aircrew were assigned to the team. Their backgrounds covered a wide range of operational roles and aircraft types, and I felt confident that we had sufficient expertise at our disposal to achieve our aims. Once they had all assembled, I briefed them on the task ahead, and then handed them over to Martin to develop the one-day Foundation Course. Shortly thereafter, I visited the Headquarters of the Army Air Corps at Middle Wallop. After briefing the senior staff on the project, I invited them to participate in the scheme by sending one of their instructors to join the team. In due course, an army Warrant Officer flying instructor was assigned to us. He not only fitted in well with the other members of the team but also provided a fund of good ideas. I also visited the Flag Officer Naval Aviation at Yeovilton where I invited the Navy's participation in the scheme, but my offer was declined. To facilitate the process of consultation we organised a one-day CRM workshop at Innsworth that was attended by representatives from front-line squadrons and other elements with an interest in the project. As a keynote speaker, we invited Roger Green, a psychologist from the Institute of Aviation Medicine, to give a talk on human factors in aviation. His wide-ranging and amusing coverage of the topic gave the workshop a promising start. As the day progressed, it was evident that there was not only a lot of interest in our proposals but also a great deal of support for the project. Furthermore, positive feedback from the assembled aircrew helped to focus and refine our ideas for the development of the training.

In developing the one-day CRM Foundation Course a significant obstacle to be overcome was the time-honoured Service view of the role of the captain of an aircraft, which could be lightly summarised in the following two rules:

Rule 1: The Captain is always right.

Rule 2: See Rule 1.

Investigations into aircraft accidents world-wide had proven conclusively that this was not always the case; and that Captains, no matter how well-trained and experienced, were not immune from human error. In the past, many accidents had been attributable to mechanical failure of the aircraft, but modern aircraft, and their engines in particular, were now so reliable that such accidents were rare. Yet accidents had continued to happen, and the resulting investigations had begun to shine a spotlight on the actions and interactions of the crew. This investigative process was greatly facilitated by the introduction of cockpit voice recorders into all modern aircraft. Far from the view that aircrew could be made infallible through training, it was becoming widely accepted that in any complex operation such as flying an aircraft, mistakes were inevitable. Some errors, such as those involving the motor skills required to fly an aircraft, could be reduced or eliminated by more or better training. Other more complex cognitive skills, such as gaining and maintaining situational awareness, decision-making and teamwork, were not only more open to error but also less amenable to what had hitherto been the standard forms of training. It was part of an attempt to mitigate accidents attributable to human factors that had led during the 1970s to the introduction of the CRM programme. The elements that comprised the CRM programmes currently in use were not new but had been recognised in one form or another since aviation began, usually under more general headings such as 'Airmanship', Captaincy', 'Crew Co-operation', etc. In the past, however, these terms had not been defined, structured or articulated in a formal way. CRM could therefore be seen as an attempt to remedy this deficiency by defining, developing and introducing a management system that made optimum use of all available resources – equipment, procedures and people – both to promote safety and also to enhance the efficiency of flight operations. Thus the first task facing my team was to bring about a paradigm shift in attitudes by introducing these concepts into the RAF's aircrew training programmes.

The available evidence suggested that these concepts could not be inculcated by didactic training methods – known colloquially as 'chalk and talk'. Instead, the training had to be orientated towards 'experiential learning', whereby those attending the course engaged as a group in some activity designed to bring out the underlying concepts and then discussed their findings. Only through this process of discovery would self-awareness, the essence of the training, and an essential prerequisite for personal development, be retained. Thus my team of instructors running the courses would act not as teachers in the conventional sense but as facilitators whose task it was to help the participants towards the aim of self-realisation.

To help the trainees gain self-awareness, we introduced a psychometric indicator known as the Myers-Briggs Type Indicator® (MBTI). Based on theories of personality developed in America, and predicated on an individual's preferred method of taking in information and acting upon it, MBTI defines 16 types of personality. Preferences are determined by a simple questionnaire that forces the person taking the test to choose between certain pairs of words. MBTI was, and still is, widely used in industry as an aid to personal development and for team-building.

Although rather sceptical about the concept at first, I was surprised in practice to find that aircrew attending the course really enjoyed the exercise and were intrigued by the results. Comparing and contrasting the different personalities within the group also led naturally into the subject of teamwork and crew co-operation. To round off the day's training, we also introduced a second indicator intended to give the participants an insight to their own performance as members of the aircrew team. Questionnaires developed by a commercial company, Human Synergistics Verax®, were distributed in advance to those attending the Foundation Course. These had to be completed not only by the individuals themselves but also by those above them in the organisational hierarchy and those below. After the questionnaires had been duly processed, the results were returned confidentially to the individual. Thus each individual received a three-dimensional picture of how they performed as a member of the aircrew team. All the members on my team, myself included, attended training courses on these programmes, so that we could not only apply them in practice but also provide insight and advice on their interpretation. We also found them highly effective in establishing greater cohesion among the members of our own team.

By the end of 1995 the Foundation Course was complete and the nine facilitators were fully trained in its delivery. The eight RAF members of the team prepared to carry out a programme of visits throughout the UK, while the army Warrant Officer returned to Middle Wallop to train aircrew of the Army Air Corps. Those of us left in the Headquarters were now able to turn our attention to the second phase of the CRM programme which involved training CRM instructors to act at squadron level. In parallel with the development of the Foundation Course, an instructor training course had been developed at Cranwell by Flight Lieutenant Rory Underwood. A pilot in the RAF, Rory had risen to fame through his prowess at the game of rugby, playing on the wing as an established member of the English national team. In developing his course, he made many liaison visits to our team at Innsworth, and his arrival always caused a stir amongst the ladies working in the Headquarters. His immense fame notwithstanding, he had a very modest and engaging personality, and much of the time during his visits was spend signing autographs for his many admirers. Despite these distractions, he put together a good instructors course which continued to run in parallel with the on-going delivery of the Foundation Course. For my part, I wrote to all the senior operational commanders in the RAF, explaining the concept of the training, and inviting them to participate in the Foundation Course, which many of them did.

Throughout 1996, as the training teams went steadily about their business, nearly all the feedback that we received was positive. I attended training sessions myself at several different RAF Stations and I was impressed by the engagement and enthusiasm of those taking part in the courses. As far as the first phase of CRM training went, I considered that we were well on the way to achieving our aim. The focus of the training was on the development of cognitive and interpersonal skills. In the context of aircrew training, cognitive skills embraced the psychological aspects of taking in information and creating an accurate mental picture of the situation on which sound decisions could be based. Interpersonal skills were important in the context of team-building and crew co-operation. Of particular importance was the concept of 'assertiveness', empowering a junior member of the crew to draw attention to a potential error in the operation of the aircraft without undermining the authority of the Captain.

On the basis of CRM training, 'airmanship' could now be defined for the first time as the optimum use of cognitive and interpersonal skills to successfully accomplish the aims of the mission. These concepts were new to the RAF, and we recognised that it would take some time and considerable repetition before they became firmly embedded in the training ethos. There was still an enormous distance yet to travel, but we had nevertheless taken the first few tentative steps along a path that would eventually see a substantial improvement in the effectiveness and safety of RAF operations.

My own involvement in these developments was, however, about to come to an end. Having reached the age of 55, and after serving for more than 37 years, I was finally due to retire. Shortly before Christmas, I was dined out of the Mess in the traditional manner by my fellow officers. Over the next few days I said my farewells to my team and all my colleagues in the Headquarters. Then, at the end of the week, I loaded my few possessions into my car and set off for the last time along the road from Innsworth to my home in Hampshire.

Reflecting on my career as I drove home, I was conscious of the extraordinary circumstances surrounding my time in the RAF. Serving during the Cold War, I had never seen a shot fired in anger. I had taken part in no campaigns, nor had I been awarded any medals, either for bravery or for any other cause. Yet I had flown all over the world, served overseas in three different countries, operated with two very different Air Forces and amassed more than 7,000 flying hours on numerous different aircraft types. Moreover, coming from a very modest home, I risen mainly by my own efforts to command an RAF Station and its complement of more than 800 men and women. Not only had I remained fit and healthy throughout this experience but I was also relatively untainted by world-weariness or cynicism. I was grateful for the life-enhancing opportunities offered to me by my service in the RAF, for the legion of friends and colleagues that my wife and I had made, and for a host of memories to reflect on in my retirement Meanwhile, as I continued my journey home, I looked forward with confidence to starting a new life in the third age.

CHAPTER 14

Flying with No 2 Air Experience Flight

DURING MY LAST year of regular service, as the time for my retirement approached, I had taken steps to prepare myself for civilian life. Being still fit and active, the prospect of a life of idleness did not appeal to me. But what was I to do? Reviewing my prospects, I recognised that I was too old to train as a commercial airline pilot. Furthermore, I was severely restricted by my age as to the types of job for which I might apply. I had no experience in the business world, nor did I have any influential connections. I did, however, have considerable experience of CRM, and I thought that there might be some commercial opportunities in this field. Accordingly, I decided to set myself up as a company designing and delivering CRM training. Now that my long-term investments had matured and I had paid off the mortgage on my house, I calculated that I would be able to live off my pension without undue hardship while I developed my contacts and established the business.

During my last year of service, to prepare myself for this new venture, I had attended a couple of resettlement courses designed to orientate me towards my new way of life. The first of these was a course on how to be a consultant, where I found myself in the company of about 30 retiring officers from the three Services who were thinking about becoming self-employed along lines similar to the path that I was intending to follow. The course was very helpful and gave me a good idea of how to set about my new enterprise. Perhaps the most useful lesson that I learned was to start in a small way and not spend too much money on office accommodation or equipment. That way, if the business failed to get off the ground, not much capital expenditure would be wasted. With this in mind, I decided that I would initially work from home, thereby saving as much as possible on overheads. I did, however, buy a new desk-top computer and, for the first time, acquired one of the new Internet connections. The second period of resettlement was a two-week course on how to set up and run a small business. Again, this proved to be very helpful in highlighting some of the hurdles to be cleared in initiating and sustaining a successful enterprise. Now, with my study at home reoriented as an office, I reviewed my list of contacts and prepared myself for this brave new world.

Before I could start work in earnest, however, I was introduced to one of the delights of being retired. At the beginning of January, my wife and I were playing with another husband and wife in a mixed golf tournament at our club in Tidworth. My opposite number in the foursome, 'Chips' Clifton-Moore, was a retired Major, who had been a helicopter pilot in the Army Air Corps. Although now getting on in years, he remained a very good golfer. His wife, Daintry, also played to a respectable handicap, and with our similar Service backgrounds we always enjoyed each other's company. While we were having a drink in the clubhouse after the game, they told us that they were going on holiday to the Algarve in Portugal the following week, where they would be staying in a time-share that they owned. They normally went with Daintry's sister and her husband, but the family had been overtaken by ill-health and had had to cry off at short notice. Would we like to take their place instead? Looking outside at the wintry weather, I asked my wife, 'Have you anything planned for the following week?'. She shook her head. 'Well, neither have I,' I replied, so why don't we do it. And so began a friendship lasting for many years in which the four of us enjoyed a regular winter golfing holiday in the sun.

I had also prepared myself for retirement by joining an Air Experience Flight (AEF). During my time at RAF Newton I had greatly enjoyed the experience of flying air cadets in the Chipmunk with 7 AEF. On making enquiries, I discovered that a sister organisation, 2 AEF, was based at Bournemouth/Hurn airport, not far from my home in Hampshire. Furthermore, the CO of the unit and I were well-acquainted. John Armstrong had been a young flying instructor when I was a student pilot as a Flight Cadet. In later years, when we were both Wing Commanders, we had for six months attended the same Air Warfare Course at Cranwell. Having retired from the regular Air Force, he was now a reservist in command of 2 AEF. 'Was there any chance that he could find a place for me on his Flight?' 'Of course there was!' In May 1995, while still serving as a Group Captain, I had visited him at Hurn and re-qualified on the Chipmunk. From then on, during my last year in the RAF, I flew with 2 AEF whenever the opportunity presented itself. I was helped considerably in this undertaking by the fact that the normal working week for the AEFs was Wednesday to Sunday, thereby enabling both the cadets and me to fly during the weekends. I was also pleased to discover, when I later attended the first of many 2 AEF Annual Dinners, that Dennis Southern, the first of my erstwhile flying instructors, was a recently-retired member of the Flight, having served previously as the CO.

Bournemouth/Hurn airport was an ideal location for an AEF. Our accommodation was located near to the western end of the main runway, so there was only a short distance to taxi to the take-off point. So close were we that often when we called for clearance to start and the airfield was not busy, the air traffic controller in the tower would reply, 'You're cleared to start. You're cleared to taxi. You're cleared for take-off.' And away we would go without further ado. Returning to the airfield there was a turn-off not far from the landing point. With a bit of judicious braking, we were back in dispersal shortly after touch-down, and ready to pick up the next cadet. It was therefore quite feasible to fly four or five cadets in a morning or an afternoon without becoming stressed or fatigued. This was just as well because 2 AEF served an enormous catchment area comprising the whole of Dorset, Wiltshire, Hampshire and the Isle of Wight, together with parts of Surrey and Sussex. Consequently, there was always a steady stream of cadets eagerly waiting their turn to fly.

Flights with the cadets were normally of 25 minutes duration and we had the choice of two routes. The first took us eastward along the coast towards Hurst Castle and the mouth of the Solent, sometimes extending as far as The Needles. This route provided awe-inspiring views of the south coast and the Isle of Wight but, because it was mostly within the Bournemouth Air Traffic Control Zone, we were restricted to 2,000 feet and were therefore not able to do aerobatics. The other route took us north-westwards towards Cranborne Chase. This area lay to the north of controlled airspace and so we could climb higher and manoeuvre to our hearts content. To fly four or five cadets in a morning, have a short break for lunch, and then fly another four or five cadets in the afternoon, made for a very pleasant and satisfying day's work.

After less than a year of this activity, change came upon us once again. Having been in service with the AEFs for nearly 40 years, the Chipmunk had come to the end of its service life. There being no replacement in the pipeline, the decision was taken to relocate the AEFs alongside the University Air Squadrons (UASs), so that both organisations could utilise the Bulldog aircraft with which the UASs were equipped. Accordingly, in the Spring of 1996, 2 AEF relocated from Bournemouth to RAF Boscombe Down, in Wiltshire, where it became collocated with Southampton University Air Squadron (SUAS). Boscombe Down was, and still is, the home of the Empire Test Pilots School. Not only was the Station responsible for training new test pilots but also for the test and evaluation of a wide range of aircraft and weapon systems. To say that the arrival of an AEF in the midst of this august establishment came as an unwelcome development would be an understatement. Notwithstanding the high professional standards maintained by all AEF pilots, we were widely regarded by the incumbent staff at Boscombe Down as a bunch of week-end joy-riders who were not fit to grace the same airspace as test pilots. Despite this initial hostility to our presence, we managed to establish a safe pattern of operations, and the task of converting all the AEF pilots from the Chipmunk to the Bulldog went ahead.

Compared with the neat and tidy operation at Bournemouth airport the AEF was less well-served at Boscombe Down. In the early stages, the aircraft were based in one hangar, SUAS in another, with 2 AEF in yet another building, and all some distance apart. In addition to these less than ideal working arrangements, the airfield was a huge, sprawling affair, with two enormously long runways and miles of taxiway. Consequently, to fly four or five sorties in succession became quite a protracted affair. The one saving grace was that part of the northern taxiway that ran parallel to the main runway was marked out as a 3,000-foot landing strip. This facility allowed light aircraft to land on the shorter northern runway, leaving the main runway free for the fast-jets and the heavies.

Separation in the circuit was achieved by having the latter aircraft fly a left-hand pattern at 1,500 feet, while the light aircraft flew a right-hand pattern at 800 feet, thereby ensuring both vertical and horizontal separation. Between the main runway and the northern runway was a grass strip that could also be used by the light aircraft when circumstances allowed. It was quite satisfying to return overhead at 3,000 feet from a cadet sortie, to simulate an engine failure by closing the throttle, and then to glide round the forced-landing pattern to a touch-down on the grass strip, thereby simulating a successful landing in a field.

In addition to the grass strip there was also a pad of reinforced concrete on a disused runway. Known as 'the diamond', by virtue of its shape, the pad was used by Harriers for hovering and vertical landings. A final complication was a public road that ran across the main runway allowing vehicular traffic to reach the southern side of the airfield. The crossing was controlled by traffic lights operated from the control tower. When the airfield was busy, with fast-jets, heavy aircraft, helicopters and light aircraft all operating at the same time, and with everyone trying to fit in their various operational and training requirements, it took considerable situational awareness on the part of both the pilots and air traffic control to keep the circuit running smoothly. Add to this a line of vehicles waiting to cross the runway when a gap occurred in the constant stream of take-offs and landings, and life could become quite hectic. For the cadets, however, these intense operations provided added interest and excitement. Indeed, there was nothing like waiting with a cadet at the holding point for departure while a pair of Tornados took off in full reheat right in front of your nose to really bring home the thrill of military aviation.

2 AEF was greatly helped in its relocation by the co-operative attitude displayed by the then Officer Commanding SUAS, Squadron Leader Steve Jarmain. Not only did he go out of his way to make us all feel welcome, but he played a significant part in smoothing a path for our operations with the rest of the station. In the early stages, following our arrival at Boscombe Down, he worked tirelessly to secure more cohesive working arrangements, with the result that SUAS and 2AEF were eventually housed next to each other on the first floor of a large hangar, with the aircraft parked just alongside. He was also quick to see the advantages of having veteran pilots with wide operational experience mixing with his university cadets and with his own young and enthusiastic flying instructors. On this basis, good relations were established from the outset between the two very different organisations, a state of affairs that was maintained during the entire time that I was a member of the Air Experience Flight.

Another source of strength for the new organisation was the engineering support. The Chipmunks at Bournemouth had been maintained by a small team of civilian engineers who were responsible not only for servicing the aircraft but also for preparing and equipping the cadets for their flight. In view of the intensity of operations when cadet flying was in progress, it was inevitable that a close working relationship had grown up over the years between the aircrew and the groundcrew. When the AEF moved from Bournemouth to Boscombe Down, many of the groundcrew came with us, carrying out a short training course on the Bulldog so that they could continue to support the flying programme. One of the longest-serving engineers was Mrs Maria Copeland, known to all as 'Titch' because of her diminutive stature. Not only was she a very good engineer but she was also an excellent supervisor, so accomplished in fact that her ability was recognised by her supervisors, and for most of the time that I flew with 2 AEF she was in charge of the engineering support.

While John Armstrong worked his way steadily through the task of converting all the AEF pilots from the Chipmunk to the Bulldog, cadet flying was suspended for several months. Because of my previous experience on the Bulldog, I was one of the first to re-qualify. In the absence of any cadets at Boscombe Down, I arranged to fly for a week at Newton , where Bill Purchase, still in charge of 7 AEF, made me welcome. Newton was some way ahead of Boscombe Down in the conversion programme and had already resumed cadet flying on the Bulldog. Consequently, I managed to accomplish a very productive week's flying. The visit also confirmed what I already knew from my former days flying with EMUAS at Newton, that the Bulldog was a much better aircraft in the air experience role than was its predecessor, the Chipmunk. Compared with the Chipmunk's 145 bhp Gipsy Major engine driving a fixed-pitch propeller, the Bulldog was powered by a 200 bhp Lycoming engine with fuel injection that drove a variable pitch propeller. This gave the Bulldog a much better rate of climb than the Chipmunk; meaning that, in a 25-minute sortie, more time could be spent in the cruise. The controls were very well harmonised and the aircraft was easy to handle. So easy to handle, in fact, that it was possible to teach the more experienced cadets to fly a few simple aerobatic manoeuvres in the space of a 25-minute sortie. Its greatest advantage, however, was the side-by-side seating that allowed the cadet to see everything that was happening. It also enabled the pilot not only to point out things in the cockpit but, more importantly, to make eye contact with the cadet and observe his or her body language. At the first signs of airsickness, the sortie could be curtailed, thereby preventing illness and loss of self-esteem on the part of the cadet.

It was strange visiting the Station where I had previously served in command, although I am glad to say that the people who were still there seemed genuinely pleased to see me again. The Station itself, however, was a sad sight. All the major units had now left the Station and moved to their new locations, leaving the domestic sight looking like a ghost town. The Officers Mess and the Airmen's Mess had been closed down and the former Sergeants Mess turned into an All Ranks Mess. Many of the buildings that had once housed busy and active units now stood empty, and the windows of the house that had been my former residence were boarded up to protect the place against vandalism. Only the airfield retained its former vitality, with EMUAS and 7 AEF keeping up a busy flying programme. Not long after this pleasant sojourn, cadet flying restarted at Boscombe Down.

As the end of my service in the regular Air Force approached, I arranged to re-muster in the Volunteer Reserves. There is only one substantive rank in the RAF Volunteer Reserve (Training) Branch and that is Flying Officer, although those with long service or holding executive responsibility can rise to the dizzy heights of Acting Flight Lieutenant. Thus it was that when SUAS and 2 AEF closed for the Christmas vacation, I was wearing on my flying suit the four bars of a Group Captain, but when we resumed operations in the New Year I was adorned only with the single stripe of a Flying Officer. I was not myself unduly concerned with this change in status. I was, after all, the same person inside the uniform, with the same level of experience and acquired degree of interpersonal skills that I had on retirement. Furthermore, several of my AEF colleagues were in the same boat. Irrespective of our former status, we all now held the same rank. We had joined 2 AEF for the flying and we operated on a first name basis in a relaxed and congenial atmosphere. However, for the SUAS instructors, who were all Junior Officers, the situation was not quite the same. While I was a Group Captain, they treated me with the respect appropriate to my rank. When I appeared almost overnight as a Flying Officer, they did not quite know how to handle the situation.

As I passed Steve Jarmain's office he called me in.

'Sid, Sid,' he said. 'We have a bit of a crisis on our hands. The chaps don't know what to call you.'

I thought about it for a moment, recognising their dilemma.

'Why don't they call me "Sid"?,' I replied. 'That's what everyone else calls me.'

With that the tension was diffused and we all got on together in a most amiable and enjoyable fashion. Some time later I received through the post a second commissioning scroll to add to the one I had been awarded when I graduated from Cranwell as a Pilot Officer some 35 years previously.

In the meantime, I was having some small success with my new CRM training business. Attending a CAA-sponsored CRM workshop at Oxford Airport, I met up with John Barker, an established CRM trainer, who ran his own business from a base at Fairoaks, a small airfield to the west of London. John and I knew each other from previous workshops and we had always been on good terms. He told me that the was seeking to expand his business and asked me if I would like to work with him. We agreed that I would work not as an employee but as an independent consultant, and that I would be paid a daily rate for my services.

This arrangement suited me perfectly, as it provided a regular source of employment but left me free to pursue any other opportunities that might eventually come along. John had established contact with several of the smaller airlines operating from regional airports, and soon I was travelling on a regular basis to Southend, Luton and Stansted airports delivering one-day CRM refresher courses in line with CAA requirements. With my extensive experience in the design of CRM training I was able to put together an interesting and stimulating programme. The crews from the different airlines arrived for their day of ground training expecting the worst, as aircrew tend to do, but once they were engaged in the experiential learning process they quickly became engrossed. As the day progressed, and they gained new insights into their performance, both as individuals and as members of a crew, lively and entertaining discussions took place in a good-humoured atmosphere. They enjoyed the training and I gained enormous satisfaction from acting as a facilitator to the discussions throughout the day. It was not unknown for the end of the day to be marked by a round of applause, which was not only very gratifying on a personal basis but also a good indication that the CRM training programme that I had devised was on the right lines.

After I retired from the regular Air Force my wife and I gave some thought as to our future lifestyle. We had owned our house in Penton Mewsey now for some 25 years, but we had lived in it only occasionally when it fitted in with my various tours of duty. For much of our period of ownership it had been let out to various tenants. We liked the village for its charm and its convenient location, but neither of us was over-fond of the house in which we lived. We had bought it at a time when house prices were rising at an astronomical rate and gazumping was rife. For example, we had looked at a house in Charlton, a small village just outside Andover, which we thought would suit us nicely. The owners, however, were asking rather more than we were prepared to pay. We said we would think about it over lunch and let them know our decision. Having agreed between ourselves that we would go the extra mile, we telephoned the owners some two hours later, only to be told that the house had already been sold to a cash buyer.

In this frenetic seller's market, we were glad to succeed in the purchase of a property in Penton Mewsey, even if the house was not our first choice. What had started out as a small dwelling had been gradually extended by various previous owners who had at different times added on various ground floor extensions. We, too, had done our share over the years by adding on an extra bedroom and bathroom over some of the existing ground-floor extensions, and a double garage at the end of the garden. Although the house now had four bedrooms and two bathrooms, and plenty of space on the ground floor, it was a higgledy-piggledy affair, and we both felt that no amount of further tinkering with it would ever turn it into a cohesive home.

Eventually, after much soul-searching, we came to the conclusion that we would look for a new and better home in the local area. After months of hope and disappointment, and with the help of a retirement mortgage, we finally managed to purchase a substantial newly-built property in the village of Compton Chamberlayne, some 10 miles to the southwest of Salisbury. In the summer of 1997, on my wife's birthday, and in pouring rain, we moved into our new home.

For the next two years I enjoyed the pleasant lifestyle of a retired officer. I worked when the opportunity presented itself, I played golf two or three times a week, I adapted my house and my new garden to suit our needs, and with my wife I went from time to time on holiday. I also flew with 2 AEF on a regular basis.

That summer, I went again for a week's flying at Newton, not in my former rank of Group Captain but now as a newly-minted Flying Officer. This change of status was a source of much amusement among the staff who still remembered me from my days as the Station Commander and I was subjected to a great deal of good-natured ribbing.

On my way home at the end of the week, I called in at Addenbrooke's Hospital in Cambridge to see my first grandchild. Chloe, born to James and Sarah, was just one-day old. Both mother and daughter were doing well. Returning to Boscombe Down, I joined the Bustard Flying Club and arranged to be checked out on the club's two aircraft. The Cessna-172 I had previously flown at the Scott AFB Aeroclub in the USA, and the Robin with the Air Cadets Gliding Centre at Syerston, so my re-familiarisation did not take long. After that I was able to fly my family, friends and visitors around the local area whenever the opportunity presented itself.

Meanwhile, John Armstrong had finally retired as the CO of 2 AEF, his place being taken by Mike Williamson. Mike's home, however, was near Woodbridge in Suffolk, so working at Boscombe Down meant that he had to live in the Mess during the working week and commute over a long distance at the weekend. Consequently, when the CO's post of 5 AEF at Wyton, near Cambridge, became vacant, he arranged a transfer to the more convenient location. The last thing he did before leaving Boscombe Down was to thrust into my hand an application for the now vacant post of OC 2 AEF saying, 'I think you should apply for this job.'

At some time in the distant past the OC AEF posts had, along with many other posts in the RAF, been civilianised as a cost-saving measure. The incumbents were therefore recruited and paid by the Civil Service, although holding the rank of Squadron Leader in the RAF Reserve of Officers. While the recruiting process ground slowly into action, there was a hiatus at 2 AEF, since without a CO the Flight could not function. To fill the gap, Mick Rogers, a Deputy Flight Commander on 2 AEF, and I, took on the job between us, alternating on a daily basis, and under contract as temporary civil servants paid for the days that we worked.

In deciding whether to apply for the job or not I was torn between retaining my independence and freedom to do much as I pleased and the challenge of having one last opportunity to be in charge of a flying unit. To fill the post, however, would mean having to re-qualify as a flying instructor, and I was mindful of the difficulties I had faced a few years earlier during my time with CFS at Scampton. On the other hand, my sources of work as a CRM instructor were drying up. My colleague John Barker had had to give up his business due to ill health, and many airlines had by now developed their own in-house CRM training programmes. Bearing in mind that I still had a new mortgage to pay off, and urged on by my colleague, Mick Rogers, I decided to apply for the job. It was, therefore, somewhat to my surprise, that I found myself at the age of 59, more than 40 years after I first joined the RAF, before an interview board at Cranwell applying for a job as an AEF Flight Commander. I rather hoped that my vast previous service experience and the fact that I was already holding down the CO's job, albeit on a temporary basis, would give me an edge over any other applicants. And so it proved to be, because in due course I was offered the post. Shortly afterwards, I attended a two-week flying course at Cranwell where I re-qualified as a flying instructor and flight examiner without undue difficulty.

In order to take up the post I had to resign my commission in the RAF Volunteer Reserve and, after joining the Civil Service, accept a new commission as a Squadron Leader in the RAF Reserve of Officers. My reappearance at Boscombe Down wearing my new badges of rank, having been promoted directly from Flying Officer to Squadron Leader, caused some consternation among the flying instructors on SUAS.

As I passed Steve Jarmain's office, he called me in.

'Sid, Sid,' he said. 'We have a bit of a crisis on our hands. The chaps don't know what to call you.'

I thought about it for a moment, recognising their dilemma.

'Why don't they just call me "Sid", I said.

And from then on, that is what they did.

Some time later, another commissioning scroll arrived, my third.

Apart from myself, a full-time officer in the Reserves, my new Flight comprised some 25 part-time volunteer pilots, most of whom were Flying Officers in the RAF Volunteer Reserve. In addition, I could call upon several pilots who were still serving but were holding non-flying posts in their regular jobs. We kept a diary in the office, and members of the Flight would book a day or a half-day of flying when their primary employment permitted. They came from a wide variety of service backgrounds and most of them were highly experienced. Quite a few were former service pilots who were now working for the airlines but had joined the AEF to retain or recapture the thrill of military flying. Several of them had previously trained as test pilots at Boscombe Down. At that time, we were not connected to the Internet, so any cancellations or changes to the programme had to be communicated by telephone. We were often stretched for pilots at the weekend, so if someone on the programme had to drop out at short notice it invariably involved a lot of telephoning around to find a replacement.

Flying for the cadets was booked in advance by the Public Schools or ATC Squadrons in our catchment area. On Wednesdays, Thursdays and Fridays we flew members of the Combined Cadet Force, who were given leave by their respective schools to attend on a weekday. On Saturdays and Sundays we flew ATC cadets, usually from one squadron in the morning and another in the afternoon. Mondays and Tuesdays were my days off. Cadet flying was carefully regulated and my biggest problem in running the AEF was uncertainty caused by the vagaries of the British weather. If the weather was totally unfit for flying it was an easy decision to call up the unit concerned and cancel the programme before they set off. It the weather was fine we ran the programme and thought no more about it.

The worst times were when the weather was bad first thing with a promise of a clearance later. Then the cadets would sit in their crew room watching films on video, bursting meanwhile with suppressed excitement, until the weather improved and I could safely get them airborne. The pilots, too, would pace up and down gazing out of the window and reporting favourably on every positive sign that the anticipated clearance was on its way. On one particular autumn morning we had had early morning fog that was slow to clear. About mid-morning the visibility showed some improvement and pressure began to mount on me from all sides to launch the fleet.

Knowing as I did from experience that there was always the danger in these circumstances of a 'sucker gap', I was reluctant to do so, but eventually I succumbed to the blandishments of my pilots and authorised the flights. I was the last of the three aircraft to get airborne that morning and as I climbed to height I saw that the entire surrounding area was covered by an endless sea of fog, with just a small hole sitting right over Boscombe Down. I recalled the fleet. We descended in a tight spiral overhead the airfield to a successful landing, and that was the end of flying for the day.

After I had been in post for some two years the Bulldog came to the end of its service life and was replaced by an aircraft built in Germany by the Grob Aerospace Company and named by the RAF as the 'Tutor'. Like its predecessor, the Bulldog, the Tutor was powered by a Lycoming engine delivering 180 bhp to a 3-bladed constant speed Hoffman propeller. Consequently, the aircraft had an excellent rate of climb. It was fully aerobatic, although its long wings made it rather ponderous in roll. In the landing phase, when the throttle was closed prior to touchdown, there was a significant nose-down change of trim, and this had to be countered as the airspeed decreased by a progressive backward movement of the control column. Failure to effect this manoeuvre correctly could result either in the aircraft landing heavily on its main undercarriage or ballooning into the air with the attendant risk of a pilot-induced oscillation. Add to this a propensity for some of the airline pilots, who were used to flying large aircraft, to start the flare a long way above the ground, and all the ingredients were present for some exciting landings. The Tutor was also fully equipped with modern flight instruments and navigation aids, including a Global Positioning System (GPS). With its clean lines and smart, modern appearance, it proved to be a favourite with the cadets.

A team came to Boscombe Down from CFS at Cranwell and converted the SUAS instructors and me to the new aircraft. The conversion course consisted of five sorties of which three were dual and two were solo. After the CFS team departed I was left to convert the 25 or so pilots on the AEF to the new aircraft. This was a formidable undertaking that, because of the intermittent availability of the pilots and the vagaries of the weather, extended over a period of about 6 months. Having sought help from other AEFs in the vicinity, I was fortunate to obtain assistance with the conversion task from Flight Lieutenants Don Merriman and Mike Neal, both from 6 AEF at Benson. The two pilots enjoyed their sojourn with 2 AEF to such an extent that Don Merriman continued to fly with us on an ad hoc basis until his retirement several years later.

Meanwhile, Steve Jarmain had been posted to a ground appointment following a well-deserved promotion to Wing Commander. He too joined the AEF and flew with us whenever his primary duties permitted. Another pilot to join us was my son, Brian. Having carried out a tour as a helicopter pilot at Yeovilton, he had now left the Royal Marines to set up his own business as an Event Manager. He had hoped to continue flying with the Royal Marine Reserve but, when that fell through, I offered him a place on 2 AEF. In due course I had the pleasure of converting him onto the Tutor, and he continued to fly with us for about a year until his business commitments became too pressing. Some two years earlier, my wife and I had had the pleasure of attending Brian's marriage to Caroline (Caz) Southern at Hever church in Kent. Not long before Brian joined 2 AEF, Caz gave birth to a little girl named Florence. Eventually, they were to have two more children, Arthur and Esther, while my other family had another girl, Niamh, making five grandchildren in all.

As a flying instructor and examiner on the Tutor I was obliged to return to CFS at Cranwell every year for a standardisation check. By judicious timing, I was able to arrange this visit to coincide with the annual meeting of the Old Cranwellians Association. This long-standing and traditional event took place over a weekend in July. Matches in various sports between the cadets and the old boys were played on Saturday afternoon, my own preference being to play in an event at the nearby Rauceby Golf Course, where I once been a member many years before. In the evening the Annual General Meeting of the Association was followed by a dinner in College Hall. The next morning the cadets would parade after returning from a church service and then the guests would take sherry in the College rotunda before dispersing to their respective homes.

There was always a good turn-out at these reunions, providing as they did an excellent opportunity to catch up with old friends and acquaintances. One of the entries that had graduated from the College while I was still a Junior Cadet had the bright idea of commemorating Flight Sergeant Holt, the famed drill instructor, now deceased, who had done so much to instil a sense of discipline and pride into the cadets who passed through his hands. A memorial stone with appropriate wording was inserted under the window of his former office, which overlooked the parade ground, and unveiled by his surviving wife after one of the church parades. A sum of money was collected by subscription and used to fund the annual award of a ceremonial pace-stick to the Senior NCO who had made the greatest contribution to cadet training in the course of the previous year. As the first award was being presented, I couldn't help but hear a faint echo of the words that Flight Sergeant Holt had said to me all those years ago, 'You don't bounce back, Mr Adcock. You don't bounce back.' After the reunion, I would stay on at Cranwell for another couple of days to carry out my annual flying commitment.

Now that I was in my early 60s, the stresses and strains of running the AEF were taking their toll, and my annual flight medical check revealed that I was beginning to suffer from high blood pressure. Between the Aviation Medical Examiner at Boscombe Down and my local GP, the situation was brought under control by medication, and I was able to continue flying. I took the view, however, that the time was approaching when I ought to relinquish my command and adopt a more relaxed life-style. I let it be known that after some three years in the post I would like to retire in the near future, and the recruiting process was put in hand to find a successor. After some considerable time, I was able to hand over command of the AEF to Mike Brooke and stand down from my duties. As a former Wing Commander, Mike had at one time been OC Flying at Boscombe Down, so he was well versed in operations from the Station. Having now re-mustered as a Flight Lieutenant in the Volunteer Reserve, he was entirely new to the world of air experience flying. Furthermore, his home was in the Cotentin Peninsular in France, and it was his intention to commute on a weekly basis from Cherbourg to Portsmouth. Given the circumstances, I suggested to Mike during our hand-over period that I stay on flying with the AEF in a subordinate capacity to provide additional support until he found his feet in the organisation. He agreed to this suggestion, and in the end I reverted to being a Deputy Flight Commander, relinquishing my commission in the RAF Reserve of Officers and re-enrolling once more in the RAF Volunteer Reserve (Training) Branch as a Flying Officer (Acting Flight Lieutenant). Retaining my flying instructor/examiner status, I was able to help out as necessary with some of the supervisory aspects of the job as well as continuing to fly cadets. Over time, Mike Brooke and I developed a close and productive relationship, and the task of flying the cadets continued without any break in continuity. After two years in command, Mike Brooke was forced by ill-health to give up the job and his place was taken by Steve Jarmain, the former Commanding Officer of SUAS, who had since retired from the regular Air Force and taken a commission in the reserves. Meanwhile, yet another commissioning scroll - my fourth – had arrived. I had it framed and mounted on the wall of my study with the three others.

Now that I was no longer in command of the AEF I was free to take up one of the singular pleasures of being an AEF pilot and that was to fly with another unit during the period of the ATC summer camps. Accordingly, I arranged to fly for a week with 10 AEF at RAF Woodvale in Lancashire, the CO and I having been fellow-students on the Staff College course many years previously. Woodvale is a coastal airfield located about half-way between Liverpool and Southport, so the flying presented some spectacular views for the cadets. A favourite sortie was to fly southwards from the airfield and along the River Mersey to the centre of Liverpool. A left turn brought you over the three famous waterfront buildings, past the two cathedrals and the football grounds of Liverpool and Everton, with an exit from the Liverpool Control Zone via the Aintree racecourse. As the latter part of this route was over a heavily built-up area, there were very few sites for a successful forced landing in the event of an engine failure, so a close eye had to be maintained on your progress. A flight from Woodvale to the north took you to Blackpool, with a splendid view of its famous promenade and tower. Compared with Boscombe Down, Woodvale was a fairly small airfield. Surrounded on all sides by various obstacles, it was not the place to suffer an engine failure just after take-off. Taking off from the main westerly runway, Formby golf course presented the most promising area for a forced landing. Fortunately, neither I nor anyone else had to put it to the test. The dispersal where the aircraft were parked was not far from the take-off point, so you could be airborne within a few minutes of starting the engine, and back in dispersal shortly after landing. Because of this, it was not too demanding to fly six or seven cadets in the course of a day, with just a short break at lunchtime for rest and refreshment. Being on the coast, the airfield was subject to rapid changes in the weather. One morning, as I took off on my first sortie of the day, I saw low cloud lying ominously just off-shore. However, the weather inland was fine, so I climbed with my cadet on a north-easterly heading into a relatively clear sky. No sooner had we settled down in the cruise than I heard over the radio a general recall of all aircraft as the weather at the airfield was deteriorating rapidly. Turning back towards Woodvale, I saw that the low cloud that had been sitting just off-shore when I took off had now encroached on the coast, and the airfield was nowhere to be seen. Fortunately, I could still see the top of a large gas holder located a few miles north of the airfield. Keeping the gas-holder in sight I descended to 500 feet, putting us just below the cloud base, then I followed the road southwards until the airfield came in sight. After a low-level circuit and a successful landing I shut down in dispersal with a sigh of relief, bringing to an end flying on that particular day. Having been made most welcome during my stay at Woodvale, I enjoyed my detachment immensely, and for several years running I returned for my annual summer break.

Another detachment that I enjoyed shortly before my retirement was a trip to Jersey as one of a flight of three Tutors. Coasting out in a loose formation from the Isle of Wight at the Needles, we flew over the Channel at 2,000 feet, passing overhead Alderney and then on to Jersey. Prior to our visit, the air cadets of Jersey had always had to travel to the mainland for their air experience flying, so our visit provided them with a rare treat. We were kept hard at it during the weekend and by the end of our stay we had flown some 60 or 70 cadets. As the island is so small, the flying was spectacular, with much of it taking place just off the coast. It was a unique experience, carrying out aerobatics over the sea, and one that provided an added thrill for the cadets and their pilots alike. It also provided a challenge for the air traffic controllers, who normally handled only a few commercial flights each day, having three light aircraft zooming in and out and carrying out take-offs and landings every few minutes. All three aircraft on the detachment had carried two pilots, so we were each able to take some time off to explore the island during our stay. In addition, some of the wives had travelled to Jersey by high-speed ferry or on a commercial flight. We were exceptionally well looked after by our hosts, and it all made for a very sociable weekend indeed. Some days after our return to Boscombe Down, Steve Jarmain and I, together with some of the other senior pilots who had been on the detachment, reviewed the operation. After some discussion, we all agreed that Jersey, with its small fields surrounded by high stone walls, provided very few opportunities for a successful forced landing in the event of an engine failure, and the island was not therefore really a suitable place for air experience flying. Further more, the long over-water crossing in a single-engined aircraft posed an unacceptable risk of having to ditch in the sea. It had been a great adventure and a most enjoyable weekend, but the exercise was not to be repeated.

By now I was well past the age of 60, when all AEF pilots were supposed to retire. In certain circumstances, selected pilots could be extend to the age of 65, but only with specific permission and on a year-by-year basis. Each year, as my birthday approached, I put in a request for an extension, and every year it was granted. I passed the 65 landmark, and still my applications continued to be approved. With my 70th birthday not far away, I set my sights on one final goal - to become the oldest pilot in the RAF. Not knowing for sure whether or not there were any other competitors for this achievement, and not daring to ask, I reasoned that, if I went on flying until 364 days after my 69th birthday, I would then undoubtedly on that day be the oldest RAF pilot still flying.

As my 69th birthday approached, I put in one final application for a year's extension, and to my great delight it was approved. But alas, it was not to be. Shortly before my birthday, I went with my wife on a two-week golfing holiday in Turkey, and when I returned I found a cryptic message from Steve Jarmain on my answerphone. Arriving at the AEF a few days later as planned, I discovered that in my absence a new directive had been issued to the Air Force at large prohibiting pilots over the age of 65 from flying unless accompanied by another pilot qualified on type. I saw at once that this would immediately prevent me and others in my age group from flying with cadets. In my capacity as a Flight Examiner, I would still be able to carry out proficiency checks on qualified AEF pilots, but that would be about the limit of my involvement. On 1st April 2010, accompanied by a suitably qualified officer cadet from SUAS, I carried out my monthly continuation training on a beautiful Spring day. Although I did not realise it at the time, this turned out to be my very last flight as the pilot in command of an RAF aircraft.

Above all else in the final phase of my military career, I had enjoyed flying the cadets. Now that this was no longer possible it was evident that I had reached the end of the road as far as flying with RAF was concerned. Consequently, after a few days for reflection, I submitted a letter rescinding my application for an extension and tendering my resignation instead.

Both requests were approved.

EPILOGUE

IN 50 YEARS of flying with the RAF I had accumulated more than 8,600 hours in a wide variety of military aircraft. Nearly 5,000 of those hours had been in command. I had been commissioned or re-commissioned on four different occasions, and it had been an immensely satisfying and fulfilling career; but now it was at an end. I was not entirely cut off from the world of aviation, as I still held a valid Private Pilot's Licence and could, therefore, continue to fly from time to time at Boscombe Down with the Bustard Flying Club. I also kept in contact with many of my former colleagues in the RAF. I had no regrets about my retirement, as other activities and events came to fill my days. But neither could I put my past entirely out of my mind. Even now, several years after my final military flight, I observe the ever-changing weather patterns and assess how they would affect me if I were to be flying that day. Seeing a light aircraft, hearing the scream of a jet in the distance, or observing the formation of contrails high up in the stratosphere, I cannot help but feel a twinge of nostalgia for those former days of glory. On the other hand, by way of compensation, I have now joined that illustrious band of brothers who have known aviation as a way of life. I am also aware that, until my dying day, I shall be forever looking up at the sky.

APPENDIX 1

Equivalent Military Ranks

Royal Navy	Royal Air Force	Army/USAF
Admiral of the Fleet	Marshal of the Royal Air Force	Field Marshal
Admiral	Air Chief Marshal	General
Vice Admiral	Air Marshal	Lieutenant-General
Rear Admiral	Air Vice-Marshal	Major General
Commodore	Air Commodore	Brigadier/Brigadier General
Captain	Group Captain	Colonel
Commander	Wing Commander	Lieutenant-Colonel
Lieutenant-Commander	Squadron Leader	Major
Lieutenant	Flight Lieutenant	Captain
Sub-Lieutenant	Flying Officer	Lieutenant
Acting Sub-Lieutenant	Pilot Officer	Second Lieutenant

Appendix 2

Abbreviations Used

AAA Automobile Association of America
ACAS Assistant Chief of the Air Staff
ACAS Ops Assistant Chief of Staff Operations
ACLO Air Cadet Liaison Officer
ADC Aide-de-Camp
ADF Automatic Direction Finding
AFB Air Force Base (USAF)
AFRAeS Associate Fellowship of the Royal Aeronautical Society
AFSD Air Force Staff Duties
AMF Allied Command Europe Mobile Force
AOC Air Officer Commanding
ASET Aircrew Standardisation and Evaluation Test (USAF)
ATC Air Traffic Control
ATC Air Training Corps
BA Bachelor of Arts
BX Base Exchange (USAF)
CGI Computer-Generated Image
CFS Central Flying School
ETA Estimated Time of Arrival
FAA Federal Aviation Authority
FEBA Forward Edge of the Battle Area
FGS Fancy Goods Store
GCA Ground Controlled Approach
GEAF German Air Force
GMT Greenwich Mean Time
GPS Global Positioning System
HF High Frequency (Radio)
IALCE International Airlift Co-ordination Element
ILS Instrument Landing System
IP Instructor Pilot (USAF)
MCSU Mobile Catering Support Unit
NATO North Atlantic Treaty Organisation
NCO Non-Commissioned Officer
NDB Non-Directional Beacon
NEAF Near East Air Force
OCU Operational Conversion Unit
PAR Precision Approach Radar
PC Personal Computer
PCF Passenger cum Freight
PMC President of the Mess Committee
PPL Private Pilot's Licence
PRT Periodic Refresher Training
PTI Physical Training Instructor
PX Post Exchange (US Army)
QFI Qualified Flying Instructor (RAF)
RAF Royal Air Force
RAFRO RAF Reserve of Officers
RAFVR(T) RAF Volunteer Reserve (Training)
RPM Revolutions Per Minute
SHAPE Supreme Headquarters Allied Powers Europe
SUAS Southampton University Air Squadron
STANIVAL Standardisation and Evaluation
TACAN Tactical Air Navigation System
UAS University Air Squadron
TGIF Thank God It's Friday
UDI Unilateral Declaration of Independence
USA United States of America
UTC Co-ordinated Universal Time
VGS Volunteer Gliding School
VHF Very High Frequency (Radio)
VIP Very Important Person
VOR VHF Omni-Radial
WPPG War Plans Policy Group

Acknowledgements

IN WRITING THIS account, I have relied heavily on the half-a-dozen logbooks that I completed during my 50 year of flying with the RAF, in which is recorded every single sortie that I completed. The log-books therefore provide not only a complete and accurate record of all my military flying but also contain a treasure-house of memories relating to my career. I have also referred to the large collection of photographs and memorabilia that I still have in my possession.

The account could not have been written, however, without the generous assistance of other people. I am particularly grateful to all those individuals and organisations who agreed to the reproduction of their photographs in this book. In this context, I would like to add a special word of thanks to Group Captain Tony Stephens and his colleague Lee Barton of the Air Historical Branch, who went to considerable lengths to unearth pictures of aircraft now long since retired from the RAF inventory. Finally, I would like to thank my editor, Nick Shepperd, and his staff at Woodfield Publishing, not only for taking on this project but also for creating such a professional product.

INDEX

The
End